The EDUCATION GAP

The EDUCATION GAP

Vouchers and Urban Schools

WILLIAM G. HOWELL

PAUL E. PETERSON

with

PATRICK J. WOLF *and* DAVID E. CAMPBELL

BROOKINGS INSTITUTION PRESS
Washington, D.C.

ABOUT BROOKINGS
The Brookings Institution is a private nonprofit organization devoted to research, education, and publication on important issues of domestic and foreign policy. Its principal purpose is to bring knowledge to bear on current and emerging policy problems. The Institution maintains a position of neutrality on issues of public policy. Interpretations or conclusions in Brookings publications should be understood to be solely those of the authors.

Library of Congress Cataloging-in-Publication data

Howell, William G.
    The education gap : vouchers and urban schools / William G. Howell and Paul E. Peterson with Patrick J. Wolf and David E. Campbell.
        p.   cm.
    Includes bibliographical references and index.
    ISBN 0-8157-0214-0 (cloth : alk. paper)
    1. Educational vouchers—United States.   2. School choice—United States.
3. Education, urban—United States.   I. Peterson, Paul E.   II. Title.
    LB2828.8 .H69   2002
    379.1′11—dc21   2002002839

9 8 7 6 5 4 3 2 1

The paper used in this publication meets minimum requirements of the American National Standard for Information Sciences—Permanence of Paper for Printed Library Materials: ANSI Z39.48-1992.

Typeset in Adobe Garamond

Composition by Betsy Kulamer
Washington, D.C.

Printed by R. R. Donnelley and Sons
Harrisonburg, Virginia

For the many teachers, public and private,
to whom we are indebted, including
Richard Adelstein, Joan Buckley, Anne Frayda,
Ernest Huckle, Michael Mullin, Marcella Smith,
Stan Taylor, *and* Sally Watson

Contents

Figures

Tables

Preface

I n the fall of 1990, the nation's first publicly funded urban school voucher program was launched in Milwaukee, Wisconsin. Disturbed by rising dropout rates and a long history of student underachievement in Milwaukee's public schools, an unusual alliance of conservative Republicans and civil rights leaders won passage of state legislation that allowed about 1 percent of the city's public school population, roughly 1,000 students, to attend secular private schools. By the close of the decade, the number of voucher recipients participating in public and privately financed programs nationwide had climbed to 60,000 and a national debate was raging over the future of American education.

Our own involvement in the voucher issue took hold just as quickly. In the early 1990s, Paul Peterson was immersed in a study of federalism and preparing a textbook on American government. The other authors were still engaged in their undergraduate and graduate training. The subject of urban schools was, for the most part, far removed from the authors' intellectual agendas. Peterson, however, had agreed to write a concluding chapter for an edited volume on Milwaukee's public schools, which was later published by the University of Wisconsin Press. The other contributors to the collection had documented the state of disrepair into which the city's public schools had fallen, and Peterson became interested in the city's voucher program as a possible remedy. On reviewing the program's evaluation, he was intrigued to find data from a de facto randomized field trial, the best research design for evaluating social interventions. He and some of his colleagues then conducted a secondary analysis, which found that vouchers had a positive impact on student test scores. These findings, released in the summer of 1996, received widespread attention and generated no small controversy, in part because they differed from earlier reports. Many suggested, quite correctly, that the Milwaukee voucher intervention, which involved only a few secular schools, was too small to yield decisive results. The lack of sufficient information about students and their families at baseline, before the vouchers were awarded, also contributed to uncertainty about the findings.

An opportunity to conduct a new evaluation with an improved research design arose in the fall of 1996. A group of philanthropists in New York City was considering a private voucher initiative and planning to announce the program within a matter of months. Vouchers would be awarded by lottery to interested families with children in the city's public schools, making it possible to conduct a randomized field trial. When Peterson proposed that a research team carefully evaluate the intervention, the group agreed to cooperate, provided that the researchers could quickly raise the necessary funds. Since Peterson was at the time directing the Program on Education Policy and Governance (PEPG) within the Taubman Center on State and Local Government at Harvard's Kennedy School of Government, a vehicle for launching a major research project was available. Fortunately, several foundations supplied the funds needed to collect and analyze information about the educational experiences and family backgrounds of voucher applicants.

No sooner was the New York City evaluation under way than separate groups of philanthropists in Washington, D.C., and Dayton, Ohio, indicated to PEPG that they, too, were interested in having their voucher initiatives evaluated as randomized field trials. It also became possible to conduct evaluations of the voucher programs in Cleveland, the CEO-Horizon program in the Edgewood school district in San Antonio, and the Children's Scholarship Fund's program, which offered vouchers to 40,000 students nationwide. What had begun as a mere secondary analysis of a small voucher program in Milwaukee blossomed almost overnight into a massive research enterprise. In our opinion, the data that we have collected constitute the most comprehensive evidence currently available on the likely consequences of using school vouchers.

As PEPG's research agenda grew, so too did the number of scholars involved. William Howell, then a graduate student in political science at Stanford University, joined the research team during the 1996–97 academic year, when Peterson was on leave at the Center for Advanced Study in the Behavioral Sciences in Palo Alto, California. Howell quickly assumed major responsibilities associated with the manifold tasks of data collection, storage, analysis, and presentation. A couple of years later, Patrick Wolf, an assistant professor at Georgetown University, agreed to take primary responsibility for the evaluation of the Washington, D.C., program, while David Campbell, then a graduate student at Harvard University, helped evaluate the national CSF program.

Unless motivated by strictly mercenary considerations, few scholars could work on a topic for years and not develop a personal point of view. We are no exception. Our perspectives have been shaped by our research, to be sure, but also by our own life experiences. Two of our mothers taught in public schools, and one was principal of a parochial school. Two of us attended public schools in Minnesota and California; one attended a public school in Canada; and another attended a private school in Minnesota. One of us had children in a central-city public school, an eye-opening experience; another currently has a child in a suburban public school; and another has a child in a parochial school. Some of us began this research hopeful that school choice could substantially alleviate the educational problems of inner-city students from low-income families. Others were more skeptical. From our differing points of departure, each of us urged that certain information be collected and, once collected, not ignored. As we explored the data together, the facts that emerged began to alter our thinking. The more hopeful of us now realize, more than ever, that not all the expected gains from choice are certain to occur. The more skeptical now concede that focused choice programs have important benefits for those who use them.

While our life experiences and opinions differed, all of us were surprised by a number of things we discovered during the course of these evaluations. None of us expected to find that the effects of school vouchers would vary so dramatically for students from different ethnic backgrounds. Early on, it did not even occur to us to look for ethnically differentiated effects, and so our early reports make no mention of the education gap. One day, quite by accident, we tried to solve a data-collection puzzle by examining voucher effects separately for African Americans. The results jumped off the page. We think you will be as intrigued by the particulars as we were.

Chapter 1 of this book introduces a differential theory of school choice. In the existing public education system, this theory notes, most families' schooling options are defined by where parents can afford to live. Some families benefit mightily from this arrangement, while others suffer by equal proportions. The likely impact of a policy intervention such as school vouchers, then, probably depends on how each family fares within the current system. Vouchers are less likely to do as much for parents who already exercise choice within public education. To those who cannot afford the costs of moving to a neighborhood with strong public schools, however, vouchers may open up new, and valuable, private schooling options. Because race is such a potent force in housing markets that have created extraordinary inequalities in public education, a differential theory of choice predicts that the programmatic impacts of school voucher programs will differ markedly for African Americans and members of other ethnic groups.

In subsequent chapters, we examine the actual workings of inner-city school voucher programs to see whether they are consistent with our theory. Our test of this theory is based on voucher programs in several cities, which provided the most reliable, highest-quality data on the subject available. In many respects, school vouchers benefited African American students more than those of other ethnic backgrounds. Though the evidence is limited to small interventions in a few cities and to students who participated in a voucher program, the findings are quite consistent across sites. Chapter 2 summarizes the key features of the voucher programs and the design of their evaluations.

In chapter 3 we report the degree of selection or skimming among those who seek and use a voucher. Many observers have noted a strong propensity on the part of educational institutions to pick the best students available. To what extent did that occur in these voucher programs? Which low-income, inner-city families made use of the vouchers offered to them, and how successful were they in gaining admission to a preferred private school? In general, we observed a moderate, though not pronounced, amount of skimming.

Chapter 4 compares the public and private schools attended by urban, low-income students who applied for vouchers. We look at the differences in the resources available, the school climate, the amount and appropriateness of homework, and the extent of school-family communication. Students in public schools had access to a broader array of resources and programs, but those in the private sector attended smaller schools that had smaller classes and fewer disruptions. In addition, private school administrators and teachers maintained a higher level of communication with parents and assigned more homework. Many of these differences between public and private schools were especially large for African Americans.

In chapter 5 we examine some of the social consequences of school voucher programs. Proponents of vouchers imagine benefits from school choice that go well beyond improvements in student learning or parents' satisfaction with their child's school. They expect parents to become more engaged in their child's education and in their community, restoring the nation's supply of social capital. Voucher opponents tend to imagine different sorts of ripple effects. They expect students' self-esteem to suffer, their racial isolation to intensify, and political tolerance to erode. For the most part, we found few ripple effects, positive or negative.

Chapter 6 examines the impact of vouchers on student test scores. We found positive and statistically significant effects of attending a private school for African Americans. However, we did not find any evidence in any city that vouchers either increased or reduced the test scores of students from other ethnic backgrounds. Chapter 6 examines some plausible explanations for why vouchers improve the test scores of African American students but not those of students of other ethnicities. Ultimately, we were unable to identify any single magic bullet—or set of bullets. No one school characteristic or assembly of characteristics explained why the test scores of African Americans who switched from public to private schools improved—one reason to think that the underlying reason is both more general and deeply embedded in the racially discriminatory system of residential choice.

Perhaps the largest, and most consistent, impact observed in the three cities involves parent satisfaction rates. Chapter 7 shows that private school parents expressed significantly more satisfaction than their public school counterparts. We observed an especially high impact of private schooling on the satisfaction of African American parents.

In chapter 8 we conclude by considering whether large-scale programs would replicate the voucher effects we observed. The answer to that question, we note, depends both on the location of voucher programs and how they are structured. We recommend giving first consideration to well-funded, enduring voucher programs in central cities with high concentrations of African Americans. Such programs are no panacea for all the troubles in American education, but they may well help to close the education gap.

Acknowledgments

During the past six years, we have profited from the advice and assistance of a large number of talented, hardworking individuals. To begin, we wish to thank the principals, teachers, and staff of the private schools in New York City, Dayton, and Washington, D.C., who assisted in the administration of tests and questionnaires.

We also wish to thank the School Choice Scholarship Foundation (SCSF) in New York City, Parents Advancing Choice in Education (PACE) in Dayton, the Washington Scholarship Foundation (WSF) in Washington, D.C., the Children's Economic Opportunity (CEO) foundation in San Antonio, and the Children's Scholarship Fund (CSF) for cooperating fully in these evaluations. David Myers of Mathematica Policy Research served as co-principal investigator of the evaluation of the SCSF scholarship program. Daniel Mayer and other MPR staff also provided important assistance. Kristin Kearns Jordan, Tom Carroll, and other members of the SCSF staff assisted with data collection in New York City. John Blakeslee, Leslie Curry, Douglas Dewey, Laura Elliot, Heather Hamilton, Tracey Johnson, Daniel la Bry, John McCardell, Ethel Morgan, and Patrick Purtill of the Washington Scholarship Fund provided support in D.C. T. J. Wallace and Mary Lynn Naughton, staff members of Parents Advancing Choice in Education, provided valuable assistance with the Dayton evaluation.

Chester E. Finn Jr., Bruno Manno, Gregg Vanourek, and Marci Kanstoroom of the Fordham Foundation, Edward P. St. John of Indiana University, and Thomas Lasley of the University of Dayton lent valuable suggestions throughout various stages of research design and data collection in Dayton.

We thank William McCready, Robin Bebel, Kirk Miller, and other members of the staff of the Public Opinion Laboratory at Northern Illinois University for their assistance with data collection, data processing, conduct of the lottery, and preparation of baseline and Year I follow-up data. We are also grateful to Mike Gibson and Marc Tagliento for their help in securing family participation in the D.C. evaluation.

We especially appreciate the insights and assistance of co-principal investigators of the Edgewood evaluations, David Myers of Mathematica Policy Research, Jay P. Greene of the Manhattan Institute (who also was a co-investigator on the Cleveland evaluation), and Rudolpho de la Garza of Columbia University (formerly at the Tomas Rivera Institute at the University of Texas at Austin). Cara Olsen and Kathy Sonnenfeld, members of Mathematica Policy Research, made major contributions in the design, data collection, and analysis stages of the research in Edgewood. Daniel Mayer and Julia Chou, also from Mathematica Policy Research, were instrumental in preparing the New York City survey and test score data.

An earlier version of portions of this volume was presented at the Conference on Charter Schools, Vouchers, and Public Education held within the Taubman Center for State and Local Government at Harvard University's John F. Kennedy School of Government on March 9 and 10, 2000. The Program on Education Policy and Governance (PEPG) and the Manhattan Institute for Policy Research sponsored this conference. Funding for the conference was generously provided by the John M. Olin Foundation, the Annie E. Casey Foundation, the Thomas B. Fordham Foundation, and the Taubman Center for State and Local Government. We are deeply indebted to Chester E. Finn Jr. and Marci Kanstoroom for their assistance in preparing the conference. Papers presented at that conference have been published as Paul E. Peterson and David E. Campbell, eds., *Charters, Vouchers, and Public Education* (Brookings, 2001). Others who participated in the conference were Jeanne Allen, Alan Altshuler, Jeffrey Berry, Clint Bolick, John Brandl, Bruce Fuller, Howard Fuller, Charles Glenn, Scott Hamilton, Eric A. Hanushek, Mark Harrison, Bryan Hassel, Jennifer Hochschild, Caroline Minter Hoxby, Kristin Kearns Jordan, Thomas Kane, Lisa Graham Keegan, Elliot Mincberg, Michael Mintrom, Tom Mooney, James A. Peyser, David N. Plank, Richard Rothstein, Isabel Sawhill, and Kay Schlozman.

During the course of our research, we received helpful advice from William Carbonaro, Charles Franklin, Bruce Fuller, Jay P. Greene, Jeffrey Henig, Paul Hill, Jennifer Hochschild, Caroline Minter Hoxby, Christopher Jencks, Henry Levin, Jens Ludwig, George Mitchell, Terry Moe, Derek Neal, Donald Rock, Donald Rubin, Isabel Sawhill, Phillip Shively, David Weimer, and John Witte. Research assistance was provided by Samuel Abrams,

Matthew Charles, Joshua Cowen, Tina Elacqua, Brian Harrigan, Jennifer Hill, D. Zachary Hudson, Suzanne Petro, Juanita Riano, Paul Schlomer, Christine Sloper, and Martin West. Lilia Halpern, Thomas Polseno, Shelley Weiner, and Antonio Wendland provided administrative and staff assistance.

We appreciate the continuing support of Alan Altshuler, Director of the Taubman Center on State and Local Government in the Kennedy School of Government at Harvard University. We also express our gratitude to the following foundations, which have supported our research: Achelis Foundation, BASIC Fund, Bodman Foundation, Lynde and Harry Bradley Foundation, William Donner Foundation, the Thomas B. Fordham Foundation, Milton and Rose D. Friedman Foundation, Gordon and Laura Gund Foundation, John M. Olin Foundation, David and Lucile Packard Foundation, Smith-Richardson Foundation, Spencer Foundation, and the Walton Family Foundation. The methodology, data analyses, reported findings, and interpretations of findings are the sole responsibility of the authors of this book and are not subject to the approval of any of the program operators or of any foundation providing support for this research.

We wish to acknowledge the outstanding work of the Brookings Institution Press staff, with special thanks to Robert Faherty, Christopher Kelaher, Eileen Hughes, Janet Walker, and Becky Clark.

Portions of this research have appeared in the following publications: William G. Howell, Patrick J. Wolf, David E. Campbell, and Paul E. Peterson, "School Vouchers and Academic Performance: Results from Three Randomized Field Trials," *Journal of Policy Analysis and Management*, vol. 21 (Spring 2002), pp. 207–33; William G. Howell, Patrick J. Wolf, Paul E. Peterson, and David E. Campbell, "Raising Black Achievement: Vouchers in New York, Dayton, and D.C," *Education Matters*, vol. 1 (Summer 2001), pp. 46–53; William G. Howell, Patrick J. Wolf, Paul E. Peterson, and David E. Campbell, "The Effects of School Vouchers on Student Test Scores," in Paul E. Peterson and David E. Campbell, eds., *Charters, Vouchers, and Public Education* (Brookings, 2001); Paul E. Peterson and William G. Howell, "What Happens to Low-Income New York Students When They Move From Public to Private Schools," in Diane Ravitch and Joseph Viteritti, eds., *City Schools: Lessons from New York* (Johns Hopkins University Press, 2000); Paul E. Peterson, David Myers, William G. Howell, and Daniel Mayer, "School Choice in New York City," in Paul E. Peterson and Susan Mayer, eds., *Earning and Learning: How Schools Matter* (Brookings, 1999); Jay P. Greene, William G. Howell, and Paul E. Peterson, "Lessons from the Cleveland Scholarship Program," in Paul E. Peterson and Bryan C. Hassel, eds., *Learning from School Choice* (Brookings, 1998).

The
EDUCATION GAP

1

School Choice and American Democracy

Liberty, Equality, Education—the very woof of America's social fabric. All three had been spun into sturdy strands by the time the Constitution was ratified, laid down after the Civil War, and tightened by twentieth-century political discourse and social practice. Yet the tapestry that history has woven over and under these strands, though rich and colorful, remains unfinished, very much a work in progress.

The strongest—and greatest—of these strands is liberty. It was for liberty that a revolution was fought, a civil war waged, and a cold war endured. Early on, Americans freed themselves from rigid social hierarchies, excessive government constraints, and the compulsory practice of religion.[1] They created both a democratic polity and a dynamic economy of unmatched size and strength. It is no wonder that John Rawls, arguably the greatest American political philosopher of the twentieth century, placed liberty at the core of his theory of justice. In a just society, Rawls says, "each person is to have an equal right to the most extensive basic liberty compatible with a similar liberty for others."[2] The most powerful political slogans convey the same message: "Give me liberty or give me death," "Free at last," "A woman's right to choose."

The concept of political equality is almost as deeply embedded in American belief and practice. The American pilgrims spoke of equality before God. The Declaration of Independence called not only for the right to life and liberty but also to the "pursuit of happiness," a marvelously ambiguous phrase that nonetheless hints at some notion of equality of opportunity. The Constitution conferred an institutional structure on those revolutionary ideals.

Later, Thomas Jefferson gave them a material basis by purchasing the Louisiana Territory, opening up new opportunities by extending westward an agrarian republic of small, independent farmers. Under the Fourteenth Amendment to the Constitution, enacted after the Civil War to guarantee equal protection before the law, the concept of political equality was eventually enlarged to include minorities, women, and disabled individuals.

In some sense, though, inequalities are unavoidable. We cannot all jump as high as Michael Jordan; we cannot all speak as eloquently as Maya Angelou; nor can we all boast the intellect of Stephen Hawkins. Because of this, we cannot all partake in the rewards that these talented individuals enjoy. Which inequalities are acceptable and which require some kind of state correction remain a staple of public debate.

According to Rawls, a just society may tolerate inequalities that improve the lives of those who are the worst off. Rawls's "difference principle" stipulates that "social and economic inequalities are to be arranged so that they are both (a) to the greatest benefit of the least advantaged and (b) attached to offices and positions open to all under conditions of fair equality of opportunity."[3] The difference principle focuses on the welfare of the least advantaged, but it still tolerates vast differences in well-being. Even as technological change has improved the living standards of the poor, it has magnified the wealth of the privileged. The consequence? During both the nineteenth century and the closing decades of the twentieth, the welfare of the worst off steadily improved, while income inequality grew unabated. So, as the twenty-first century dawned, differences in income and wealth were wider in the United States than in most other industrial democracies.

For the most part, Americans have not felt much urgency about correcting such inequalities. The size of the American welfare state pales by comparison with that of most of its European counterparts. U.S. citizens do not have access to a state-run health-care system, nor do the unemployed receive benefits comparable to those of their peers abroad. U.S. taxpayers pay on average only one-third of their income to the government, while many Europeans pay as much as 40 to 50 percent.[4] When Americans speak of equality, they speak mainly of *equal opportunity*. Each citizen has a right to the pursuit of happiness, not a guarantee of its realization. As long as the starting line in the economic race is clearly drawn, those who can run fast or are lucky enough to find shortcuts may dash unrestrained to the finish line, well ahead of their competitors.

Equality, Education, and Race

American policymakers have settled on education as a primary tool to promote and protect the concept of equal opportunity. Though the U.S. Constitution does not mention education, the subject was very much on the mind of the nation's founders. John Adams, author of the Massachusetts constitution, inserted a paragraph requiring legislators "to cherish the interests of literature and the sciences, and all seminaries of them, especially the university at Cambridge, public schools, and grammar schools in the towns; to encourage private societies and public institutions."[5] The Northwest Ordinance, enacted in 1787, affirmed that "religion, morality and knowledge, being necessary to good government and the happiness of mankind, schools and the means of education shall forever be encouraged."[6] Judging by his tombstone inscription, Jefferson took more pride in founding the University of Virginia than he did in serving two terms as the nation's third president. Years later, the Freedmen's Bureau provided the rudiments of education to former slaves. And it was a case involving equality of education (*Brown* v. *Board of Education*) that launched the civil rights movement of the 1950s and 1960s.

Yet education's historical contribution to equal opportunity has been ambiguous at best. Although education for students between the ages of six and sixteen is now virtually universal, its quality varies markedly. Blacks and whites continue to attend very different schools. As late as 1996, for instance, approximately 70 percent of blacks remained in predominantly minority schools.[7] Education budgets also vary dramatically from state to state. In 1997 Connecticut and New Jersey spent $8,600 and $9,600 per enrolled pupil, respectively, while Mississippi and Utah got by on $4,000 and $3,800.[8] Within states, disparities among districts can be just as large. Even within big cities, more experienced teachers gravitate to more desirable schools, where they are better paid. The most disturbing gaps concern student achievement. Children of educated and well-to-do parents consistently outperform those from less advantaged backgrounds. A half-century after *Brown* v. *Board of Education*, the test scores of blacks and whites remain, on average, strikingly dissimilar—in technical language, differing by approximately one standard deviation, a statistical measure indicating that the average white student scores as high as an African American student who ranks among the top third of his or her racial group.

The differences in the test scores of blacks and whites have deep roots. Before the Civil War, very few slaves were taught to read. The Freedmen's Bureau opened schools for former slaves a few years after the war, but when Reconstruction ended in 1876, the responsibility for educating African Americans devolved to white southerners more interested in perpetuating the racial status quo than in enhancing the region's human capital. The first black high school in the South was not constructed until the 1920s. Nationwide, only 6 percent of young black adults in 1920 had received a high school education, compared with 22 percent of white adults of the same age.

Nearly 45 percent of young black adults had less than five years of elementary school, compared with 13 percent of whites of comparable age.[9]

Between 1910 and 1970, the percentage of African Americans living outside the South increased steadily. With the move northward came new opportunities. High school completion rates among young black adults jumped from 12 percent in 1940 to 58 percent in 1970 and, if official statistics are to be believed, continued upward to 88 percent by 1998.[10] But while educational attainment rates have improved, school quality has lagged behind. Most blacks continue to attend predominantly minority schools that have a greater incidence of violence and fewer opportunities to participate in extracurricular activities than their predominantly white counterparts.

Despite the transformations wrought by the civil rights movement, many schools today remain just as segregated as they were three decades ago. According to one study, 69 percent of African Americans attended predominantly minority schools in 1997, a 5-point increase since 1973. For Hispanics, the increase was even steeper—from 57 percent to 75 percent.[11]

The problems have not been confined to the South, the initial focus of both the civil rights movement and federal judicial and administrative efforts to integrate schools and neighborhoods. When civil rights activists turned their attention to Chicago and other cities of the North, they encountered strenuous opposition, and this time they lacked the backing of federal judges and marshals. The legal focal point was the predominantly African American Detroit public school system and the predominantly white suburban schools that surrounded it. Civil rights groups contended that the division was no less unconstitutional than the segregation outlawed in the South. But in 1974, in *Milliken* v. *Bradley,* the Supreme Court distinguished *de facto* segregation in the North from *de jure* segregation in the South. Suburban school districts in the North had never practiced the legalized racial segregation of the South; the segregation that had occurred was simply the result of families' private choices about whether to live in cities or suburbs. The Court ruled that the Constitution did not require integration across district lines,[12] and further integration of northern schools subsequently stumbled to a halt.[13]

If schools do a decent job of promoting equal opportunity, one would expect early gaps in the test scores of blacks and whites to attenuate over time. In fact, there is little sign that this happens. According to one careful analysis, test-score gaps increase as children progress through school: "About half of the total black-white math and reading gap at the end of high school can be attributed to the fact that . . . blacks learn less than whites who enter school with similar initial skills."[14] Nor do family background characteristics account for all the differences. During the 1990s, when black children were growing up in better-educated families, their test scores continued to fall, and the gap between blacks and whites continued to widen.

The economic benefits of eliminating the gap in test scores are substantial. As Christopher Jencks and Meredith Phillips have pointed out, young adult blacks in 1993 who scored above the median on test scores earned fully 96 percent as much as their white peers. The wage gap remained larger for blacks with lower test scores, but even those scoring between the 30th and the 50th percentile earned 84 percent of the amount earned by whites with similar scores. (By contrast, in 1964 these blacks earned only 62 percent of the income of similar whites.)[15] In other words, a key, perhaps *the* key, to solving the gross inequalities between blacks and whites in the Unites States is to narrow the racial gap in educational achievement.

Education and Liberty

While education may be a cornerstone of a free society, it remains compulsory for most children between the ages of six and sixteen. Other than the requirements to pay taxes and to register for military service at age 18, it is one of the few duties that the U.S. government imposes on its citizens. Americans need not vote, fill out census cards, notify the government of their address, or obtain a national registration card—but they must see that their children are schooled.

To do so, most Americans send their children to the public schools assigned to them by their local government. That is striking when one considers the emphasis that Americans place on the principle of freedom of choice in other areas. High school graduates choose their university, even though the government provides grants, loans, and tax breaks to defray the costs. Preschool services are tax deductible, but families can choose their care provider. Although the federal government pays the lion's share of Medicare costs, beneficiaries choose their doctors and hospitals. Yet when it comes to sending a child to primary or secondary public school, families—especially poor families—have not been allowed the prerogative to choose.

Origins and Development of Public Schools

Contrary to common belief, compulsory public education did not originate with the liberal ideals expressed during the American Revolution. The Land Ordinance of 1785 did set aside one section of land in sixteen for "the maintenance of public schools within the said township." But rather than signifying state operation, the word "public" simply implied communal instruction outside the home.[16] Benjamin Rush, an early advocate of public education, made that explicit when he proposed that "free, public" schools, funded in part by parental fees, be organized so that "children of the same religious sect and nation may be educated as much as possible together."[17] Thomas Paine went further. In *The Rights of Man*, Paine proposed compulsory, publicly financed education but recommended vouchers so that parents would have a choice of schools. To ensure compliance, "the ministers of every . . . denomination [would] certify . . . that the duty is performed."[18] As late as the 1830s, state-funded schools in Connecticut still charged tuition.[19]

Not until the 1840s did public schools become synonymous with state-funded and state-operated schools. The man usually credited with founding public education as we now know it in the United States, Horace Mann, a Massachusetts secretary of education and practicing Unitarian, expressed great concern about the papist superstitions of immigrants pouring into American cities. "How shall the rising generation be brought under purer moral influences," he asked, so that "when they become men, they will surpass their predecessors, both in the soundness of their speculations and in the rectitude of their practice?"[20] His answer, the public school, won the curious praise of the Congregationalist journal, the *New Englander*: "These schools draw in the children of alien parentage with others, and assimilate them to the native born . . . . So they grow up with the state, of the state and for the state."[21]

Although public schools originally were designed to impart a moral education to new immigrants, they quickly became an integral feature of American democracy. Locally elected school boards, whose members shared a single-minded commitment to education, were a key factor in their expansion. Unlike most other local governments, school boards had just one specific public responsibility and therefore one distinct mission: to promote public education. Many of the boards could collect taxes, and all had the power to campaign on behalf of local schools. The boards won widespread public support, in part because quality schools became bragging points for those eager to attract new residents to their growing communities.

The U.S. educational system soon became the world's largest. By 1910, more than three-quarters of the adult population had attended elementary school for at least five years, despite the fact that undereducated immigrants continued to pour out of Ellis Island. A secondary-education system quickly emerged, and by 1940 nearly 40 percent of young adults had graduated from high school.[22] Even as late as 1985, 84 percent of sixteen-year-olds in the United States attended high school, compared with 67 percent of their peers in France, 52 percent in Germany, 42 percent in the Netherlands, and 31 percent in Denmark. Not until the 1990s did high school completion rates in these countries surpass those in the United States.[23]

Southern schools, it is worth noting, lagged considerably behind U.S. national trends. During the antebellum period, most young people in the South received little formal education. While public schools flourished in other parts of the country, the Civil War and Reconstruction left the southern states despoiled and demoralized. Even today, educational attainment in the South—among whites as well as blacks—trails well behind that in other parts of the country. Only 65 percent of whites in Kentucky had a high-school diploma in 1990, compared with 77 percent of whites in Ohio, just across the Ohio River. And only 67 percent of adults in Arkansas had a high-school diploma, compared with 78 percent of those in the similarly rural but midwestern state of South Dakota.[24]

Private Schools

American private schools date from the colonial period. During the seventeenth and eighteenth centuries, Congregationalists, Presbyterians, and Episcopalians opened boarding schools to initiate young men into the ministry. Some grew into Ivy League colleges; others became exclusive secondary schools. While these early educational pioneers have attracted much attention and envy, in raw numbers they represent but a blip on the private education screen. The major expansion of private schools occurred in the middle of the nineteenth century, when Catholics, eager to maintain old-country practices and suspicious of the Protestant-dominated public schools, decided to establish their own system of education. By the opening of the twentieth century, approximately 11 percent of all students attended a private school, almost the same percentage as at the beginning of the twenty-first.

While the proportion of students enrolled in private schools as a whole has remained quite stable, the religious affiliations of the schools themselves have changed noticeably. The Catholic share of private school students, once 80 percent of the total, has slipped considerably. After Vatican II and the Kennedy presidency, Catholicism entered the religious mainstream, and public school practices no longer had as explicit a Protestant patina. In the parochial schools, meanwhile, many teaching nuns were replaced by salaried lay teachers, driving up Catholic school costs and tuition. Offsetting the decline in the number of Catholic schools has been a growing Protestant school presence—primarily in the form of self-designated "Christian schools"—which now accounts for nearly 20 percent of all private school enrollments.

Whether Catholic or Protestant, private schools typically are modest in size and limited in their resources. Nationwide, public schools spent, on average, $6,900 per pupil in 1998, while private school expenditures totaled just under $4,000.[25] In 1998–99, private schools paid their teachers, on average, only $25,000 a year, while public schools paid their teachers more than $40,000—over one-third more.[26] Exclusive, well-endowed private schools, which often are affiliated with mainline Protestant churches, are a rarity. In Washington, D.C., Sidwell Friends, a Quaker school, and the Episcopalian St. Albans enjoy great reputations, having educated the children of such political leaders as President Bill Clinton, Vice President Al Gore, and civil rights leader Jesse Jackson. But such schools are the exception. Most private schools historically have enjoyed very little prestige, so little, in fact, that at one point some states, such as Nebraska and Oregon, attempted to shut them down.[27]

Public-School Philosophy

Though a small, stable private sector holds steadfast, many Americans share what Stanford scholar Terry M. Moe refers to as a "public-school ideology."[28] They have an abiding faith in the idea of public education. They do not see public schools as interfering with personal liberties or constituting a burdensome part of a welfare state; rather, whether liberal or conservative, they cast their lot in favor of the expansion of state-financed and state-operated public schools. But while most Americans embrace public schools without much forethought, it is the duty of philosophers to square a nation's institutions with its political traditions. In the United States, it was John Dewey, America's most influential philosopher of education, who provided the rationale.

   Dewey realized that public schools fit uncomfortably within the liberal tradition inherited from the Declaration of Independence and the American Revolution. "In the eighteenth century philosophy we find ourselves in a very different circle of ideas," he wrote in *Democracy and Education*. Previously it was thought that "to give 'nature' full swing," inquiry had to be "freed from prejudice and artificial restraints of church and state." Admitting the force of those concerns, he posed a question: "Is it possible for an educational system to be conducted by a national state and yet the full social ends of the educative process not be restricted, constrained and corrupted?" Although he knew that the state was constrained by "tendencies . . . which split society into classes," he nonetheless suggested that the public school could "balance the various elements in the social environment, and . . . see to it that each individual [received] an opportunity to escape from the limitations of the social group in which he was born."[29] Democracy, according to Dewey, required that the government run schools in order to limit social and economic inequalities.

Dewey's hope that schools would minimize the effects of social hierarchies made little sense, however, at a time when public schools were controlled by local school boards. Communities shaped local schools, and community opinion, or at least its dominant element, was homogenous enough that the two were intimately intertwined. Critics charged that schools did little to change the social order,[30] and those critics were much closer to the nub of the matter than was Dewey with his hopeful philosophizing. But, over time, control of schools shifted from local school boards to more centralized and professional bureaucracies. By the end of the twentieth century, the public school better approximated the kind of state-run institution Dewey envisioned, capable of acting independently of the local social context in which schools, for good or ill, had once been embedded.

Centralization and Professionalization of American Education

Just as Dewey had hoped, the American school system became, in the years following his writings, increasingly uniform, centralized, comprehensive, and professional. Basic statistics reveal the powerful effects of that transformation: in 1900, 72 percent of all children ages five to seventeen who were not enrolled in a private school attended a public school; by 2000, 92 percent were enrolled. More telling, perhaps, is the average amount of time students attend school each year, which nearly doubled from 86 days in 1900 to 161 days in 1980. The number of students graduating from high school increased from 62,000 in 1900 to 2,341,000 in 1997.[31] Financial commitments to education increased just as dramatically, even when adjusting for inflation. Between 1920 and 1996, per-pupil expenditures climbed from $535 to $6,400.[32] Teacher salaries rose from less than $7,300 to more than $34,000. Between 1955 and 1998, the pupil-teacher ratio tumbled from 27:1 to 17:1.

The trend toward professional control of the education system proved no less impressive. In the 1920s, the mother of one of the authors taught public school in rural Minnesota, despite the fact that she had received only one year of "normal schooling" beyond her graduation from high school. In that time and place, her training was typical. In the 1980s, the mother of another author had to complete several years of graduate training in an accredited school of education in order to teach at a California public elementary school. She subsequently attended training sessions to keep abreast of the latest and most fashionable pedagogical theories and techniques.

Classroom teachers are not the only professionals in education receiving specialized training today. Curriculum designers, guidance counselors, psychologists, school librarians, and special educators are found in abundance.

Principals now are expected to have advanced degrees, and professionally trained superintendents, doctorate in hand, take the helm of most school districts.

As Americans moved from towns to metropolitan areas, smaller rural school districts were quickly consolidated. There were nearly 120,000 school districts in the nation in 1937; by 1998, the number had dropped to less than 15,000. Even through the 1990s, districts continued to steadily grow in size. In 1989, 650 school districts enrolled more than 10,000 students; a decade later, the number of such districts had increased to more than 800. Along with school districts, the financing of schools grew increasingly centralized. While schools relied on their local government for fully 82 percent of their funding in 1920, by 1997 only 45 percent of their funds came from the local government, the rest coming from state and federal coffers.

As school systems became larger and more centrally controlled, conditions became ripe for the emergence of strong teachers unions. The American Federation of Teachers (AFT), which was affiliated with the larger labor union movement (American Federation of Labor–Congress of Industrial Organizations, known as the AFL-CIO), struck big-city school systems in New York, Chicago, Detroit, and elsewhere in the 1960s and early 1970s. As the AFT won one collective bargaining victory after another, its enrollment swelled. Responding to the competition, the National Education Association (NEA), which for years had been dominated by administrators, dropped its antistrike, antiunion philosophy and became a powerful force working on behalf of teachers' rights and prerogatives. Ultimately, most large and moderate-sized school districts signed collective bargaining agreements with one of the two organizations. These contractual agreements formalized relationships among teachers, administrators, and other school personnel, further isolating schools from the communities in which they had once been embedded.[33]

The informal, lay-controlled, decentralized school system of John Dewey's day was further eclipsed by the actions of legislators and judges. Beginning in the 1970s, courts asked state legislatures to minimize funding inequalities among school districts. In 1974 a new federal law reinforced court orders demanding that schools address the particular educational needs of disabled children. Shortly thereafter, a combination of legislative and court actions spawned new programs for students who spoke little English. State legislatures, meanwhile, continued to give other schools new tasks, asking them to teach students to drive, guard their health, practice safe sex, and engage in public service. Courts ruled that schools could not ask students to salute the flag, pray in school, or conform to a dress code that infringed on their beliefs.

While parents and local school boards exercised significant control over public schools at the beginning of the twentieth century, by its end, they had to
compete with legislators, state and federal judges, teachers unions, and professional bureaucrats.

Varieties of Choice in American Education

As public schools became more centralized and more professional, many
groups, parents, and commentators began to criticize the education system
for limiting opportunities for individual choice. Public school systems have
responded by offering magnet schools, interdistrict public school choice,
charter schools, and tax credits for private education expenses.[34] In addition,
a number of publicly and privately funded school voucher initiatives have
been undertaken in various parts of the country. Before turning to vouchers,
the main focus of this book, we consider a variety of alternatives to conventional schooling arrangements.

The first major choice initiative emerged from the conflicts surrounding
desegregation in the 1960s. So unpopular was compulsory busing with many
Americans that the magnet school was developed as an alternative way of
increasing racial and ethnic integration. According to magnet school theory,
families could be enticed into choosing integrated schools by offering them
distinctive, improved education programs. Although the magnet idea was
initially broached in the 1960s, it was not until after 1984 that the magnet
school concept, supported by federal funding under the Magnet Schools
Assistance program, began to have a national impact. "Between 1984 and
1994, 138 districts nationwide received a total of $955 million" in federal
funds to implement this form of school choice.[35] By the early 1990s, more
than 1.2 million students attended 2,400 magnet schools in more than 200
school districts.[36] The magnet school concept, if taken to its logical conclusion, opens all public schools in a district to all families, allowing them to
select their preferred public school, subject to space constraints. Such programs, generally identified as open-enrollment programs, can be found at the
high-school and middle-school level in a few school districts.

Most studies of magnet schools and open-enrollment programs find positive effects on student learning.[37] Although scholars have questioned many of
these findings on the ground that the apparent effects were due to the prior
ability of students selected to attend magnet schools,[38] two studies that carefully addressed this issue still found positive effects.[39] In the East Harlem
community school district within New York City, the magnet school pro-

gram was expanded to give most parents within the community a choice of schools. Test scores climbed both within the magnet schools and within traditional neighborhood schools competing with the magnet schools.[40]

Although most magnet-school programs limit parents' choice of public schools to those within a particular school district, in a number of places public institutions outside the local school district are included. As early as 1985, Minnesota gave local school boards permission to allow students from outside their district to attend their school, although the program was restricted to students who would not adversely affect the racial integration of participating school districts.[41] By 1997, nearly 20,000 students were participating in the Minnesota program;[42] and similar programs operated in another sixteen states. Although many of these programs are too new to lend insight into the long-term effects of interdistrict choice, preliminary evidence from the Massachusetts program indicates that school districts losing students often make significant efforts to upgrade their curriculum in order to curtail their losses.[43]

While magnet schools and interdistrict enrollment programs limit parents' choice of schools to those operated by school boards, charter schools have expanded the options to include government-financed schools operated by nongovernmental entities. By 2000 thirty-four states and the District of Columbia had enacted charter-school legislation, and more than 400,000 students were attending nearly 1,700 charter schools.[44] Although the percentage of students in charter schools nationwide is still a small fraction of public school enrollment, in some places it is quite significant. For example, 4.4 percent of the students in Arizona were attending charter schools in 1997, and in the District of Columbia, 15 percent of all students attended charters in 2000.[45]

Charter school terminology varies by state, as does the legal framework under which these schools operate. Charter schools have two common characteristics: First, the entity operating the school is ordinarily not a government agency, although it may receive most of its operating revenue from the state or local school board. Second, charter schools do not serve students within a specific attendance boundary; instead, they recruit students from a large catchment area that may encompass traditional public schools. As a result, they must persuade parents that their offerings are superior to those provided by traditional public schools in their vicinity.

Studies have found that, on average, students attending charter schools are fairly representative of the general school population.[46] Most charter schools are popular with parents and substantially oversubscribed, although some have been closed for violating safety and education standards. Charter schools have been more successful than traditional public schools at attracting teachers who were educated at selective colleges and who received higher education in mathematics and science.[47] Whether students learn more in charter schools than traditional public schools has yet to be ascertained.

Some states allow tax deductions or tax credits that can be used to help pay the cost of a private education. In Minnesota, families earning under $33,500 per year can claim a tax credit of up to $1,000 per child ($2,000 per family) for such school-related expenses or the purchase of books and other educational materials, but not for private school tuition. Nearly 38,000 Minnesotans claimed the tax credit in 1998, averaging $371 per credit. Small state tax deductions for both tuition and educational expenses also are available for higher-income families.[48] In Arizona, taxpayers may receive a tax credit of up to $500 if they contribute to a foundation that provides scholarships to students attending private schools. In 1998, the program's first year, 5,100 Arizonans claimed the credit.[49]

That there are so many different varieties of school choice suggests that many Americans have become uncomfortable with the growing centralization and bureaucratization of their educational system. Yet all choice initiatives have provoked controversy, and none have been widely adopted. Still, school vouchers, the main focus of this book, remain the most far-reaching—and controversial—of all proposals to expand choice in education. It is therefore worth examining the theoretical underpinnings for what might, if fully implemented, constitute a fundamental restructuring of the country's educational system.

Theories of Choice

The nineteenth-century English philosopher John Stuart Mill suggested the first fully developed voucher proposal. Although he favored compulsory, publicly financed education, he insisted that families retain the right to choose their schools. His resolution of the conflict between society's need for an educated public and the individual's right to remain free of state compulsion is worth citing at length:

> Is it not almost a self-evident axiom, that the State should require and compel the education . . . of every human being who is born its citizen?
> . . . Were the duty of enforcing universal education once admitted, there would be no end to the difficulties about what the State should teach, and how it should teach, which now convert the subject into a mere battlefield for sects and parties, causing the time and labor which

should have been spent in educating, to be wasted in quarreling about education. . . . It might leave to parents to obtain the education and how they pleased, and content itself with helping to pay the school fees.[50]

Nearly a hundred years later, economist Milton Friedman, a future Nobel-prize winner, made much the same proposal:

Governments . . . could finance [education] by giving parents vouchers redeemable for a specified maximum sum per child per year if spent on 'approved' educational services. Parents would then be free to spend this sum and any additional sum on purchasing educational services . . . of their own choice.[51]

Friedman's ideas initially were put to ill use. In the wake of the *Brown* v. *Board of Education* decision, white southerners fought school desegregation with every legal means at their disposal—not only through delay, redistricting, and tokenism, but also by withdrawing white students from predominantly black public schools and placing them in white private schools. Courts, however, eventually struck down those practices, and today it is clear that publicly funded voucher schemes cannot pass constitutional muster if they permit private schools to discriminate on the basis of race or national origin.[52]

Tainted by their proposed use as a segregationist tool by Southern legislators in the 1950s and 1960s, vouchers languished until the 1970s when liberals proposed them as an antidote to overly bureaucratized big-city schools. Christopher Jencks, a Harvard University sociologist who worked on contract with the Office of Economic Opportunity, the agency charged with overseeing much of the War on Poverty, initially requested federal funding to establish six experimental choice programs.[53] Eventually, however, only one watered-down version, limited to public schools within a single district, was attempted—in Alum Rock, California.[54] Even there, teachers union opposition crippled the program, which eventually was abandoned. Another decade passed before the idea was resurrected.

Politics and Markets

In the early 1990s, Brookings Institution scholars John Chubb and Terry M. Moe revived public interest in school choice.[55] Their point of departure, however, was slightly different from that of Friedman, who was principally concerned with market efficiencies, and Jencks, who was interested in empowering society's least advantaged citizens. For Chubb and Moe, the problem with public education lay in its connection to politics. They found problematic what John Dewey took for granted. Concerned about the need to alleviate inequalities arising from birth or accident, Dewey, like many other progressives at the time, demanded that public schools operate independently from political forces. But in imagining how they would actually function, Dewey, ironically enough, fully expected schools to interact with and receive direction from their community. "What the best and wisest parent wants for his own child, that must the community want for all of its children. Any other ideal for our schools . . . destroys our democracy."[56]

But how, in practice, do communities express their will? Through group struggle, competitive elections, and political compromise, all forces that undermine school productivity, say Chubb and Moe. Schools perform best when they have a clear mission and the autonomy and flexibility to pursue it. When politics intrudes, which necessarily occurs when governments run schools, that mission is subordinated to narrow rules drafted by interest groups and school employees. The likely result, Chubb and Moe conclude, is school failure.

The problem may be particularly severe in big-city school systems. In the words of Howard Fuller, a former Milwaukee school superintendent, "The only way to change a large system is through pressure from the outside—for instance, by controlling the flow and distribution of the money. Otherwise, the internal dynamics of the system will make change impossible. It isn't a matter of individual teachers and administrators being unprofessional; it's the system itself, and how it is organized—unions, boards, federal and state regulations, mandates, court orders."[57]

In the marketplace, Chubb and Moe point out, businesses are free to define their mission as they see fit. Though consumers exert considerable influence on business decisions, they have no direct control of company operations.[58] Even in publicly held corporations, stockholders concede most operational authority to managers, holding them accountable only for the bottom line. While these managers must abide by laws and regulations, they have a strong incentive to search for the most efficient way of satisfying the consumer.

With vouchers, parents can choose schools that best address the needs of their child. Meanwhile, schools will compete with one another and come under consistent pressure to improve their services and develop more effective techniques for meeting customer demand. Bad schools, presumably, will lose customers—unless they quickly find ways to adapt and improve. Good schools, meanwhile, will flourish, and over time new schools will appear. In short, the promise of vouchers is the introduction of autonomy, flexibility, and innovation into public education.

Social Capital Theory

As the Friedman and Chubb-Moe formulations make clear, school choice proposals derive from a well-established theory of markets. Yet the argument for school vouchers is also rooted in another more recently developed set of ideas, known as social capital theory.[59] Social capital is generally understood as consisting of the resources generated by the routine interaction among people in a well-functioning community.[60] Social capital was once so abundant that it, like the air we breathe, was taken for granted. Dense social networks once thrived in small-town America and in ethnically homogeneous urban neighborhoods. Residents regularly saw and spoke with one another in shops, churches, and community recreation halls. Young people congregated under the supervision of an active and vibrant adult community. Schools forged close connections with parents, and parents communicated frequently among themselves. All of that, presumably, redounded to the benefit of students.

Indiana University political scientist Elinor Ostrom argues that social capital helps public servants perform their duties more effectively. The police can do a better job of preventing crime if citizens, too, monitor the goings-on in their community.[61] Sanitation engineers find it easier to collect the garbage if citizens check to see that their neighbors toss trash in cans instead of the gutters. And students learn more if parents and teachers work together. For services that are coproduced by government employees and citizens, social capital is a vital resource.[62]

It is a matter of some concern, then, that the nation's reserves are being depleted. According to Harvard political scientist Robert Putnam, adult engagement in community-building activities has steadily decreased over the past fifty years. Not only are groups such as the Elks and Kiwanis on the decline, but people rarely get together to play cards, share a meal, or attend ice-cream socials. Televised professional sports, long bouts on an exercise machine with headphones blaring, and video games have replaced community baseball and local theater productions. Suburban shopping malls and megastores supplant Main Street, where neighborhood connections once occurred. The consequences, according to Putnam, include mounting public distrust of one another and government ineffectiveness, especially when services depend on mutual cooperation.[63]

The decline of social capital may have particularly deleterious consequences for education. As urban neighborhoods have become increasingly anonymous and suburbs have replaced small towns, schools have grown increasingly disconnected from the neighborhoods they serve. Schools' financial base has shifted from local property taxes to state income and sales taxes. Government regulations, bureaucratic requirements, and court orders have established a more defined relationship between school officials and parents, pushing the latter to the periphery of the educational process. Out of concern for student safety, many schools allow parents in school buildings only under carefully controlled circumstances. And all of these developments have been particularly pronounced in urban schools serving low-income communities.

If declining social capital is the problem, then school choice may provide a solution. If private school communities are voluntarily constructed as parents and schools choose each other, then a commonality of interest may provide a basis for mutual support and continuing interaction. Indeed, the very term "social capital" was coined in a study that found private schools to be more effective than public schools.[64] University of Chicago sociologist James Coleman and his colleagues accounted for the higher performance of students in Catholic schools by noting the social capital generated when parents gather at religious services, bingo parties, Knights of Columbus meetings, fundraising events, and other gatherings. Although those communal occasions had no ostensible educational content, they provided a positive foundation for student learning.

School Choice: Key Questions

Although both market and social capital theorists present persuasive arguments on behalf of school choice, vouchers remain extremely controversial. The resistance they have encountered is due in part to citizens' long familiarity with public schools as well as the opposition of various interest groups, most notably teachers unions. There also remain important questions about how school choice might work in practice. The five concerns that will receive the most attention in the ensuing chapters are as follows:

—Parents lack the information necessary to choose schools wisely.

—Choice will increase educational stratification.

—Choice precludes adequate attention to the needs of disabled students.

—Choice does not improve student achievement.

—Choice will contribute to racial isolation, political intolerance, and the unconstitutional establishment of religion by government.

Information about Schools

In a well-functioning market economy, most consumers are able to make intelligent choices. People usually buy shoes that fit, food that is edible, and cars that do not immediately break down. One need not be a cobbler, a farmer, or an auto mechanic to make sensible choices among the alternatives available. But schools may be different. Education is a slow, painstaking process that takes years to complete; only in the long run can one discern the depth of knowledge gained. At any given point in time, parents may not know what is happening in the classroom, whether their children are learning, or how to tell if they are not.

When useful information is unavailable, parents may divine the quality of a school from the appearance of the students attending it, the exhibition of new computers, the quality of the sports team, or some other consideration that may have little academic content. According to education sociologist Amy Stuart Wells, when parents in the St. Louis area were given a chance to send their child to a school outside the central city, "not one of the [eleven] transfer" parents she interviewed "actually went to visit a county district before listing their top three choices." She concluded that their choice of school was based more "on a perception that county is better than city and white is better than black, not on factual information about the schools."[65]

Statewide testing and accountability schemes can help current and prospective parents learn about the quality of a school by providing detailed information on the performance of the school's students. Nonetheless, summary statistics can be quite deceiving—a school may work well for average students but not for those with special needs or with advanced aptitudes— and annual changes in test scores may be influenced as much by random fluctuations from one year to the next as by the instruction provided.[66]

Even if families have adequate information about their options, others may not. According to a group of British scholars, the "unequal sophistication of parents as choosers in the educational marketplace bodes ill for educational equality."[67] Such concerns may be exaggerated. Not everyone needs to be fully informed in order for all to benefit from an education system based on parental choice. Busy people buy their groceries hurriedly, paying little attention to price, while a neighbor with more time painstakingly examines quality and price. Because producers in a competitive market price their products for the marginal customer, busy folk enjoy the benefits of their persnickety neighbors.[68] Some empirical studies suggest that markets become competitive when between 10 percent and 20 percent of consumers are informed.[69] After examining school-choice programs in New Jersey and New York, Mark Schneider and his colleagues concluded that it requires only "a subset of parents" to "be informed about . . . their schools" in order for an effective educational market to emerge.[70]

Even if families had access to reliable information, would they choose schools for the right reasons? A Carnegie Foundation report argues, "When parents do select another school, academic concerns are not central to the decision."[71] The problem may be particularly severe with low-income families. A Twentieth Century Fund report observes that low-income parents are not "natural 'consumers' of education . . . [Indeed], few parents of any social class appear willing to acquire the information necessary to make active and informed educational choices."[72] Writer Nicholas Lemann made much the same point more provocatively: when a major impediment to the achievement of poor children is "their parents' impoverishment, poor education, lax discipline and scant interest in education," it is absurd to think that the same parents will become "tough, savvy, demanding education consumers" once they have the right to choose.[73]

The issue is important, because parents need to select schools for the right reasons if their choices are to enhance school productivity. In the ensuing chapters, we provide extensive information about the reasons why parents initially choose and stay with a school and, more generally, about how low-income parents assess the public and private schools their children attend.

Selection and Stratification

More problematic than the possibility that parents will make ill-informed decisions is the possibility that schools, rather than parents, exercise choice in an education marketplace. If so, vouchers may further fragment and stratify the country's educational system as a handful of private schools attract the best and brightest students while leaving public schools to contend with an especially unmotivated and disadvantaged population. According to Richard Kahlenberg, "privatization under most circumstances will only further segregate the schools by race and class because the 'choice' that advocates talk about ultimately resides with private schools rather than with students."[74] Some schools will attract hordes of applicants, and they may cull their list to select the most talented. Less reputable schools, forced to accept the remainder, may spiral downward. "The incentives are clear," says Harry Brighouse: when British schools have a choice, they "are all pursuing . . . able, well-motivated, and middle-class students."[75]

Examining a school-choice program in New Zealand, Edward Fiske and Helen Ladd observe a movement of students to high-status schools from those with high proportions of minorities and economically disadvantaged students. "Just as parents have seized upon their new right to select the schools their children attend, so individual schools have taken advantage of their self-governing status to become more aggressive in marketing themselves."[76] But defenders of the New Zealand choice program say that the country's schools are no more stratified than they were under the previous neighborhood school system.[77]

Whatever the situation in New Zealand, the seriousness of the problem depends on the specific features of a school-choice program. If vouchers are made available only to low-income residents and if new schools form in response to changes in parent demand, the problem may be mitigated. Chapter 3 considers whether choices by parents and schools in voucher programs serving low-income families contribute to a more stratified education system.

Needs of Disabled Students

To the extent that the selection process in a choice system adversely affects lower-performing students, disabled children would seem to be at the greatest disadvantage. According to federal law, disabled students must be educated in a setting that suits their needs. It is unclear, however, how the law might be enforced in an education system based on parental choice. If disabled children are not accepted into many schools, the private choices of parents and school administrators may only reinforce their isolation. "Choice programs often operate in a way that is either directly or indirectly exclusionary" of those with disabilities, says Laura Rothstein.[78] Such students, if taught separately, are expensive to educate, and they may distract other students and teachers if taught in regular classrooms. As a result, "schools face a disincentive to provide well for [these] students."[79] Even if a school opens its doors to disabled students and serves them well, it may encounter new problems. As one educator argued, "You work hard, you develop an area, you get known as a good school for [special needs students] and so what happens?—you're flooded with [special needs] kids."[80] Yet some moderate learning disabilities may be as much the result of a poor match between a student and a particular school as an inherent characteristic of the student. If so, school choice may help meet the needs of such students. Chapter 3 explores the impact of school choice on children with special needs.

Student Achievement

Market theories predict that students will receive a better education when schools are forced to compete; social capital theory predicts a higher level of educational coproduction by schools and families when schools foster close relations with their community. In practice, though, school choice may yield few, if any, gains in student productivity. Some researchers think that learning is more a function of genetic inheritance, family environment, and the influence of a child's peer group than of any instruction teachers provide, no matter how adequately outfitted a school may be.[81] Others argue that private schools are no better at educating students than public schools; observed differences in the test scores of the two instead derive entirely from self-selection mechanisms. In chapters 4 through 7, we review that debate, present new evidence regarding the kinds of schools that voucher users attend, and estimate the effect of a private education on student achievement.

Racial Isolation, Intolerance, and Constitutionality

Schools do more than teach math and reading; they also prepare citizens to participate in a democracy. School choice, however, may only encourage racial isolation and intolerance. Says former *New Republic* editor Michael Kelly, "Public money is shared money, and it is to be used for the furtherance of shared values, in the interests of *e pluribus unum*. Charter schools and their like . . . take from the *pluribus* to destroy the *unum*."[82]

In the words of David Berliner, dean of Arizona State's college of education, "Voucher programs would allow for splintering along ethnic and racial lines. Our primary concern is that voucher programs could end up resembling the ethnic cleansing . . . in Kosovo."[83] Some of this rhetoric may be dismissed as scare tactics. Elected officials are no more likely to turn over school dollars to extremist groups than they are to allow airlines to fly unregulated or meat to be marketed without inspection. As RAND scholar Paul Hill points out, "In the long run, schools in a publicly funded choice system will be public because they'll be regulated."[84] Still, some believe the government needs to operate schools directly, to ensure that democratic values are taught. Princeton theorist Amy Gutmann puts it this way: "public, not private, schooling is . . . the primary means by which citizens can morally educate future citizens."[85] Or, in the words of Felix Frankfurter, writing the Supreme Court majority opinion in *Minersville Board of Education* v. *Gobitis* in 1940, "We are dealing here with the formative period in the development of citizenship . . . . Public education is one of our most cherished democratic institutions."[86] We examine this question in chapter 5.

Regardless of their impact, vouchers may simply be unconstitutional. Some have argued that any kind of financial aid to religious schools contravenes the First Amendment's prohibition on the "establishment of religion"; others reply that no "establishment" occurs as long as parents can choose between secular and religious schools. Lower courts have reached inconsistent decisions on the question, and the Supreme Court has yet to issue a definitive ruling. In chapter 8, we discuss how our empirical findings bear on constitutional issues.

School Choice by Residential Selection

These topics—the capacity of parents to make informed decisions; selection effects; the needs of disabled students; student achievement; and tolerance, racial isolation, and constitutional requirements—provoke impassioned debate. But despite the energy brought to the discussion, a simple fact often goes unmentioned: most Americans already have a choice of schools. Families pick schools when they decide where to live. School choice is not an abstract vision of the future; it is deeply embedded in contemporary practice. School vouchers would not so much introduce choice in education as reduce its dependence on housing markets.

Thus we offer in this book another way of thinking about school choice—a differentiated theory of choice, so to speak, one that expects new forms of school choice to have different impacts for different groups in society. According to this theory, new educational opportunities will most benefit those groups that cannot exercise choice in the residential market.

Both sides in the debate on school choice have a vested interest in overlooking school choice by residential selection. It is convenient for many choice advocates to ignore the choice of schools that families make every time they purchase a home or rent an apartment. If choice already exists, why should vouchers be expected to produce large productivity gains? Many of those critical of school vouchers are no less reluctant to admit that the U.S. education system, as currently structured, is a choice-based system. Many defenders of public education presume the existence of common schools in which all children are educated together regardless of their race, creed, household income or parents' occupations. But public schools in fact serve highly differentiated populations. What is similar about the types of education offered in New York's New Rochelle and South Bronx? California's Palo Alto and East Palo Alto? Massachusetts's Concord and Dorchester?

Because space in the United States is plentiful, at least by European and Asian standards, school choice by residential location is especially potent. Americans have always moved to get what they wanted—whether it was Daniel Boone, with his constant urge to move still further West to avoid the settlers arriving just behind him; the Mormons in their flight to the Salt Lake desert to escape persecution; the multitudes of immigrants who passed through Ellis Island on their way to destinations throughout the country; or city residents who shifted to suburbia to avoid urban grit and decay.

School choice by residential location is more prevalent today than ever before simply because families now have more options about where to live. A half-century ago, proximity to work, more than any other factor, influenced the attractiveness—and thus the average cost per square foot—of residential locations, especially within metropolitan areas. But when highways replaced railroads as the primary mode of transportation, employment opportunities spread to the suburbs. As job opportunities dispersed, local amenities became the primary determinant of housing prices, and one of the most important amenities was the neighborhood school.[87] In 1993, 39 percent of parents with children in school said they considered the local school when selecting a place to live.[88] Actual behavior seems consistent with parental responses to survey questions. Communities with exceptional schools command relatively high housing prices; as the quality of local schools deteriorates, housing prices fall.[89]

The degree of school choice by residential selection varies across metropolitan areas. In the Miami area, for example, choice is restricted by the fact that one school district serves the entire metropolitan area, whereas more than 100 school districts serve the Boston metropolitan area. When residential choice is greater, schools are better. In metropolitan areas with more school districts, students take more academic courses and spend more time on homework, and in addition, classes are more structured and disciplined. Moreover, parents are more involved with schools, student test scores are higher, and sports programs are given less emphasis.[90]

Although choice by residential selection conforms to market theory, promising efficiency and productivity gains, it does not guarantee equal educational opportunity. Only those willing and able to pay the price receive the educational benefit of better schools. Low-income families do not have the earning power to buy into a neighborhood with high-quality schools. Quite the opposite—they often can afford a home or apartment only because it is located in a poorer neighborhood with lower-quality schools. Ironically, when a neighborhood serving a low-income community improves, land values rise and poor families often are displaced.

Since housing purchases constitute a large capital investment, residential selection is especially inegalitarian. When Britain created comprehensive schools in place of academically selective grammar schools in the 1960s, "selection by mortgage replaced selection by examination." The results may be unfortunate, researchers worry, because access to a college preparatory education is now "closed for many bright working class boys and girls."[91]

Residential Selection and the Education Gap

In the United States, African Americans have the least residential choice. To begin with, they generally earn less than other groups. In 1998, black families with two children had a median annual household income of $25,351, compared with $28,330 for Hispanic households and $40,912 for white households.[92] Income, however, only partially determines access to credit markets, which is necessary to maximize residential choice. Wealth, the accumulated assets of the household, also is critical, and there the differences are even more dramatic. In 1995, the median net worth for white households was nearly $50,000, compared with little more than $7,000 for black and Hispanic households.[93] The net effect is to relegate blacks more than any other ethnic group to more racially homogeneous neighborhoods.[94]

Still other signs indicate that African Americans often get the short end of the stick in the residential marketplace. Fully 72 percent of whites own their home, compared with just 47 percent of African Americans.[95] African Americans also are less likely to secure mortgage loans. During the 1990s, African Americans nationwide were twice as likely as whites and 33 percent more likely than Hispanics to be denied a loan.[96] In New York, 29 percent of the loan applications of African Americans are turned down, compared with 15 percent of applications of whites; in Washington, D.C., the figures for the two groups are 14 and 6 percent, respectively.[97]

African Americans also pay considerably higher housing costs, as a percentage of their incomes, than do whites. Nineteen percent of African Americans, compared with 13 percent of whites, devote more than 40 percent of their income to housing costs.[98] Their returns on their housing investments, meanwhile, are much lower. Minority populations are especially likely to live in urban and suburban areas that are substandard and burdened by crime, environmental degradation, and inferior schools. Amenities that middle-class people take for granted, such as banks, supermarkets, and stores that provide basic goods and services, are scarce in low-income minority neighborhoods. Simply put, it is difficult to enjoy a middle-class lifestyle in a poor minority neighborhood.[99]

African Americans are four times more likely than whites to report physical problems with their housing unit;[100] they are more likely to report noise and traffic problems near their home;[101] and they are almost twice as likely to claim that crime is a problem in their neighborhood.[102] According to one careful study, "race is still an important factor that influences housing options and residential choice. No matter what their educational or occupational achievement or income level, all blacks are exposed to higher crime rates, less effective educational systems, higher mortality risks, and more dilapidated surroundings because of their race."[103]

Surely, part of the reason that African Americans live in less desirable neighborhoods is that their economic resources are more limited. But racial discrimination by real estate agents, local residents, and banks also can influence the residential choices presented to African Americans. Studies suggest that banks are less likely to offer loans to blacks than whites with comparable financial portfolios. According to an examination of lending practices in Boston, for example, "minority applicants with the same economic and property characteristics as white applicants would experience a denial rate of 17 percent rather than the actual white denial rate of 11 percent."[104]

The net result of economic factors and racial discrimination is a highly segregated housing market. Eight in ten African Americans live in neighborhoods where they are the majority, despite the fact that they constitute just 12 percent of the population nationwide.[105] Residential segregation is especially pronounced in metropolitan regions. On one "segregation index" that ranges from zero (indicating perfectly representative proportions of African Americans and whites) to one hundred (indicating complete segregation), in 1980 Washington, D.C., scored 79 and New York City scored 75.[106] In all U.S. metropolitan areas, two-thirds of African Americans live in central cities, compared with just 40 percent of whites; one-third of African Americans, compared with 60 percent of whites, inhabit surrounding suburbs.[107]

How do such factors affect African Americans' ability to exercise school choice through residential selection? According to one national survey, 45 percent of white parents said that they "moved into [their] neighborhood at least in part because of the quality of the public schools."[108] In contrast, only 35 percent of Hispanics and just 22 percent of blacks did so. What is more, white and Hispanic parents were better able than African American parents to leverage their economic resources to send their child to a desired public school. Whereas roughly 40 percent of whites and Hispanics with lower incomes claimed to have moved to a neighborhood because of the quality of its public schools, 60 percent of those with higher incomes said that they did. The percentage of blacks who chose their neighborhood because of its schools, however, did not increase with income. At both high and low income levels, only about one-quarter of African Americans stated that they selected their neighborhood because of its public schools. For many black Americans, school choice by residential selection simply does not exist.

It should be no surprise, then, that public schools inherit the racial inequality that pervades the housing market. "A considerable portion of existing school segregation in metropolitan areas is associated with segregated housing patterns," notes Duke University professor Charles Clotfelter. "Combined with the Supreme Court's decisions in the 1974 *Milliken* v. *Bradley* case, this residential segregation virtually guarantees public school segregation in urban America for the foreseeable future."[109] The educational consequences can be devastating. According to one national survey, only 23 percent of students at urban high-poverty schools read at the basic level, compared with 46 percent of students in high-poverty nonurban areas. Nationwide, the black-white test-score gap, historically large, widened even more during the 1990s. As columnist William Raspberry put it, "Poor children desperately need better education. Yet the schools they attend—particularly in America's overwhelmingly black and brown inner cities—may be the least successful of all public schools."[110]

Most Americans, meanwhile, remain committed to a system of educational choice based on place of residence. Attempts to cut the link between the two provoked some of the greatest turbulence in American educational history: the school busing controversy of the early 1970s. Since school choice by residential selection gave white families access to better schools while relegating black students to relatively poor schools, some state and federal judges ruled that educational equality could be achieved only by busing children across neighborhood lines.[111] The ensuing uproar, and occasional violence, revealed the extent to which school choice by residential selection and an enduring belief in the value of neighborhood schools are embedded in the American political ethos.

The political advantages of school choice by residential selection are considerable. Not only does it serve the interests of the prosperous, but it does so without offending their political sensibilities. Were the children of the rich explicitly directed to good schools and the children of the poor to rotten ones, it would be both unconstitutional and a political embarrassment to those who profess the public schools to be the main vehicle for achieving equality of opportunity. Like the formally segregated school system of the South, such an arrangement eventually would break down. But when school choice derives from residential choice, the pretense of equal educational opportunity is preserved. Schools, at least in principle, remain open to all children—rich and poor, black and white, immigrant and native, healthy and disabled, capable and challenged. All that is required is that a child's family live within the appropriate community.

For all these reasons, new forms of choice may be expected to have differential effects by racial group. Among those families that already live in a neighborhood with good public schools and enjoy a broad array of education options, the marginal benefits of—and political support for—school vouchers should be quite small. But where residential patterns yield poor educational options, the demand for vouchers should escalate and the impact of a voucher program may prove to be much larger.

Perhaps that is the reason that, according to many polls, blacks are more likely to support school vouchers than other ethnic groups. In one 1995 survey, African American parents were 4 percentage points more likely to support vouchers than Hispanics and 12 percentage points more likely than whites.[112] Those findings were confirmed by a 2000 national survey of black and white Americans conducted by the Joint Center for Political and Economic Studies. Fifty-seven percent of African Americans, compared with 49 percent of the adult population generally, said that they supported school vouchers; 74 percent of blacks with children and 75 percent of blacks under the age of 35 supported the policy.[113] Furthermore, 67 percent of low-income, inner-city parents said that they would be interested in leaving their public school to attend a private school, compared with 52 percent of public school parents in general.[114]

In the following pages we offer another way of thinking about school choice in American public education. Contrary to what is often assumed, school choice is not new, but, for most white Americans, an integral part of the existing educational system. Middle-class families, which have the financial wherewithal to move to better school districts, enjoy a considerable range of options. Even if their choice of school does not conform to the ideal prescribed by market theorists, they have many more options than the African American poor, who generally are consigned to schools that serve highly segregated low-income neighborhoods. Because racial inequities pervade the U. S. housing market, this system of educational choice through residential selection operates contravenes the ideal of equal opportunity that the nation espouses. Because vouchers can break the link between place of residence and schooling options, we should expect African American families, who fare worst in housing markets, to be the most pleased with and to receive the greatest benefits from school choice.

In the pages to follow, we look at the manifold ways in which the workings of school voucher programs affect low-income families. In some respects we find similar results across ethnic groups. For example, we find that low-income families of all ethnic groups report a better educational climate when they have a choice of school. But in other important respects, particularly with regard to student achievement, we find that school choice has the greatest impact on African American students. Our findings, we believe, are of particular interest because they derive from the results of randomized experiments. The importance of that fact and the details of our research methodology are the subjects to which we now turn.

2

Evaluating Voucher Programs

In 1990, the only data available on school choice came from an experimental public program conducted during the early 1970s in Alum Rock, California; and even this program did not give families a voucher to attend private schools. But in the next few years, new publicly and privately funded voucher programs for low-income families began in Milwaukee, Cleveland, New York City, Dayton, Charlotte, Indianapolis, San Antonio, Washington, D.C., and the state of Florida. In addition, another private program offered nearly 40,000 vouchers to students across the nation. Between 1990 and 2000, the number of students using vouchers to attend private schools climbed from about 5,000 to more than 60,000.[1] Nearly 50,000 of these students currently participate in 68 privately funded voucher programs and another 12,000 participate in three publicly funded programs.[2] Table 2-1 describes key characteristics of several of these programs.

Evaluations of some of the programs, especially those that are privately funded, provide answers to questions that have long been matters of speculation. Free of many of the political constraints that limit the flexibility of public programs, the design of several private programs allows researchers to conduct rigorous evaluations. In this chapter we summarize the current array of pilot programs and discuss the methodologies employed to evaluate them. Although the research reported in this book focuses mainly on privately funded initiatives, we first describe the main features of the better-known, publicly funded programs in the cities of Milwaukee and Cleveland and the state of Florida.

Table 2-1. *Characteristics of School Choice Programs for Low-income Families*

Location	Sponsor	Religious schools included	Grades	First school year	Initial enrollment	2000–01 enrollment	Number of schools 2000–01	Maximum payment in 2000–01 dollars	Selection method
Milwaukee	State of Wisconsin	Yes	preK–12	1990–91	341	9,638	103	5,326	Lottery
Indianapolis	ECCT[a]	Yes	K–8	1991–92	746	2,387	82	1,000	First-come[b]
Milwaukee	PAVE[c]	Yes	K–12	1992–93	2,089	819	52	1,000 (elementary) 1,500 (high)	First-come
San Antonio	CEO[d]	Yes	1–8	1992–93	930	1,319	62	4,000	First-come
Washington, D.C.	WSF[e]	Yes	K–12[f]	1993–94	30	1,300	116	2,000 (elementary) 3,000 (high)	Lottery
Cleveland	State of Ohio	Yes	K–8	1996–97	1,996	3,900	67	2,500[h]	Lottery
New York City	SCSF[g]	Yes	1–5	1997–98	1,200	1,650	216	1,400	Lottery
Dayton	PACE[h]	Yes	K–12	1998–99	542	680	42	1,785 (elementary) 2,300 (high)	Lottery
Florida	State of Florida	Yes	K–12	1999–00	146	52	2	3,500	Lottery
Charlotte	CSF[i]	Yes	2–8	1999–00	388	438	52	1,700	Lottery
U.S.	CSF[i]	Yes	K–12[j]	1997–98	1,000	40,000	7,000	1,700	Lottery

a. Educational Choice Charitable Trust.
b. Program enrollment in Indianapolis is supplemented with periodic lotteries.
c. Partners Advancing Values in Education.
d. Children's Educational Opportunity.
e. Washington Scholarship Fund, Inc.
f. Students must be in grades K through 8 to begin the Washington Program.
g. School Choice Scholarships Foundation.
h. Parents Advancing Choice in Education.
i. Children's Scholarship Fund.
j. Once awarded a scholarship, all students are guaranteed continued assistance for three additional years. However, the first-year scholarship must be awarded while the student is enrolled in grades K through 8.

Publicly Funded Voucher Programs

No publicly funded voucher program offers all students within a political jurisdiction the opportunity to attend the private school of their choice. All are limited in size and scope, providing vouchers only to students who come from low-income families, who attend "failing" public schools, or who lack a public school in their community. Nonetheless, these programs have created tremendous political controversy in courts, legislatures, and the media—an indication that major interests are at stake.

Milwaukee

In 1990, the Wisconsin state legislature authorized the first state-funded, urban school voucher initiative, the product of an alliance of Republican officials and black leaders in Milwaukee.[3] Previously, Republican governor Tommy Thompson had introduced several voucher proposals in the legislature, only to see them fail in the face of opposition from teachers unions. Black leaders in Milwaukee had been seeking a separate school district for inner-city neighborhoods, but that too had been blocked by teachers unions and the Milwaukee school board. Thompson and black leaders in Milwaukee found common ground in a law that allowed low-income families to receive vouchers to attend private, secular schools.[4]

The result was a very limited venture. To be eligible, families had to qualify for the federal food stamp program. The amount of the voucher was limited to $2,500, which families could not supplement with their own resources. Only secular private schools could participate, despite the fact that nearly 90 percent of the private schools in the city had a religious affiliation. No more than half of the student body attending any private school could receive a voucher. Initially, only 1 percent of the public school population in Milwaukee could participate in the program; two years later, the cap was raised to 1.5 percent. If the number of applicants to a school exceeded the number of available spaces, the school was required to admit students by lottery. Because of such restrictions, six years after its inauguration the program included only 1,600 voucher students attending twenty private schools. A research team at the University of Wisconsin evaluated the first four years.[5] A Harvard-based research team and a Princeton economist conducted secondary analyses (see page 42).[6]

In 1996, Wisconsin expanded the program. Not only did it lift various technical restrictions and allow the distribution of vouchers to up to 15 percent of the public school population, it also opened the program to religious schools. The inclusion of religious schools was challenged in court, delaying implementation of the expanded program. In 1998, in a 4-to-2 decision, the Wisconsin Supreme Court ruled the expanded program constitutional, and in November of that year the U.S. Supreme Court allowed the decision to stand without explicit review.[7] After passing constitutional muster, the larger-scale voucher intervention began in the fall of 1998. By 2000, approximately 10,000 students were receiving as much as $5,326 each to attend more than 100 private schools. The Legislative Audit Bureau of the state of Wisconsin conducted a limited evaluation of the larger program, and other research has assessed the program's impact on Milwaukee public schools.[8]

Cleveland

The Cleveland Scholarship Program, established by the state of Ohio in 1996, incorporated religious schools from the beginning. By the time the state legislature considered the voucher bill, the reputation of Cleveland's public schools had fallen to an unprecedented low. In 1995 a state judge had declared the local school board unfit to govern the schools and handed direct control to the state. Not until 1999 did the state give authority back to the city. It was in this context that David Brennan, an energetic Republican party fundraiser who headed a state school-reform commission, lobbied Republican governor George Voinovich for a voucher program. Key bipartisan support was secured when a black Democratic city council member, Fannie Lewis, endorsed the pilot program.

Despite its path-breaking inclusion of central-city religious schools, the Cleveland voucher program had important limitations. Only children entering kindergarten through the third grade were eligible. The initial maximum value of the voucher was $2,250, although by 2000 this had increased to $2,500. Vouchers could cover only 90 percent of tuition. Although initial appropriations were expected to cover the tuition of no more than 1,500 students, private school tuition did not always amount to 90 percent of the maximum voucher value, so funds were available to support another 500 students in the program's first year. In 2000, approximately 3,900 students used vouchers to attend more than sixty-seven schools.

In July 1996, the Ohio Federation of Teachers, together with other groups, challenged the constitutionality of the Cleveland voucher program in the state's Court of Common Pleas.[9] The Ohio Supreme Court found the program to be consistent with the establishment clause of the U.S. Constitution, but it ruled that enactment of the program as part of the overall budget package violated the "single subject" rule of the Ohio state constitution. Subsequently, the state legislature reenacted the program as part of legislation dealing only with education.

During the summer of 1999, the legal challenges moved to the federal courts. Just days before the beginning of the new school year, a U.S. District Court judge, Solomon Oliver, issued a preliminary injunction that suspended the voucher program pending legal review, a move that prompted widespread criticism. Oliver quickly backtracked, allowing students already in the voucher program to continue attending private schools but forbidding any new enrollments. Two months later, in a 5-to-4 decision, the U.S. Supreme Court intervened, calling for the continuation of all aspects of the program until the constitutional question was resolved.[10] Since the Supreme Court usually does not intervene on a procedural matter unless it believes that there are substantial grounds for reversal on the merits of the case, many observers, while cautioning against making firm predictions, expected the Supreme Court majority would find the law constitutional.

Nonetheless, at the trial court level, Judge Oliver ruled in December 1999 that Cleveland's voucher program violated the U.S. Constitution.[11] The following year, a federal circuit court of appeals affirmed the district court order.[12] Thereafter, the U.S. Solicitor General urged the Supreme Court to hear the appealed case, and in October 2001 the Court granted a hearing. Oral argument was heard in February 2002, and a decision is expected in July. Two research teams have assessed the Cleveland program's impact on the education of participating students.[13]

Florida

When running for governor in 1998, Jeb Bush campaigned on behalf of his A+ education plan, which offered vouchers to children attending public schools that were "failing," as partially determined by average student performance on statewide math, reading, and writing tests. The plan further required private schools to admit students randomly when they received more applications than they had spaces available. The plan won the support of the Miami chapter of the Urban League, although the national Urban League remained opposed. With the additional backing of some key black legislators, Bush's proposal was enacted into law in 1999. That September, students at two "failing" schools were offered the chance to switch to another public school or to receive vouchers worth up to $3,389 to attend a private school.[14]

Because schools serving some 40,000 students had received failing grades once, and those students would become eligible to participate in the voucher experiment if the schools failed again, observers expected that the size of the voucher program would increase substantially in 2000. That year, however, all the public schools that had received an F in 1999 received passing grades.

Although other public schools also improved, one evaluation suggests that the voucher threat generated positive educational effects on public schools in Florida; average test scores in the poorest public schools facing the threat of vouchers improved more between 1999 and 2000 than did scores in roughly equivalent schools that did not face this threat.[15]

Evaluations of Publicly Funded Programs

The evaluations of these publicly funded programs have attracted considerable media attention—and for very good reason. For one thing, they focus on innovative government programs operating under real-life political conditions. Further, the programs can, in principle, continue in perpetuity, provided that the courts do not find them unconstitutional and the legislatures that created them do not reverse their actions. Whenever appropriate, therefore, we report results from these evaluations.

Still, researchers conducting these evaluations confronted a variety of challenges. Because the programs were created in the heat of political struggle, they had features—restrictions on the types of school that could participate, controversy surrounding their constitutionality, and so forth—that limited their scope. Moreover, when enacting the programs, legislators paid little attention to how they might best be evaluated; substantive policy questions, rather than issues of research design, were their principal concerns. As a result, the findings from these evaluations, however interesting, are rife with uncertainty.

Privately Funded Voucher Programs

Nonprofit organizations funded by grants from private foundations often experiment with ideas too untried and controversial for most governments to implement. In 1965, the Ford Foundation sponsored the "gray areas" program, which became the model for the community action program associated with the War on Poverty.[16] Privately funded preschool programs provided the impetus for Head Start, and private organizations served disabled students long before the federal government required special education programs.[17] In all cases, privately funded programs informed policymakers about the potential value of these social interventions.

School voucher research has proceeded in much the same way, as several privately funded programs have afforded vital opportunities for research. These voucher programs differ from traditional private scholarship programs in two important ways. First, a student's chance of winning a voucher was not tied to his or her academic performance; vouchers generally were awarded by lottery or on a first-come, first-served basis. Second, vouchers were not tied to a particular school or religious denomination. Instead, families could choose from a wide variety of participating secular or religious schools with any number of different affiliations.

The urban programs for which we have the most information are located in Dayton, Ohio; New York City; Washington, D.C.; and the Edgewood school district in San Antonio, Texas. In addition, we evaluated the nationwide program operated by the Children's Scholarship Fund. We also report results from evaluations of other voucher programs in Indianapolis, San Antonio, and Charlotte, North Carolina.[18] As mentioned, table 2-1 summarizes the basic characteristics of most of these programs, as well as the programs in Cleveland and Florida and two programs (public and private) in Milwaukee.

This book pays particular attention to the nationwide program and to the programs in New York City, Dayton, and Washington, D.C., where we conducted randomized field trials, an evaluation technique described later. All four programs gave students a full choice of private schools, religious and secular. All four held lotteries and provided fairly small vouchers—somewhere between $1,200 and $1,800 dollars. Given that the vast majority of voucher recipients attended religious schools that charged relatively modest tuition—the average tuition in New York City, Dayton, and Washington was $2,100, $2,600, and $3,100, respectively—even these small vouchers went a long way toward covering private schooling costs. Nonetheless, all four programs expected parents to supplement the vouchers with their own funds.

New York City

The New York City program, sponsored by the School Choice Scholarships Foundation, is the oldest and largest of the four lottery-based voucher programs that we evaluated. Announced in February 1997, the program invited applications through late April. Students who previously attended public school could apply for a voucher—which could be worth as much as $1,400—if they were entering grades 1–5 and were eligible to participate in the free-lunch program. More than 20,000 students expressed interest. The lottery was held in May 1997, and that fall approximately 1,200 students began using their vouchers to attend more than 225 different private schools. Vouchers initially were guaranteed for three years and subsequently were extended for longer periods. During the program's first year (Year I), 82 percent of families that were offered vouchers and participated in the follow-up testing session actually used the vouchers to send their children to private schools; after the second and third years (Years II and III), 79 and 70 percent of evaluation participants offered a voucher, respectively, continued to attend private schools.[19] During all three years, a small percentage of those not offered a voucher also found alternative funding sources to pay the cost of a private education.

Dayton, Ohio

The Dayton program, sponsored by Parents Advancing Choice in Education, was established at the same time as the one in Washington, D.C. Students in grades K–12 whose family income was less than twice the federal poverty-level income were eligible; depending on family income, the voucher could be worth as much as $1,200 or 60 percent of tuition, whichever was less. Approximately 3,000 students initially applied, roughly 800 students in both public and private schools were offered vouchers, and 530 students used their vouchers to attend private schools. (Students already in private school could win vouchers, but those students were not included in the evaluation.) Vouchers could be used in public schools, provided they were not within the district in which the student resided. Most public schools refused to participate, however, and only a very few students exercised that option.[20] In Years I and II, 78 and 60 percent of those offered vouchers, respectively, used them to attend private schools. Eighteen and 10 percent of those not offered a voucher nonetheless attended private schools during Years I and II.

Washington, D.C.

The Washington, D.C., voucher program, sponsored by the Washington Scholarship Fund, developed out of an ongoing scholarship program that previously had operated on a first-come, first-served basis.[21] Following widespread advertisement of the program in early spring of 1998, approximately 7,500 parents applied. That April, program operators conducted a lottery, and that fall roughly 1,000 students entering grades K–8 used vouchers to attend local private schools. (Again, students already in private schools could enter the lottery, but they were excluded from the evaluation.) Only those families with an income of less than 2.7 times the poverty-level income were eligible, and the value of the vouchers varied depending on income. For families at or below the poverty line, the voucher was worth as much as $1,700 or 60 percent of tuition, whichever was less. During Year I, 68 percent of the treatment group attended private schools; during Years II and III, only 48 and 29 percent, respectively, remained in private schools. Over the first three years of the program, the percentage of control-group students attending private schools dropped from 11 to 3 percent.

Types of Schools Students Attended

Most of the students who made use of the voucher offered to them attended religious schools. As can be seen in table 2-2, in Year I in all three cities, a clear plurality of students offered a voucher attended Catholic schools. Sixty-eight percent of those offered a voucher in New York City initially chose a Catholic school; the figures in Dayton and Washington, D.C., were 59 and 49 percent. Most of the others attended Protestant private schools: 8, 13, and 14 percent in Year I in New York City, Dayton, and D.C., respectively. In all three cities, another 5 percent attended either a secular private school or a private school from another religious tradition.

Over time, the percentages of students who did not use the voucher but instead attended public school gradually increased. Although the topic is discussed in more detail in chapter 3, it is worth noting here the differences among the three cities in the varying propensity of voucher students to return to public school. In New York City the percentage in public school increased from 18 percent in Year I to 30 percent in Year III. In Dayton, the shift was from 20 to 33 percent between Years I and II. By far the biggest shift occurred in Washington, D.C., where among those offered a voucher, 29 percent returned to traditional public schools in Year I and fully 46 percent returned in Year III. Moreover, many of those offered vouchers in Dayton, and especially in Washington, D.C., attended publicly funded charter schools (which charged no tuition) instead of remaining within the voucher program. In Dayton, the percentage of students in charter schools increased only from 3 to 5 percent, but in D.C., the percentage grew from 3 percent in Year I to 13 percent in Year II to 17 percent in Year III. As we shall see, in D.C. the increasing use of charter and public schools among those offered vouchers weakened our capacity to estimate precisely the effects of shifting from public to private schools in this city. In New York City, however, the charter school option was barely available to students during the course of the evaluation, and as a result a higher percentage of students remained in private schools, making it possible to estimate more precisely the educational effects of vouchers on students and families.

Children's Scholarship Fund Program

The mission of the nationwide voucher program administered by the Children's Scholarship Fund (CSF) is "to maximize educational opportunity . . . by offering tuition assistance for needy families." To that end, in 1999 CSF announced that it would award scholarships enabling low-income families across the United States to send their children in grades K–8 to the private

Table 2-2. *Type of School Students Attended*[a]

Percent

Type of school	Offered a voucher			Not offered a voucher		
	Year I	Year II	Year III	Year I	Year II	Year III
New York City						
Public school	18	26	30	94	92	96
Charter school	0	0	0	0	0	0
Catholic school	68	62	59	5	7	4
Protestant school	8	8	9	1	1	0
Other private school	5	4	2	0	0	0
Total	100	100	100	100	100	100
Dayton						
Public school	20	33	. . .	82	83	. . .
Charter school	3	5	. . .	2	6	. . .
Catholic school	59	43	. . .	8	6	. . .
Protestant school	13	14	. . .	6	5	. . .
Other private school	5	4	. . .	3	0	. . .
Total	100	100	. . .	100	100	. . .
Washington, D.C.						
Public school	29	38	46	77	72	66
Charter school	3	13	17	12	18	24
Catholic school	49	34	27	6	7	6
Protestant school	14	9	6	3	2	2
Other private school	5	5	3	2	1	2
Total	100	100	100	100	100	100

a. Percentages of types of schools attended by students who showed up for Year I, Year II, and Year III testing sessions, as reported on parent surveys.

school of their choice. Parents of more than 1.25 million children applied for vouchers; 40,000 were awarded. Recipients were chosen by lottery, again enabling the conduct of a randomized field trial.

To qualify for a voucher, CSF applicants had to have at least one child in grades K–8 (although the evaluation includes only families with children in grades 1–8) and to qualify for the federal free and reduced-price lunch program. The voucher amounts were determined on a sliding scale, ranging from 75 percent of tuition for families at or below the federal poverty line to 25 percent of tuition for families at 270 percent of the poverty line. According to CSF administrators, the average income of recipient families was $20,663. The average scholarship totaled $1,030 per child, with the family contributing an additional $1,100 toward tuition.[22] If a family was selected in the lottery, all of its children were offered a voucher. Vouchers were awarded in April 1999, and that fall 29 percent of lottery winners used their voucher to attend a local private school. (Issues surrounding voucher usage are explored in chapter 3.)

Edgewood School District Program, San Antonio, Texas

Although the San Antonio program is not lottery based, it is of special interest because, unlike the other four privately funded programs we have discussed, it offers vouchers to all public school students, grades K–12, from low-income families residing within a particular school district. The program operates within the Edgewood school district in San Antonio, which serves a predominantly Hispanic population. The Texas Department of Education classified as economically disadvantaged 90 percent of the 13,490 students who attended Edgewood's public schools in 1997–98.[23] The Children's Educational Opportunity (CEO) Foundation sponsored the voucher program, known as the Horizon program.

Announced in April 1998, the program provided vouchers for the 1998–99 school year. To receive a voucher, families needed only to qualify for the free or reduced-price federal lunch program at the time of application; they did not need to requalify for the program each year they used the voucher. Families were guaranteed financial support for as long as they lived in Edgewood and their child remained in a participating school. Vouchers could be used to attend public schools outside the Edgewood school district or local private schools, religious or secular. CEO imposed no restrictions on the private schools' admissions policy. All elementary students who attended private schools within Edgewood received scholarships worth $3,600; high school students who went to private schools in Edgewood received scholarships worth $4,000.[24] The average private school tuition paid by students during the program's first year was $1,982.[25] As a result, although they did not always cover fees and supplies, the vouchers were sufficient for most tuition costs.

Horizon officials announced that in the first semester of the 1998–99 school year 837 students used vouchers to attend one of fifty-seven private schools in Edgewood or elsewhere in the San Antonio metropolitan area. Two students used their voucher to attend a public school outside the Edgewood school district.[26] In 2000, approximately 1,300 students attending sixty-two different schools participated in the program. The program is projected to continue for ten years or until a publicly funded program is established.

Randomized Field Trials

We evaluated the privately funded voucher programs in New York City, Dayton, Ohio, and Washington, D.C., and the nationwide CSF program by means of randomized field trials (RFTs), a research design that is well known in the medical field. The Food and Drug Administration (FDA), for example, requires proposed prescription drugs and other medical treatments to be evaluated by means of an RFT prior to their widespread dissemination. In an RFT, subjects are randomly assigned to a treatment or control group. Those in the treatment group are offered the drug or therapy being evaluated; those in the control group receive a conventional drug or therapy. If outcomes are more favorable for those in the treatment group than for the controls and if those in the treatment group do not suffer serious side effects, the FDA usually allows the product to be disseminated on a wider scale, although monitoring of product safety and effectiveness continues.

In a perfectly controlled experiment in the natural sciences, the researcher is able to control for all factors while manipulating the variable of interest. Consider, for example, an experiment designed to determine whether deer can distinguish between red and green (they can!). To ensure the credibility of the finding, the experimenter must vary the color of the signal while controlling for all other factors. If the green signal is always on the right, for instance, and the red signal on the left, the deer may simply perceive the difference between right and left, not the difference in color. Much of the work that goes into scientific research design involves devising ways to vary only one factor while holding all others constant.

Experiments with humans are much more difficult to manage. Researchers cannot give out pills or placebos and then ask subjects not to change any other aspect of their lives. To conduct an experiment in the social sciences that nonetheless approximates the natural-science ideal, scientists have come up with the idea of random assignment—drawing names out of a hat (or, today, by computer) and putting subjects into a treatment or control group. When individuals are assigned randomly to one of two categories, one can assume that the two groups do not differ from each another systematically, except in the one respect under investigation.

The principle of random assignment is common in everyday life—captains of pick-up baseball teams, for example, have long recognized its virtues. Simply numbering people off, one and two, usually produces two teams of roughly equivalent ability. Of course, if a pool of only eighteen people is involved, random fluctuations can produce unbalanced teams and, as a result, dull, one-sided games. But if the pool is enlarged somewhat—even to a few hundred people—random assignment usually will generate the desired balance. One then can assume that subjects, on average, do not differ except with respect to the one element deliberately allowed to vary between the two groups. In the words of mathematician William Mendenhall, randomization "produce[s] substantial increases in the quantity of information in an experiment by reducing nuisance variation."[27] Analysts then can concentrate on the variation that matters: whether a group received the treatment under study and what happened as a result.

Having generated two groups that are equivalent at baseline—the beginning of the experiment—investigators can meaningfully attribute to the intervention any differences between the two groups that are subsequently observed. Statistical tests tell investigators whether they can be confident of obtaining the same results if they run the study many times. When the statistical test passes a certain threshold, the results are said to be statistically significant. Unless otherwise indicated, we discuss only results that would pass the test of statistical significance—that is, only if there is less than a 10 percent probability that random chance produced these particular results.

It is the very simplicity of random assignment that makes such studies so eloquent and their findings so compelling. Simply by comparing what happens to members of the treatment and control groups, analysts can assess whether an intervention makes any difference, positive or negative. Of course, complications inevitably arise. People in the treatment group refuse treatment. People in the control group discover alternative ways of getting the treatment. People fail to report back, or move away, or provide inaccurate information. Still, statisticians have found a variety of ways to correct for such eventualities; such adjustments are discussed in greater detail below.

Of late, analysts have used RFTs to study the programmatic impacts of a number of policy interventions. For example, Lawrence Katz, Jeffrey Kling, and Jeffrey Liebman have reported initial results from an RFT of housing vouchers.[28] The program, called Moving to Opportunity (MTO), provided housing vouchers to interested Boston families that wished to move from high-poverty to low-poverty neighborhoods. Participants in MTO also received counseling and assistance in locating a new residence. Because the program was oversubscribed and vouchers were awarded by lottery, the researchers were able to evaluate the program's effects in the context of a randomized experiment. Katz and others determined that families that were offered the treatment—participation in the MTO program—realized improved outcomes on a number of measures of quality of life, including safety, health, and reduced rates of juvenile delinquency among boys.

Jens Ludwig, Greg Duncan, and Paul Hirschfield also employed an RFT to determine whether a low-income housing voucher program reduced the incidence of juvenile crime. Using information from the experiment, they quite convincingly show that "the offer to relocate families from high- to low-poverty neighborhoods reduces juvenile arrests for violent offenses by 30 to 50 percent of the arrest rate for controls."[29]

In a related study, Jens Ludwig, Helen Ladd, and Greg Duncan examined the effect of the MTO housing voucher program on student achievement.[30] The MTO program not only provided low-income families with a housing voucher, but required them to use the voucher to relocate to a more affluent neighborhood. Using analytic methods that are virtually the same as those that we employed, these researchers found "that the opportunity for public housing residents to move from high-poverty to low-poverty neighborhoods improves reading and math scores for young children by about one-quarter of a standard deviation compared to their control group counterparts."[31]

In addition to evaluating the impacts of housing vouchers, RFTs have been utilized to evaluate the efficacy of the negative income tax, welfare-to-work programs, job training programs, programs designed to reduce recidivism rates for released convicts, and a host of other social interventions.[32] But, unfortunately, they have been less widely used in the field of education.[33] The U.S. Department of Education, unlike the FDA, has never required and has seldom directly funded RFTs. The federal government's large-scale compensatory education program for disadvantaged students has never been evaluated by means of an RFT. Nor has Head Start yet been evaluated by an RFT, although a privately funded precursor was.[34] The effectiveness of increases in per-pupil expenditures has been a matter of great debate, but their impact has never been evaluated in a randomized field trial.

Nonetheless, RFTs are attracting the attention of education researchers and federal policymakers. In 1999, a conference held by the American Academy of Arts and Sciences focused on the need for—and problems attendant upon—conducting randomized experiments in the field of education.[35] In this same spirit, Harvard president Lawrence Summers reminded his education school faculty and students that "one of the five most important medical innovations in the last century" was the introduction of randomized experiments. He asked that "debates in the field . . . go beyond competing dogmas, hurling platitudes and clichés at each other, and instead be based on a rigorous assessment of facts about what works."[36] Of special significance, in 2000, a House of Representatives committee approved a bill that would require the use of RFTs in federally funded education research. [37] Although as of this writing the Senate has not taken up the bill, RFTs may well become an integral part of federal education research programs.

Although much of the newfound interest is due to an influential RFT of class-size reduction in Tennessee discussed in chapter 3,[38] school choice is an area in which RFTs are especially needed—mainly because those who exercise choice may differ markedly from those who do not, creating what is known as the self-selection problem. In the words of political scientist Jeffrey Henig,

> The thorniest problem plaguing efforts to empirically determine the educational consequences of school choice . . . concerns selection bias. . . . Those who choose . . . likely differ from those who fail to take advantage of choice opportunities, in such factors as motivation, ambition, and capacity. These factors, rather than choice and its consequences, may account for any higher levels of academic achievement that choice students subsequently reveal, and standard statistical controls for family background may not be sufficient to take this into account. . . . The selection bias . . . probably cannot be eliminated without a truly randomized experimental design.[39]

Among studies of publicly funded voucher programs, only the secondary evaluations of the initial, small-scale program in Milwaukee used the RFT research design. The original researchers collected test score information for both those who were offered a voucher and those who applied for but did not receive one. Since the law required that vouchers be awarded by lottery, the conditions for an RFT obtained, and the two secondary studies of the Milwaukee program exploited this fact.[40] One study found positive effects of vouchers on reading test scores, and both found positive effects on math scores. However, the generalizability of their findings is limited by the fact that the early Milwaukee program did not include religious schools. Moreover, school administrators, rather than experienced, independent social scientists, conducted the lottery.[41] Although there was no sign that administrators misused their authority, it is still unknown whether the lottery was truly random.

In Cleveland, an RFT never was possible. Although vouchers initially were awarded randomly, a variety of administrative problems precluded holding an effective lottery; in the end, vouchers were offered to all applicants. The program in Florida was too small to allow for an RFT. The results from those cities are nevertheless of interest, and we refer to them from time to time in the coming chapters. But because all of the studies of public voucher programs have significant limitations, we believe that much more can be gained from a close look at the privately funded programs.

Randomized Trials in New York City; Dayton, Ohio; and Washington, D.C.

Our evaluations of the privately funded voucher programs in New York City, Dayton, and Washington, D.C., were conducted as RFTs. In all three cities, our evaluation teams collected baseline data before the lottery was held, administered the lottery, and collected follow-up information in subsequent years.[42]

Baseline Data Collection

Before the lottery, families in all three cities were asked to accompany their children to income-verification sessions. During the sessions, which usually were held on Saturdays, students took the Iowa Test of Basic Skills (ITBS) in reading and mathematics. The sessions were held at private schools, where students could take tests in a classroom setting. Private school teachers and administrators served as proctors under the supervision of the evaluation team. Riverside Publishing, the producer of the ITBS, scored the tests.[43] Students in grades 4 through 8 also completed short questionnaires about their school experiences. As is shown in table 2-3, 1,960 students completed baseline tests in New York City, 803 in Dayton, and 1,582 in Washington, D.C.

While the children were being tested in separate rooms, their parents or other adults accompanying them completed extensive questionnaires about how the child's school was selected, the child's experiences at school, homework, school-parent communication, parents' involvement in the child's education, their satisfaction with the child's schools, and their demographic characteristics.[44] Administrators explained that responses to the questionnaire would be held in strict confidence and used for statistical purposes only. Respondents had considerable time to complete their surveys, and administrators were available to answer questions about the meaning of particular items.

To enter the lottery, families had to participate in the survey and testing sessions, ensuring the collection of relevant baseline information from nearly all parents and students in the grades that were evaluated. In Washington and Dayton, those who did not win the initial lottery became the control group. Because the New York City program received far more applicants than had been anticipated, the control group consisted of families chosen at random from the nonwinners.[45]

Table 2-3. *Patterns of Participation in Three Randomized Field Trials of School Vouchers*

	New York City (School Choice Scholarships Foundation)	Dayton and Montgomery County, Ohio (Parents Advancing Choice in Education)	Washington, D.C. (Washington Scholarship Fund)
First school year under study	1997–98	1998–99	1998–99
Entry grades	1–4	1–8	1–8
Number of students from public schools that were tested at baseline	1,960	803	1,582
Treatment group going to private school			
First year[a]	82%	78%	68%
Both of first two years[b]	79%	60%	47%
First three consecutive years[c]	70%	. . .	29%
Control group going to private school			
First year	4%	18%	11%
Both of first two years	1%	10%	8%
First three consecutive years	2%	. . .	3%

a. Percentage of the treatment group that attended the first-year follow-up testing session that used a voucher to attend a private school during the first year of the program. Actual take-up rates are lower than those reported here.

b. Percentage of the treatment group that attended the second-year follow-up testing session that used a voucher to attend a private school during the first two years of the program. Actual take-up rates are lower.

c. Percentage of the treatment group that attended the third-year follow-up testing session that used a voucher to attend a private school during the first three years of the program. Actual take-up rates are lower.

After verification sessions were completed, our evaluation teams conducted the lotteries, usually in mid-April. Program operators informed lottery winners in early May. If a family was selected, all children in that family entering the eligible grades were offered a voucher to attend a private school that fall. A total of 1,500 vouchers were offered to public school students in New York City, 811 in Washington, and 515 in Dayton.[46] Because vouchers were allocated randomly, the characteristics of those offered vouchers did not differ significantly from members of the control group.

Follow-up Data Collection

To estimate the impact of attending a private school, our evaluation teams collected follow-up information from all three programs for two consecutive years after baseline data collection; in New York City and Washington, D.C., follow-up information was collected for a third year as well. The procedure used to obtain follow-up data was essentially the same as that used at baseline. Students again took the ITBS in mathematics and reading. The adults accompanying the children completed surveys that asked a wide range of questions about the educational experiences of each child. Students in grades 4 and above completed questionnaires that asked about their experiences at school.

Only students who had been tested at baseline and were entering grades 2 through 5 in New York City and 2 through 8 in Dayton and Washington were included in the test-performance portion of the evaluation. (Those entering first grade were excluded because it was not feasible to collect baseline test score information from children in kindergarten.) Parent survey information, however, was collected from all participating families.

Since students required more time to finish their questionnaire and the ITBS than parents needed to complete their survey, our evaluation teams were able to conduct recorded but anonymous focus group sessions with some parents. Parents' comments and anecdotes in the chapters that follow are from the transcripts of those sessions.[47] The recordings were made during separate focus group conversations with members of three groups—families that were offered and used a voucher, those that were offered but did not use a voucher, and those that were not offered a voucher. In general, focus groups consisted of roughly six to eight randomly chosen parents and lasted about thirty to forty-five minutes. Parents were not required to participate, although most who were asked did so. Because anonymity was promised, all identifying information—such as names of schools and children—has been removed from the statements quoted.

The purpose of the focus group conversations is different from that of the statistical results we report. The conversations do not constitute a rigorous test of differences between the private and public school populations. Instead, they provide texture and detail that help to illuminate the brief responses to questions on the written surveys.

Response rates

In research, obtaining a high response rate is always a challenge. The National Election Studies, for instance, which is one of the most important and frequently cited data sets used by political scientists, has panel response rates that have fallen as low as 59 percent.[48] Because of the normal movement of students from one school to another, researchers who conducted the Tennessee STAR study on class size reduction were unable to follow many children for the duration of the study. After one year, just 71 percent of the students in the original sample were retested; after two and three years, 60 percent and 48 percent of students were retested, respectively. Furthermore, because baseline data were not collected in the STAR study, it is impossible to verify whether students from the original sample who were included in follow-up testing differed markedly from those who were not.[49] The state-sponsored evaluation of the Milwaukee voucher program had even lower response rates. After one year, the response rate for the treatment group was 43 percent and the rate for the control group was just 30 percent. Although exact figures were not reported, response rates in subsequent years appear to have dropped considerably lower.[50]

In order to encourage high rates of participation in the collection of follow-up data in New York City, Washington, D.C., and Dayton, we compensated both those who had declined a scholarship offer and those who were members of the control group (families usually were given between $50 and $150) and informed them that they would automatically be included in a new lottery.[51] In most cases, those who had been receiving a voucher were told that renewal depended on participation in follow-up sessions.[52]

As a result, the response rates achieved were comparable to those in the Tennessee STAR study and higher than those in Milwaukee. Of those participating in the baseline evaluation, 56 and 63 percent of students returned for testing in Year I in Dayton and Washington, respectively (table 2-4); in Year II, 49 and 50 percent returned, respectively. In New York, the response rates were somewhat higher: 82 percent for Year I, 66 percent for Year II, and 67 percent for Year III.[53] In all three cities and all years, approximately equal numbers of students in the treatment group (those who were offered a voucher) and control group (those who did not win a voucher) were tested. [54]

Comparisons of baseline test scores and background characteristics revealed minor differences between respondents and nonrespondents in all three cities.[55] To account for those differences, we generated weights based on the probability that students, according to their baseline demographic characteristics, would attend follow-up sessions. Students who were more likely to attend follow-up sessions were weighted downward somewhat; students who were less likely to attend the sessions but nevertheless did attend were weighted upward. Because only slight differences existed between the groups of respondents and nonrespondents, the weights had little effect on the results of the analysis. Appendix A provides information on weighting procedures.

To generate the weights we could use only observable characteristics as recorded in parent surveys. The weights did not necessarily eliminate bias

Table 2-4. *Response Rates in Three Randomized Field Trials of School Vouchers*[a]

City	Baseline	Year I	Year II	Year III
New York City[b]	100	82	66	67
Dayton[c]	100	56	49	. . .
Washington, D.C.[d]	100	63	50	60

a. Percent.
b. School Choice Scholarships Foundation.
c. Parents Advancing Choice on Education.
d. Washington Scholarship Fund.

associated with unmeasured, or unobservable, characteristics that may have influenced patterns of participation in follow-up sessions. However, the weights partially adjusted for unmeasured characteristics that were correlated with measured ones. (See discussion in appendix A.)

Evaluation of the Nationwide CSF Program

Our RFT evaluations in New York City, Dayton, and Washington, D.C., were supplemented by a fourth, of the nationwide CSF program.[56] Because this evaluation differs significantly from the other three, a separate discussion of both its strengths and limitations is required. Two positive qualities are worth noting. First, it provides valuable information about a nationwide voucher program, facts that pertain to the country as a whole, not just to those in particular cities. Second, it provides valuable information about observed differences between those who apply for vouchers and those in the eligible population. With this information, it is possible to ascertain the unique qualities of applicants to school voucher programs.

The nationwide evaluation nonetheless has certain limitations. We were unable to estimate the impact of a voucher on student test scores, because it was not feasible to administer the same test nationwide. Also, we (as in the Tennessee STAR evaluation) were unable to gather baseline data, so it can only be assumed—it cannot be shown—that treatment and control groups resembled one another at baseline.[57] Fortunately, in our study at least, this is not a particularly restrictive assumption, because the lottery assigning students to test and control groups was conducted by an independent research organization. Finally, only 29 percent of the families offered a voucher actually used them. Although this does not bias our results, it makes our estimates less precise. Only those impacts that were very large could be observed with sufficient certainty.

To conduct the nationwide CSF evaluation, two types of surveys were conducted. First we interviewed by telephone a sample of all families that applied for a CSF scholarship—including both families that were offered a voucher and families that were not. Families were contacted in the summer following the first year of the program.[58] With their parents' permission, students in grades 4 through 8 also were interviewed. A total of 2,368 adults participated in the telephone surveys: 464 from families that were offered and used a voucher, 1,116 from families that were offered but declined a voucher, and 788 from families that were not offered a voucher. Of the 872 students surveyed, 177 students were offered and used a voucher, 411 were offered but did not use a voucher, and 282 were not offered a voucher.

The parent survey was administered to "the parent or caretaker" of the child or children in the family.[59] The response rate to the telephone survey was 46 percent, comparable with response rates of other national telephone surveys and relatively high for a low-income population. Response rates were almost identical for treatment and control groups.[60] Despite random assignment to the treatment and control groups and the similar response rates for the two groups, small differences remained between the two groups in the racial composition, education level, and religious affiliation of their members. All results, therefore, were weighted to adjust for differences in the demographic characteristics of the two groups.[61] Because the differences were small, the weights had only a minimal effect on the results.

To compare those who applied to the CSF program with all those who qualified, we administered a similar survey to a nationwide sample of families that met the CSF program's eligibility criteria. These families had children in grades 1 through 8, had low-to-moderate incomes (less than $40,000), and lived in cities with a population of 200,000 or more. CSF requirements set the income ceiling at 270 percent of the federal poverty level, which is lower than the ceiling we set in conducting our surveys. Consequently, the relevant findings reported in this book may overestimate the actual differences between applicants and the eligible population.

Under our direction, Knowledge Networks Inc. administered the survey in July and August 2000 over Web TV, a device that connects a television set to the Internet. Knowledge Networks's panel was constructed using a probability sample of the U.S. population; subjects initially were contacted by telephone, and data were weighted to account for nonresponse, either to the initial invitation to join the panel or to the request to complete this particular survey. Although the exact wording of the questions on the Internet survey varied slightly from those used in the telephone survey, the content of the questions was essentially the same, facilitating direct comparisons between the various groups of families interviewed. Other research has shown that differences in how a survey is administered has little substantive effect on the answers given.[62]

Data Analysis

The analyses reported in chapters 4 through 7 take advantage of the fact that a lottery was used to award vouchers. As a result, it is possible to compare two groups of students who were similar, on average, except that members of the control group were not offered vouchers. As mentioned previously, many of those offered a voucher did not use it, while a small percentage of students who were not offered a voucher nonetheless attended private schools. Because of the low usage rate, comparisons between those who were offered a voucher and those who were not will understate the true effect of actually switching from a public to a private school. Yet if one compares only those who accepted the voucher with all of the members of the control group, bias may be introduced into the analysis because those who accept and use the voucher may differ in important ways from those who do not use it.

To obtain the best estimate of the effect of switching from a public to a private school, we compare those who used the voucher to attend private school with those in the control group who would have used the voucher had it been offered to them. This comparison is made by means of an instrumental variable analysis widely employed in RFT research.

James Heckman of the University of Chicago, a Nobel-prize-winning economist, first developed the analytical approach. Building on his ideas, statisticians have shown that a consistent and unbiased estimate of the effects of an independent variable (in our case, attendance at a private school) on a dependent variable (for example, student test scores) can be obtained if a third variable—the instrument—can be identified. To work, our instrument must do a good job of predicting the likelihood that a student attends a private school; it also must be completely uncorrelated with the error term in regressions that estimate outcomes such as student test performance.

The benefits of this approach may be best illustrated by taking two examples from the literature on a quite different subject, campaigns and elections. The first study, which estimates the impact of spending on election returns, is creative, but the results remain uncertain. The second, which estimates the effect of canvassing on voter turnout, is more successful.

For many years researchers have struggled to find a way to estimate the effect of campaign spending on the outcome of an election. The difficulty arises from the fact that high-spending candidates are a selected population.

That is, most incumbents and many strong challengers can raise large sums of money simply because contributors know that they have a good chance of winning. As a result, simple comparisons between spending and election outcomes are likely to make it appear that money is more important than it really is. To address this problem, political scientist Alan Gerber used the instrumental variable technique that Heckman and others developed.[63] Gerber used a candidate's personal wealth as one instrument on the assumption that rich candidates could easily spend money whether or not they were going to win and that their wealth, by itself, would have no direct effect on the election. He predicted campaign spending in a regression that included the wealth of the candidate; he then used the predicted values from this regression in a second regression that estimated election outcomes.

A major improvement on previous research, the instrument provides unbiased and consistent effects of campaign finance as long as the wealth of a candidate has no direct effect on the outcome of an election. However, this assumption may be questioned. Steve Forbes probably suffered politically for being a rich man's son. Conversely, Jay Rockefeller, despite his personal wealth, may have had a special appeal to West Virginians because of his demonstrated commitment to those in need. More generally, rich people, because of their wealth, may receive special attention from the media that affects their appeal to voters.

The second example of an instrumental variable analysis is more compelling. In this case, Gerber, together with a Yale colleague, Donald Green, found a more powerful instrument when they designed an RFT to estimate the effect of door-to-door canvassing on voter turnout.[64] They used a lottery to randomly assign New Haven households to one of two categories: targets and nontargets of a nonpartisan canvassing campaign. A selection problem arose because some people targeted for an appeal were never contacted, either because they were not at home or refused to answer the door. As a result, the people actually canvassed were a selected population, more connected to home and community and therefore more predisposed to vote in the first place.

Fortunately, in this case, an ideal instrumental variable was available. Gerber and Green used the lottery itself to predict whether a person would receive the door-to-door, nonpartisan appeal, because most of the New Haven residents who "won" the lottery were in fact contacted while none of those who "lost" the lottery were contacted in this manner. The lottery itself was not related to any factor that had a direct effect on voter turnout in New Haven (independent of the canvassing effort), and thus represented an ideal instrument. Using the instrumental variable technique, Gerber and Green then demonstrated that door-to-door canvassing increased voter turnout—at least in one New Haven election.

More generally, whenever an RFT is conducted, it is possible to use the lottery results as an instrument for estimating the impact of actually receiving treatment—in our case, attending a private school. The lottery fulfills both requirements of an instrument: it has a pronounced impact on the likelihood that a student will attend a private school, and it is completely uncorrelated with the error term in regressions that predict educational outcomes. The technique has been widely used to estimate, among other things, the effect of class size on student performance, military training on future earnings, and housing vouchers on educational outcomes.[65]

The instrument yields consistent and unbiased estimates, but their precision varies, depending upon the sample size, the variance of the distribution, and, importantly, the voucher use rate. If most students offered a voucher attended a private school and most students who were not offered a voucher remained in a public school, then the use of the offer as an instrument for estimating private school effects can generate estimates that are quite precise. But if only a minority of the treatment group used vouchers and many of those not offered vouchers found alternative means to finance a private education, the instrument, though still unbiased, will generate estimates with higher standard errors, making it more difficult to detect impacts unless they are large.

Whether large or small, the size of an impact may be measured in standard deviations. Although a technical term, one can grasp its rough meaning by considering the fact that on most tests of student achievement, the scores of African Americans fall one standard deviation below that of white Americans. As mentioned in chapter 1, most people feel that if this gap could be eliminated, we would take a major step forward in providing for equal educational opportunity. But the effect sizes of most policy innovations are much smaller than one full standard deviation. Ordinarily, an effect size of 0.1 standard deviations, one-tenth of the education gap, is thought to be rather slight. An effect size of 0.25 to 0.4 is thought to be moderate; an effect of 0.5 to 0.8 is usually said to be large; and an effect size of 1.0 is quite remarkable.

Effect sizes can be applied to other educational outcomes besides test scores. In the pages that follow, we will calculate in effect sizes many different consequences of the voucher program—the seriousness of problems at school, class size, homework, school-parent communication, parents' satisfaction, and other things as well. We do so not to be technical and obscure but to allow the reader to compare readily the size of impacts on various kinds of outcomes.

When impacts are large, they can be estimated even when the measurement tools at hand are clumsy. But when impacts are smaller, one needs more precision. In the case of student test scores, precision is especially desirable, because test score changes from one year to the next are likely to be modest. After all, education is a long, multiyear process, and rapid test score gains for large numbers of individuals in the span of just one year, or even two or three, are unlikely. Further, given the random volatility of test scores, it is easy for researchers—and policymakers—to arrive at incorrect conclusions about the efficacy of different educational interventions.[66]

When estimates are imprecise, one of two types of errors can occur: the analyst can estimate a positive or negative impact of a treatment, even when one did not actually occur (what statisticians refer to as a Type I error), or fail to attribute such an impact, even when one in fact did occur (usually labeled a Type II error). Table 2-5 shows, for each city, the size that an effect must achieve before the analyst is no longer at risk of making a Type I error, that is, before he or she can be sure, at the 0.95 confidence level, that the effect estimated actually occurred. The table also shows the size of an effect that if not obtained places the analyst at risk of making a Type II error, that is, of falsely concluding at the 80 percent confidence level that no effect occurred.[67] Generally speaking, the smaller the effect size needed to avoid these two kinds of error, the more precise the estimate.

As can be seen in table 2-5, the precision of the estimates varies from year to year and city to city. In Year I, effects that attain the size of 0.19 in New York City are not at risk of being subject to either Type I or Type II error, but by Year III, the effects must be 0.25 to avoid the same level of risk. In Dayton and D.C., meanwhile, the required effect sizes are much larger. In Dayton, Year II effects must be 0.63 to avoid making either a Type I or a Type II error. In Washington, D.C., a Year III effect size must reach 0.71 to do the same. In short, among the three cities, impacts are most precisely estimated in New York.

In chapters 4 through 8, we use this technique to estimate the impact of attending a private school on a wide variety of outcomes—parent and student descriptions of the student's school experiences, students' test performance, parents' satisfaction, and parents' involvement in their child's school and education. This statistical procedure compares those in the treatment group who attended private schools with those in the control group who would have attended private school had they been offered a voucher.[68]

Evaluation Procedures in San Antonio

Our evaluation in San Antonio differed from the RFTs in New York City, Washington, D.C., and Dayton in important respects.[69] Because vouchers

Table 2-5. *Effect Sizes Necessary to Avoid Estimation Error*[a]
Standard deviations

City	Year I	Year II	Year III
To avoid Type I error			
All students			
New York City	0.13	0.16	0.17
Dayton	0.31	0.45	...
Washington, D.C.	0.22	0.41	0.51
African Americans			
New York City	0.21	0.24	0.28
Dayton	0.38	0.42	...
Washington, D.C.	0.22	0.44	0.54
To avoid Type II error			
All students			
New York City	0.19	0.23	0.25
Dayton	0.44	0.63	...
Washington, D.C.	0.31	0.53	0.71
African Americans			
New York City	0.29	0.33	0.39
Dayton	0.51	0.59	...
Washington, D.C.	0.32	0.57	0.76

a. For Type I errors, figures represent the minimum effect size of attending a private school one would have to observe in Years I, II, and III in each city in order to avoid rejecting the null hypothesis when the null is true at $p < .05$. For Type II errors, figures represent the minimum effect size of attending a private school one would have to observe in order to avoid accepting the null hypothesis when the null hypothesis is false with power = .80 and α = .05. All estimates are presented as standard deviations. Standard deviations for all students are set at 20.7 national percentile ranking points for all cities in all years, which is the unweighted average standard deviation of baseline test scores across the three cities; for African Americans, the standard deviation for all cities in all years was set at 19.9. Estimates vary according to the sample sizes, the variance of the distributions, and the percentage of the treatment and control groups that attended private schools each year.

were offered to all students, it was not possible to conduct an RFT here. Instead, those students between the ages of eight and seventeen who accepted and made use of the voucher to attend a private school were compared with a cross-section of students of similar ages remaining in the Edgewood public schools. Although this made it more difficult to assess the impact of a voucher program on emotional outcomes, the research design had compensating advantages. For one thing, one could ascertain what kinds of families seek and obtain vouchers when they are offered to a large population. Also, one could compare the assessments of schooling by voucher parents to those of a cross-section of all public school parents, not just those in a control group consisting of parents who were dissatisfied enough with public schools to apply for a voucher. For those reasons, results from San Antonio also deserve careful attention.

Internal and External Validity

When RFTs are conducted, questions about their internal and external validity necessarily arise. Questions of internal validity concern whether the findings reported apply to the population under investigation. Most scientists believe that internal validity is paramount, because one wants to be certain that the estimates of the effects of the intervention have been accurately calculated for the population being treated. For this reason we have discussed in detail the procedures we followed to ensure the internal validity of our RFTs.

To summarize, we have addressed the following questions regarding the internal validity of our evaluations. Were the lotteries conducted fairly? Yes, independent organizations separate from the program operators used computers to generate random numbers to select those who would be offered a voucher. Were there signs that the treatment and control groups differed significantly from one another? No, across a wide range of baseline characteristics, the two groups appeared to be virtually identical. Were the same procedures used to assess the two groups in subsequent years? Yes, both treatment and control groups were tested and questioned in the same manner at approximately the same time. Were biases introduced when only some families made use of the voucher? Yes, but a well-established statistical technique, instrumental variable analysis, allowed the investigators to address the problem effectively. Does the inability to follow all participants throughout the life of the study cast doubt on the findings? For the most part, no—not when baseline data indicate only small differences between those who continue to participate and those who do not and when statistical adjustments correct for these small differences. For these reasons, we believe that the results we report are unbiased for the populations we studied.

But what of external validity problems? The question of external validity, which arises constantly in RFT research, concerns the generalizability of the observed findings to other populations. Canvassing may increase turnout in an old city such as New Haven, but would it have the same effect in a suburb in California or a small town in the Midwest? Many medical RFTs are conducted on nurses and other hospital workers, in part because they are conveniently located and can be tracked over time without great inconvenience to either patient or investigator. But nurses tend to lead healthier lives than most citizens. Will a medical intervention that works well among healthy, resourceful, attentive professionals also be effective if given to a more diverse population?

As long as one generalizes to small-scale voucher programs serving low-income families living in central cities, the results we report are likely to hold. Of course, one cannot know for certain what might happen if vouchers are introduced in a southern or western city. But that we find quite similar results in New York City, Dayton, Ohio, Washington, D.C., and a nation-wide program suggests that comparable findings would hold for many central cities.

But can we generalize beyond the three years we followed the programs? Definitely not, although we can see whether our findings are consistent with results from other investigations which, even if not RFTs, nonetheless track students into their adult lives (see chapter 6). Ultimately, our findings apply most clearly to small-scale voucher interventions that lasted between two and three years. Impacts may differ for larger programs over longer periods of time. In the concluding chapter we consider the likely consequences of increasing the scale and duration of a voucher program. But first, we consider the evidence at hand.

3

Seeking and Using a Voucher

S kimming—the practice of recruiting and selecting talented, committed people for whatever the task at hand—is part and parcel of modern life. And for good reason. Restaurants that have lively, intelligent servers tend to thrive. High-tech firms that employ hard-working personnel with a sophisticated knowledge of the field have a better chance of beating the competition. Charities that hire capable managers generally excel when others falter.

Most Americans accept skimming as a fact of life. Few would deny that excellence should be rewarded in the workplace. But when it comes to primary and secondary education, many Americans profess a belief in equal opportunity that would seem to preclude selecting students according to their ability and background. In the words of Chief Justice Earl Warren, writing in the *Brown* v. *Board of Education* decision outlawing school segregation: "It is doubtful that any child may reasonably be expected to succeed in life if he is denied the opportunity of an education. Such an opportunity, where the state has undertaken to provide it, is a right which must be made available to all on equal terms."[1]

But despite this general belief in equality of opportunity, the practice of skimming pervades American education. The most visible examples are found in higher education. Harvard, Georgetown, and the University of Wisconsin's flagship campus in Madison all have highly selective admissions policies. Just as a farmer skims the cream off raw milk, so admissions committees shuffle applications until the strongest candidates rise to the top of the pile. For the institutions themselves, the stakes are high. Most college rankings, including those conducted by *U.S. News and World Report,* estimate a university's quality in part by the difficulty of gaining admission. The more selective the university, the higher the ranking, and thus the easier it is to secure the financial support of government agencies, industries, and private foundations.

Skimming in Public Schools

Skimming is a common feature of U.S. public schools as well. The typical student entering New Trier High School, a public school serving Winnetka, a leafy suburb north of Chicago, comes from a different family background and demonstrates greater academic competence than the typical student entering Hyde Park Academy High School on Chicago's south side. Students entering the high schools in New York's upscale New Rochelle differ noticeably from entrants at South Bronx High, which is located just a few miles to the south.

Magnet schools within central cities, which often apply strict admissions criteria, are especially prone to skimming. In 1999, Chicago's North Side College Prep accepted 400 of approximately 3,000 applicants. Fifty-seven percent of the incoming class was white, despite the fact that white students constituted just 10 percent of Chicago's public school population. Only 14 percent was African American, even though such students constituted a majority of all public school students in Chicago. By employing stringent admissions standards, North Side has achieved an outstanding reputation, enabling it to draw students not only from neighborhood public schools but from nearby private schools as well. No less than one-third of the school's freshman class had attended a private school the previous year. "This place is top-notch and it's free," pointed out one North Side student who had been attending a Lutheran school. "It's pretty simple. You can get a better education here than at Luther North, and you don't have to pay $5,000 in tuition."[2]

Academically selective public schools remain the exception, however, not the rule. Neighborhood schools, open to all children residing within defined boundaries, serve more than 85 percent of public school pupils.[3] Yet another selection rule pervades public education. By requiring students to live within a specific district, school boards have created a system that is highly stratified by class and race.[4] Families that are able and willing to pay what the housing market demands can buy good schools, while those that lack sufficient resources are consigned to poorer ones.

In three New York City boroughs for which we have relevant data, a clear connection between social characteristics and educational performance is evident. In some of the boroughs' public schools comparatively few students come from families with low incomes, as indicated by the relatively small percentage of students eligible for the free-lunch program; meanwhile, in other public schools in the boroughs, most of the students come from low-income families. The average academic performance in schools is closely associated with the proportion of students eligible for free lunch. Only 55 percent of third-graders attending schools with many free-lunch students scored above the minimum on the state exam, while 75 percent of third-graders scored above the minimum in schools with few such children.[5] Quite simply, processes of selection separate students along income lines, in turn stratifying them by level of academic performance.

The common school attended by all children is, for the most part, an American myth. To be sure, many small towns still have one high school that serves the entire community. But for nearly a century, small towns have been giving way to large metropolitan areas in which whole suburbs are clearly defined in socioeconomic terms—industrial, working class, middle class, elite. In the largest metropolitan areas, ethnic and religious identity as well as socioeconomic status serve to define communities; there, suburbs are often regarded not just as rich or poor, but also as black, Hispanic, Catholic, or Jewish. Within central cities, neighborhood boundaries are equally pronounced. Such housing patterns have a direct effect on the composition of public schools. As long as public schools draw students only from specified neighborhoods, residential segregation begets school segregation.

Skimming in Private Schools

If skimming and segregation already characterize American public schools, wouldn't vouchers only make a bad situation worse? John Witte, the state-appointed evaluator of the Milwaukee voucher program, characterized such concerns succinctly: "Vouchers will (1) further reduce equal access and equal results in terms of achievement by increasing the elite selection of students by schools; and (2) accelerate the current problem of segregation of students by race, class, and educational achievement."[6]

Within a voucher system, racial and class selection may occur simply because parents are not equally adept at making informed decisions about their child's education. While some families may use their voucher to send their children to better schools, many others may lack the wherewithal to scout out and then apply for admission to adequate private schools. In the words of educational sociologist Amy Wells, "White and higher-SES [socio-economic status] families will no doubt be in a position to take greater advantage of the educational market."[7] An education system based on choice, then, may relegate African American, Hispanic, and poor students to under-funded and increasingly neglected public schools.

Not only may better-off families be in a better position to take advantage of the schooling options presented, but private schools would seem to have strong incentives to pick out the best and brightest students. Just as a univer-sity's reputation rests in part on the selectivity of its admissions standards, so too may the long-term success of a private school depend in part on its abil-ity to attract talented students from financially stable families.

Despite those possibilities, one cannot easily foresee how a comprehensive voucher system will impact the degree of class and racial separation within the country's educational system. Prima facie, private schools appear to be more selective than public schools for the simple reason that parents must pay tuition to send their children to private school, whereas a public school education, at least nominally, comes free of charge. But differences in neigh-borhood housing costs may produce public schools that are equally stratified. If it helped to level the economic playing field, a voucher-based system might actually be less selective than a system of education based on residency.

Information now available suggests that the existing differences between public and private schools are not as large as many imagine. Most private schools have little in common with the famous residential schools of New England or the academically advanced institutions attended by the children of Washington, D.C.'s political elite. Those privileged retreats do select their students from brilliant, successful, and well-connected families, and they demand high tuition for their services. But Andover and St. Albans are as much the exception among private elementary and secondary schools as Yale and Princeton are among private universities. Most private schools are known more for their religiosity than their social exclusivity. Of the 5 million-plus students who attend private school, roughly 50 percent attend Catholic schools, where the average annual tuition for elementary school stu-dents is approximately $1,600 a year; 35 percent attend other religiously affiliated schools, where the tuition is $2,600; and 15 percent attend nonsec-tarian schools, where the tuition is $4,700.[8] Of those schools, only a few cater to the country's richest citizens.

Nor are private schools mainly a byproduct of white flight from public schools. True, new private schools appeared in the South during the 1950s and 1960s in response to court-ordered desegregation plans. But elsewhere, it was not socially advantaged citizens but poor immigrants who built America's private schools. Catholics, Lutherans, and members of other religious groups constructed the vast majority of private schools in the United States. In recent years, those schools have opened their doors to increasing numbers of black and Hispanic children: in 1997, African Americans constituted 10 percent of the students attending private elementary schools, Hispanics 9 percent, and Asians and Pacific Islanders 5 percent.[9] The proportions of members of those minority groups who attend private schools come close to approximating their share of the total U.S. population. Private schools, what is more, tend to be more integrated than public schools. According to the U.S. Department of Education, nationwide 54 percent of public school students, compared with just 41 percent of private school students, attended schools whose student body came predominantly (90 percent or more) from a single racial group.[10]

This is not to say that there are no distinctions among private schools. Indeed, the amount of variation in students' economic background in private schools exceeds that in public schools, the result perhaps of variation in the tuition private schools charge. When it comes to student academic performance, however, private schools are *less* heterogeneous than public schools. According to one national survey, "despite the greater variation in socioeconomic status across private schools, there is less variation in test scores across private schools than across public schools."[11] In sum, differentiation by income is greater in the private than in the public sector, but differentiation by race and academic ability is less.

Skimming in Voucher Programs

Despite the willingness of private schools to admit students with a broad range of abilities and ethnic backgrounds, they still may not provide realistic options for low-income families, which have the greatest need for more school choice. While partial vouchers give those families some of the resources they need to attend a private school, the remaining tuition, transportation costs, and additional amounts for books, fees, and uniforms may exceed their capacity to pay. Moreover, families may lack information about available private school options, and they may be unable to fulfill expectations that they volunteer at their children's new school.

Skimming in a voucher program can occur in various ways. To start, private schools may simply deny admission to low-income minority families. National Education Association (NEA) president Robert Chase claims that "a large majority of voucher schools . . . reject two-thirds of their applicants." According to University of Wisconsin professor Michael Apple, an applicant's failure to pass entrance tests is the primary reason for not getting access to a private school: "Children who perform well on such . . . tests are welcome, but those who do not are often discouraged or marginalized."[12] Given this scenario, it is hard to imagine how a voucher program would benefit the poorest or most needy students.

More subtle selection processes also may be at work. Many low-income families lack the motivation to apply for a voucher, much less investigate private school options. As a result, according to Henry Levin, "choosers will be more advantaged both educationally and economically than non-choosers . . . thereby relegating [the latter] to their assigned [neighborhood] schools."[13] The experiences of one Washington, D.C., parent are consistent with Levin's suggestion: "I don't think that the public school is giving [my child] the challenge that he wants. He does do his work, and he's fast. . . . And that's why I'm trying to get him into a private school—because I'm sure it would be a better challenge for him."[14]

Skimming may proceed after a voucher student has enrolled in a private school. Once the school year has begun, teachers and administrators may weed out underperformers. Students who have special needs or who require additional attention may be encouraged to leave, producing higher rates of turnover among voucher recipients—either within the school year or from one school year to the next.

In the remainder of this chapter we examine who applies for vouchers and who uses them to attend private schools. We investigate selection effects throughout the first two years of voucher programs, from the initial decision to apply to later decisions to keep a child in a private school. Overall, we found little academic and only modest social skimming among younger applicants, but academic selection effects were more pronounced among students seeking a private school in grades 6 through 8.

Who Applies for Vouchers?

To determine who applies for vouchers, we compared various characteristics of a random sample of applicants for Children's Scholarship Fund (CSF) vouchers with a sample of the eligible population. (See chapter 2 for sampling and data collection techniques). For the most part, differences between the two groups were modest. As shown in table 3-1, 23 percent of the mothers of voucher applicants reported that they had a college degree, hardly more that the 20 percent of mothers of eligible public school children. Similarly, students applying for vouchers were only slightly more likely than the eligible population to live with both parents. There were no significant differences between the two groups in the average age of the child's mother or in the percentage of mothers who had been born in the United States. However, appli-

Table 3-1. *Demographic Characteristics, Applicants for CSF Voucher and Eligible Families*

Percentage except as noted

Characteristic	Voucher applicants[a]	National sample of eligible public school families[b]
Mother graduated from college	23	20**
Two-parent household	52	46***
Mother's age (average years)	37.1	37.2
Mother born in United States	82	83
Lived in current residence ≥ two years	81	71***
Black	49	26***
Hispanic	17	25***
Catholic	25	28**
Attend church at least once a week	66	38***
Number of cases	(2,303–68)	(874–971)

*p < .10; **p < .05; ***p < .01; two-tailed tests.

a. Sample of applicants not offered a voucher.

b. Data from national sample are weighted to ensure representativeness.

cant families were 10 percentage points more likely to have lived in their current residence for two years, suggesting that applicant families were less mobile than the eligible population as a whole.

The racial composition of the two groups made for the biggest—and by far the most important—difference revealed by our investigation. No less than 49 percent of voucher applicants were African American, even though they constituted just 26 percent of the eligible population. These results are consistent with another scholar's finding that minority families are especially interested in moving their children from public to private schools.[15] Apparently the demand for vouchers among African Americans is larger than what one would assume if one looked only at patterns of private school use in the absence of an external subsidy.[16]

Given the large network of relatively inexpensive Catholic private schools, it is somewhat surprising that voucher applicants were actually slightly less likely to be Catholic than the eligible population. Nevertheless, religiously observant families were especially likely to apply for a voucher. Sixty-six percent of voucher applicants reported that they attended church at least once a week, a response given by only 38 percent of eligible public school families.

Table 3-2 provides information on the level of voucher applicants' involvement in their public school compared with that of the eligible population.[17] The findings are mixed. On the one hand, voucher applicants

Table 3-2. *Parents' Involvement, Applicants for CSF Voucher and Eligible Families*

Characteristic	Voucher applicants[a]	National sample of eligible public school families[b]
Parent/teacher conferences per year	3.1	2.5***
Telephone conversations per year	2.4	2.7***
Volunteered in school (four-point scale)	0.9	0.7***
Talk to other parents (four-point scale)	1.9	1.9
Number of cases	(662–69)	(964–68)

*p < .10; **p < .05; ***p < .01; two-tailed tests.
a. Sample of applicants not offered a voucher.
b. Data from national sample are weighted to ensure representativeness.

attended more parent-teacher conferences and volunteered for longer periods of time at their child's school during the past year than did parents in the eligible population. On the other hand, applicants spoke less frequently with their child's teacher by telephone. One way of reconciling those findings is to distinguish between teacher-initiated and parent-initiated involvement. Taking advantage of parent-teacher conferences and volunteering at school may come at the initiative of parents, and our data suggest that parents who make the effort to participate in school life in this way are more likely to apply for vouchers. Telephone conversations with teachers, on the other hand, may originate with the teacher. When fewer calls go out, schools may miss opportunities to communicate with families, making them more likely to apply for a voucher.[18]

The need for special education may keep families from applying for a voucher. To examine this possibility, parents were asked whether their child had ever been diagnosed as having a learning disability. As table 3-3 indicates, no selection effects along this line were observed. The percentage of students applying for the program who had a disability did not differ significantly from the percentage reported by the eligible population as a whole. The survey responses of students also show little evidence of family self-selection. Students who applied for a voucher reported that they expected to stay in school longer than did students in the eligible population. But if this suggests that voucher applicants tended to be the more motivated students, responses to two other questions—"How difficult was your class work?" "Did you have trouble keeping up?"—indicated that voucher applicants found public schools to be challenging. When an index of school difficulty was constructed from the answers to these two items, voucher applicants,

Table 3-3. *Academic Characteristics, Applicants for CSF Voucher and Eligible Families*

Characteristic	Voucher applicants[a]	National sample of eligible public school families[b]
Parents' reports		
Student has been diagnosed with		
a learning disability	14%	13%
Number of cases	(692)	(943)
Students' reports		
How far student will go in school		
(four-point scale)	4.1	3.8***
Would read better with help		
(four-point scale)	2.6	2.4**
Class work is hard (four-point scale)	2.1	2.3
Trouble keeping up (four-point scale)	2.1	2.2
Index of difficulty in school		
(varies between 1 and 3)	2.1	2.6***
Number of cases	(223–36)	(482–526)

*p < .10; **p < .05; ***p < .01; two-tailed tests.
a. Sample of applicants not offered a voucher.
b. Data from national sample are weighted to ensure representativeness.

more than those eligible for a voucher, indicated having more academic problems.[19] In general, then, families most likely to apply for a scholarship had children with high hopes but were frustrated with their progress.

Table 3-4 addresses the concern that many white parents would use vouchers to remove their children from schools attended by large numbers of minority students, thus increasing racial segregation. Each row reports the percentage of families whose children attended schools with a minority population of 90 percent or more. Among whites and Hispanics, no differences were observed between applicants and the eligible population. However, there is evidence that African American families left public schools that had an overwhelmingly minority student body. A little less than half of African American applicants attended schools that were 90 percent minority, compared with only 32 percent of eligible African American families. Rather than contributing to white flight, the Children's Scholarship Fund program appears to have been successful in giving African American students opportunities to leave predominantly minority public schools.

In general, applicants to the CSF voucher program resembled a cross-

Table 3-4. *Attendance at Public School with a 90 Percent or More Minority Population, Applicants for CSF Voucher and Eligible Families*

Group	Voucher applicants[a]	National sample of eligible public school families[b]
Whites	8%	8%
Number of cases	(146)	(446)
Blacks	47%	32%***
Number of cases	(359)	(205)
Hispanics	23%	23%
Number of cases	(111)	(186)

*p < .10; **p < .05; ***p < .01; two-tailed tests.

a. Sample of applicants not offered a voucher.

b. Data from national sample are weighted to ensure representativeness.

section of the eligible low-income population in many respects. Notably, the need for special education was just as high among applicants as among the eligible population. Although the parents of applicants were somewhat better educated and more likely to live in two-parent families, the differences were small. Other differences, however, were more substantial: Applicants were more likely to be religiously observant, suggesting that the religious identity of most private schools affects the type of families they attract. Also, African Americans were much more likely to apply, especially if their child attended a segregated public school.

Who Uses a Voucher?

As discussed in the previous chapter, vouchers were randomly allocated to applicants. As a result, the lotteries themselves had no skimming effect. Applicants offered a voucher in New York City; Dayton, Ohio; and Washington, D.C., did not differ significantly from applicants who were not offered a voucher. Quite simply, the lotteries worked as planned.[20]

Vouchers performed as expected in another way as well: they increased the schooling options of lottery winners. Although most families had to supplement the vouchers with at least half of the tuition themselves, winning the lottery increased the likelihood that a child would attend a school that his or her family preferred. In New York City, Dayton, and D.C., parents who were offered a voucher were 15 percentage points more likely, on average, to say that they sent their child to a preferred school (see table 3-5). Clearly, vouchers expanded the school choices available to the inner-city poor.

Table 3-5. *Attendance at Preferred School by Those Offered a Voucher and Those Not Offered a Voucher, Year I*

City	Offered voucher (percentage)	Not offered voucher (percentage)	Impact of voucher offer (percentage difference)
Three-city average	73	58	15***
New York City	72	60	12***
Dayton	83	50	33***
Washington, D.C.	70	52	18***

*$p < .10$; **$p < .05$; ***$p < .01$; two-tailed tests. Three-city average weighted inversely to variance.

Still, as discussed in chapter 2, not all families were able to take advantage of the vouchers offered to them. Of those participating in the evaluation's Year I follow-up testing session in New York City, only 82 percent of those offered a scholarship used it in the first year. In Dayton and Washington, D.C., only 78 percent and 68 percent of those families, respectively, made use of them (see table 2-3 on page 44).[21] Several factors contributed to this underutilization. For one thing, the announcement of lottery winners was not made until just a few months before the beginning of the new school year; by this time many families already had made their own plans for the coming year and many private schools already were full. One D.C. parent explained why her two children did not use the voucher:

> *Parent*: I didn't do that because . . . I didn't know I was going to get it, so I wasn't prepared. When I knew all the things you had to go through to . . . it was like the end of the school year anyway.
> *Focus group moderator*: It was pretty late in the year that you had found out, right?
> *Parent*: Exactly. So I didn't bother doing it.[22]

Another parent expressed the same concerns:

> *Parent*: The scholarship—we received it too late, because the school that she wanted to attend you had to go to summer school, and it was too late to enroll in summer school, so I declined.
> *Focus group moderator*: So you are going to try to get it this year?
> *Parent*: I got the notice in time and filled out the application and paperwork now, so hopefully we'll be right in line for the summer school session.[23]

Apart from the timing of the voucher offer, other factors depressed voucher use. The most common reason lottery winners gave was the family's inability to pay the remaining school costs. Fifteen percent of those offered a voucher in New York gave this as a reason for not attending a preferred school, as did 14 percent of those in Washington and 7 percent in Dayton. Apparently, a significant number of families could not afford to pay for books, school uniforms, fees, the portion of tuition not covered by the voucher, and other costs. As one D.C. parent said, "I declined on it because I couldn't afford to pay the difference. It was just too much . . . the fees are just too much . . . a lot of things that they receive in public school, it's like an extra fee in a private school."[24]

Transportation problems also may have added to the difficulties of switching to a private school. Many private schools have no buses and certainly not the extensive transportation systems that serve public schools. In one focus group session with parents who were offered but declined a voucher, a mother commented, "A lot of private schools don't offer transportation," and went on to describe how her work schedule precluded using a voucher because she could not pick up her daughter from school until late in the afternoon. Another mother echoed her sentiments by noting that private schools were "too far, no transportation. It was kind of a turn-off. So I just said I would leave him [in a public school]."[25] Their views were not aberrations. As much as 7 percent of parents said that an inconvenient location or transportation problems were among the reasons they decided not to use their voucher.

In addition to timing, costs, and transportation problems, a variety of other factors precluded parents' use of the voucher offered to them. Some parents said that the desired school lacked space for their child. Others moved. Still others said that they had found a public school of their choice. Significantly, no more than 2 percent of parents in any of the three cities said that they could not get their preferred school because they did not share the school's religious affiliation; and only 1 percent said that their child failed the admissions test. In other words, explicit screening by schools on religious or academic grounds appears to have been rare.

Still, private schools may have been less than forthcoming when explaining to parents why they could not admit their child. Another way of assessing the extent of skimming is to compare the educational and demographic characteristics of students who used a voucher with those who declined one. If schools select the best and brightest students while rejecting those of lower ability, one would expect to find voucher users to have considerably higher initial test scores, fewer special education needs, and more advantaged family backgrounds than those who did not make use of the voucher offer. But as the following section demonstrates, only moderate differences were observed between those who used the voucher and those who declined it.

Initial Test Scores

Some parents who used their voucher clearly did so on behalf of a talented child. As one Washington parent put it, "My first daughter, she finished 6th grade in the public school, and I saw that she had a lot of potential and that she would be better off in a private school. This is her second year in the private school, and she is doing great. And they have a lot of classes, and the academics are much, much better than the public system, and they have more opportunity to go to college and more expectations for their future."[26] But other parents made use of the voucher because their child's performance in public school was well below par. Explaining her reason for looking for an alternative to the public school, a Washington mother said that her son had ". . . been suspended. . . . 'Cause he won't stay in the classroom. He disrupts everything. He won't do anything. . . . "[27]

Which of these two parents represented voucher users as a whole? Were the children who used the voucher more academically capable than those who did not? Or were voucher users having problems in public school? To assess the academic ability of students at the time of application for a voucher, all applicants in New York City, Dayton, and Washington, D.C., who were entering grades 2 and above were asked to take the Iowa Test of Basic Skills in reading and mathematics. With this information, it was possible to see whether those who used their voucher to attend private school had better initial test scores than those who did not. To the extent that the two groups differed, skimming, whether by schools or by family self-selection, was occurring.

Results depended on the age of the child. As can be seen in table 3-6, no skimming was observed among younger children entering grades 2 through 5. In New York City and D.C., no significant differences were observed between users and decliners. In Dayton, there was actually reverse skimming. Those using the vouchers scored 4 percentile points lower than those declining the vouchers—suggesting that parents of problem children were using vouchers in hopes that their children could do better in an alternative setting. Other studies have obtained similar results. In Milwaukee, for example, the initial test scores of students who applied for vouchers were lower than those of the average low-income student in the city.[28]

The picture changes somewhat for older students. Private school administrators indicated that they were more likely to scrutinize these students' aca-

Table 3-6. *Initial Educational Characteristics of Students Taking Vouchers in Three Cities*

Characteristic	Takers	Decliners	Difference
Average initial reading test scores			
Dayton[a]	25.1	22.1	3.0
New York City[b]	26.6	25.5	1.1
Washington, D.C.			
All students	32.5	28.2	4.3**
Grades 1–5	32.4	30.0	2.4
Grades 6–8	32.9	23.8	9.2**
Average initial math test scores			
Dayton[a]	24.9	29.0	–4.1*
New York City[b]	21.1	20.7	0.4
Washington, D.C.			
All students	24.8	22.8	2.0
Grades 1–5	24.1	23.5	0.5
Grades 6–8	27.2	20.9	6.3**
Percentage of children with a learning disability			
Dayton[a]	8.2	10.2	–2.0
Washington, D.C.	9.2	13.4	–4.2
New York City [c]	10.0	15.0	–5.0**

*p < .10; **p < .05; ***p < .01; two-tailed tests. Test scores represent national percentile ranking points.
a. Grades 1–8.
b. Grades 1–5.
c. Grades K–4.

demic capabilities. One D.C. administrator indicated that she admitted students without regard to ability at an early age but was more wary of admitting older students. A Catholic superintendent of schools in a central city that was not part of our evaluations mentioned to one of the authors that older voucher students entering the schools under her supervision had more serious adjustment problems than did younger ones. As shown later in this chapter, her observations seem to be borne out by the reports of students themselves.

In most places data limitations prevented us from observing whether skimming on the basis of ability regularly occurred when older students—those in grades 6 through 8—tried to switch from public to private school.[29] In Washington, however, we received enough applications from older students to examine this question, and we did observe skimming on the basis of test scores for those students. Voucher users performed 9 national percentile points higher in reading and 6 percentile points higher in mathematics than those who declined a voucher.

Family Background

When deciding whom to admit, private schools may give greater consideration to students' family background than to their test scores. Administrators, for instance, may wish to verify that parents are financially committed to their child's education and that they are willing to support schools' educational programs. How different were the family backgrounds of those who used their voucher and those who did not?

Family backgrounds of voucher users and decliners in the three cities closely resembled one another. The two groups were similar in the likelihood that the mother and father lived together, the number of siblings in the family, the birthplace (United States or abroad) of mothers, and the length of time that the family lived at its residence. Some differences were observed, but they were, on the whole, both moderate and inconsistent from one city to the next (see table 3-7). Consider income, for example. In Dayton, the average income of voucher users was $3,000 *lower* than that of decliners. In Washington, D.C., however, the average income of users exceeded that of decliners by roughly $2,000. Similar inconsistencies emerged in examining other socioeconomic measures. In Dayton, mothers of users were less likely to work full time than mothers of decliners, but in New York City, mothers of users were more likely to work full time. In D.C., the two groups did not differ significantly. Welfare recipients were more common among users in New York and Dayton, but not in D.C. Mothers of users had somewhat less education in New York City but modestly more education in Dayton and D.C. In New York, whites were somewhat less likely to use a voucher; in the other two cities there were no statistically significant differences in the ethnicity of users and decliners.

We also asked parents about their involvement in their child's education—whether they volunteered at school, joined the PTA, helped their child with homework, or attended a wide variety of social and academic events with their child. In most cases, users and decliners closely resembled one another. Where differences were detected, parents who used the voucher tended to have been *less* involved in their child's education before they entered the program than parents who declined the voucher.

In the national CSF program, however, we detected clearer socioeconomic and other differences between users and decliners. Although they were nearly equally likely to come from two-parent households, the two groups differed in other respects, including household income and mother's education, labor

Table 3-7. *Demographic Characteristics of Families Taking Vouchers in Three Cities in Year I*

Characteristic	Takers	Decliners	Difference
Average family income			
Dayton	$17,681	$20,597	–$2,916**
Washington, D.C.	$17,774	$15,781	$1,993*
New York City	$9,583	$9,538	$45
Family receives welfare			
Dayton	17.2%	16.7%	0.5
Washington, D.C.	34.6%	41.6%	–7.0*
New York City	59.1%	54.1%	5.0
Family receives Social Security			
Dayton	4.1%	7.0%	–2.9
Washington, D.C.	13.3%	14.3%	–1.1
New York City	12.4%	5.7%	6.7
Average years of mother's education			
Dayton	13.6	13.2	0.5**
Washington, D.C.	12.9	12.6	0.3***
New York City	12.2	12.3	. . .
Mother employed full time			
Dayton	46.6%	55.2%	–8.6*
Washington, D.C.	56.8%	55.6%	1.1
New York City	20.7%	13.0%	7.7
Mother employed part time			
Dayton	17.7%	16.3%	1.4
Washington, D.C.	15.3%	10.5%	4.8**
New York City	15.4%	7.4%	8.0
Percent white			
Dayton	67	73	–6
Washington, D.C.	1	1	0
New York City	3	13	–10***
Percent Hispanic			
Dayton	1	1	0
Washington, D.C.	3	2	1
New York City	45	46	–1
Percent African American			
Dayton	32	26	6
Washington, D.C.	95	95	0
New York City	48	36	12***

$*p < .10$; $**p < .05$; $***p < .01$; two-tailed test.

Table 3-8. *Demographic Characteristics of Families Offered Vouchers in the National CSF program*
Percentage except as noted

	Takers	Decliners	Difference
Two-parent households	53.7	51.8	1.9
Average household income	$30,700	$33,000	–$2,300**
Mother lived at current residence			
at least two years	85.3	79.4	6.9***
Mother's age (years)	36.8	37.2	–0.4
Mother's ethnicity			
White	30.1	24.8	5.3***
African American	38.0	51.9	–13.9***
Hispanic	13.5	17.4	–3.9*
Mother's religious affiliation			
Catholic	31.3	24.1	7.2***
"Born Again" Christian	38.2	40.5	–2.3
Mothers who			
Have a college degree	29.4	22.4	7.0***
Attend church at least once a week	74.2	64.4	9.8***
Work full time	50.3	59.6	–9.3***
Students with learning disabilities	13.4	13.4	0.0

$*p < .10; **p < .05; ***p < .01$; two-tailed tests.

force participation, and frequency of church attendance (table 3-8). Also, whites were more likely than blacks and Hispanics to make use of the voucher offer. While these differences were statistically significant, they were not overwhelmingly large. For example, 29 percent of mothers in user households had a college degree, compared with 22 percent in decliner households. Thirty percent of users were white, compared with 25 percent of decliners. However, only 38 percent of users were African American, compared with 52 percent of decliners.

Special Needs

Even if private schools do not rigorously select students on the basis of test scores or family background, they might exclude those with special needs. Voucher programs did not provide larger vouchers for students with special needs, and given that students with physical or learning disabilities may require extra attention, private schools may only reluctantly admit them. To understand the way that vouchers may affect those with special needs requires a review of existing programs for disabled students.

During the 1997–98 school year, roughly 5.9 million of the nation's children were served by federally supported programs for students with disabilities.[30] Those programs cover a broad range of services; some require specialized facilities while others do not. In administering these programs, the U.S. Department of Education has established numerous classes of disabilities, which can, at the risk of oversimplification, be lumped together into two broad categories—severe and moderate. By labeling a disability moderate—a learning disability, speech or language impairment, or emotional problem, for example—we do not mean to suggest that it is insignificant. For many students, families, and schools, even moderate disabilities present serious challenges; they appear moderate only in comparison with severe, often life-long disabilities such as mental retardation, deafness, blindness, autism, traumatic brain injury, and developmental delay.

Educating severely disabled children not only is costly and demanding, but it also often requires special facilities. Even if children are mainstreamed—taught in regular classrooms alongside other students—specialized personnel must devote considerable time and effort to ensure their academic progress. As expensive as these services can be, the greater controversy in special education surrounds the provision of special services for children with moderate disabilities—in part because the number of children so classified nearly doubled between 1977 and 1998, from 5.4 percent to 9.2 percent.[31] Today, students with only moderate learning disabilities represent at least 70 percent of the total number of disabled students. One pair of analysts has estimated the percentage with only "mild disabilities" to be as high as 90 percent.[32] Some feel that many of those with moderate disabilities can be taught effectively within regular classrooms, in either public or private schools. Others feel that specialized services are necessary. Still others think that some public schools use the designation indiscriminately, thereby contributing to the special education classification of a disproportionate number of minority students.[33] Whether partial vouchers can help such students depends very much on whether their needs can be met within regular classrooms, because the monies made available by these partial vouchers are unlikely to be adequate to cover major additional expenditures.

For this reason, one might expect that most students with learning disabilities would refuse the vouchers offered to them. And, in fact, for some families this concern proved decisive. One Washington focus group participant, for example, said that concerns about special education were the primary reason she turned down the voucher: "We didn't want to [use the voucher] because we got the public schools to act. He's a special ed student."[34]

To get a better sense of the overall pattern of participation in the voucher program by students with special needs, we asked parents whether their child had a "learning disability." In the national CSF program, 13 percent answered yes (see table 3-8), a percentage that is roughly equivalent to U.S. Department of Education estimates of the overall incidence of disabilities nationwide. In New York, Dayton, and D.C., the percentage of students with learning disabilities (as reported by parents) hovered around 10 percent (see table 3-6).[35]

In the national CSF program, users and decliners were equally likely to have learning disabilities. In the three cities, however, small differences emerged. In New York, 10 percent of users had disabilities, compared with 15 percent of decliners. In Dayton, 8 percent of users and 10 percent of decliners had disabilities. In Washington, 9 percent of users and 13 percent of decliners had disabilities. Only the difference in New York was statistically significant, however.

Since the vouchers themselves did not cover additional services, it is possible that many students with learning disabilities were placed in regular classrooms. If so, this would conform to the recommendations of the many professionals who believe that students with moderate disabilities should not be isolated. We did not ask parents the precise manner in which the school addressed their child's special needs, but we did ask them "how well" their needs were addressed. In the national CSF evaluation, 73 percent of the private school parents responded positively, but only 30 percent of public school parents did. In two of the three cities, private schools also appeared to have the advantage (see table 3-9). In Washington, D.C., 49 percent of the private school parents said that their school was addressing their child's special needs "very well," compared with only 23 percent of the public school parents. In New York, 33 percent of the private school parents and 17 percent of the public school parents gave the same response. In Dayton, however, 48 percent of the public school parents but only 40 percent of the private school parents said that the school attended very well to their child's special needs. Only the D.C. results were statistically significant, however.

In Year III, New York parents were asked to indicate the biggest obstacle keeping their child from advancing academically at school. Among the items they were invited to consider was the "lack of facilities and programs needed to address their child's special needs." Parents with children in private school were much less likely than control-group parents to say that their school lacked such facilities and programs. Only 7 percent of the parents with children in private school expressed this concern, compared with 17 percent of the control group, a statistically significant difference.

Table 3-9. *Schools' Ability to Address Students' Learning Disabilities*

	Year I			Year II		
Program	Private school (percentage)[a]	Public school	Impact (percentage difference)	Private school (percentage)[a]	Public school	Impact (percentage difference)
Dayton	40	48	–8	95	0	95***[b]
Washington, D.C.	49	23	26**	28	14	14
New York City	33	17	16	26	16	10
National CSF	73	30	43	. . .	. . .	. . .

*p < .10; **p < .05; ***p < .01; two-tailed tests.

a. Percentage of families claiming school does "very well" in addressing learning disabilities. Percentages expressed in terms of those students who have the relevant special need, *not* in terms of the total population.

b. This impact is based on a very small number of observations.

Focus group conversations helped explain why parents appreciated the special education programs offered by private schools. When one recipient of a voucher in Dayton was asked how she liked her child's private school, she responded:

Love it. They are wonderful people. I walked into a meeting the other day for my daughter, who is having a hard time in math. They laid out the testing. There were two psychologists at this meeting, and both her teachers—two psychologists were at this meeting and another special education person. Five people showed up at this meeting for my one daughter who is doing poorly in math. . . . They did all this testing. They said she is a brilliant child. We need to boost her confidence. She can do this, we just have to work with her. They invited her tutor in who works with her—there were seven of us around the table to discuss one child with a "D" in math. It was awesome. I said, "You can't get this anywhere else."[36]

Another parent discussed the way special education worked at a D.C. private school:

They [name of private school] got counselors here to help the children with slow disabilities. They have groups . . . where . . . she, maybe, comes in one or two times out of the week and she sit with the children who have . . . reading comprehension problems and stuff like that . . . and . . . get a chance to really express themselves within a group, so that help them come off when they get in a group of other kids in the classroom.[37]

Private schools, then, appeared to have played a positive role in the education of voucher students who were in need of special education. While students in New York City were less likely to use a voucher if disabled, usage rates were similar in the other evaluations. Moreover, among those families that used their vouchers, private schools seem to have served student needs more effectively than public schools did—according to the parents surveyed.

Voucher Use in San Antonio

Since the Edgewood program offered vouchers to all low-income families living in the school district, it was possible to compare the characteristics of those who used vouchers with a cross-section of students and families who remained in the district's public schools. Comparison of the two groups provides an additional estimate of skimming that occurs in school voucher programs.

In many ways, the opportunities in San Antonio for skimming could hardly have been greater. For one thing, because the program was not announced until mid-April 1998, just a few months before the beginning of the new school year, the program clearly benefited the quick-footed. The need to move quickly was all the greater given limitations in the number of available places in private schools. Only 837 of the nearly 14,000 eligible students actually attended a private school in the fall of 1998. Quite apart from these practical realities, the program was bitterly attacked by public school officials, possibly discouraging all but the most energetic and committed parents from applying.

Many education leaders in Texas fully expected the Edgewood voucher program to produce "cream" as rich and thick as the clotted cream that the British spread on Devonshire scones. An officer of the Texas Federation of Teachers predicted that the private schools would "cherry pick" desirable students so as to "shorten the honor roll" in public schools.[38] The Edgewood school superintendent, Dolores Munoz, speaking on national television, said, "Right now, I don't have the profile of every child" using a voucher, but she was willing to "guarantee . . . that at least 80 percent will be the high-achieving students. They will be. The private schools are having the choice of the best students around, because they have a criteria, and not every child is taken into consideration, and their doors are . . . not open for every child."[39] Concerns about skimming were not directed only at children. According to a

Houston Chronicle editorial, "a large student exodus could shift support of the most able parents away from neighborhood schools."[40]

Conversations with parents in focus groups illustrated how skimming might occur in the San Antonio program. One savvy parent previously had found a way to place her seventh-grade daughter in a neighboring school district; with the arrival of the voucher program, it was possible to send her to a private school closer to home. "She is an honor student . . . she's real good, she's real smart. She talks about going to college, she already picked out a college. She wants to go to Notre Dame." The same mother decided to keep her son in an Edgewood public school because he lacked the ability that her daughter exhibited. "I don't think that the private schools have a lot of programs—the Edgewood district has a lot more programs for kids that need extra help and after-school care. They have a lot of tutoring where you don't have to pay. [At the private school] you have to pay for tutoring."[41]

But another Edgewood parent reported making the switch to private school because her child had performed poorly in school: "My daughter "didn't bring me no homework, I didn't see nothing. When I changed her . . . here [to the private school] . . . , she was not used to the discipline. . . . [Now] I see a lot of changes in my daughter. . . . She's outspoken, she likes to read, she likes to talk."[42]

To see whether selection was a general phenomenon in Edgewood, we used a variety of indicators to compare voucher recipients with those who had remained in public school. Given the widespread expectation that only the best and brightest students would take advantage of the voucher, we were quite surprised by the findings. Initial math test scores of voucher recipients were virtually the same as those of students remaining in public schools, and initial reading scores were only somewhat higher (see table 3-10). In addition, the two groups of families earned roughly equivalent incomes. The percentages of two-parent homes in the two groups were similar, and voucher students were no more likely to have enrolled in programs for gifted children.

In other respects, however, voucher students were better off. They were less likely to have participated in programs for students with learning disabilities. Their mothers were somewhat better educated—on average, voucher mothers said that they had received twelve years of education, compared with the eleven years reported, on average, by the public school population. Voucher parents also were somewhat more likely to be employed, and they were slightly less likely to receive government assistance.

These findings do not differ substantially from those obtained by researchers who worked for the Edgewood public school system. Because they also were interested in the amount of skimming that had occurred, they

Table 3-10. *Initial Test Scores, Voucher Students and Public School Students, Edgewood*

Initial average test scores	Voucher students (NPR points)	Public school students (NPR points)
Math	36.6	34.8
Reading	35.0***	28.3

*p < .10; **p < .05; ***p < .01; two-tailed tests conducted.
NPR = national percentile ranking.

compared the test scores of voucher students in grades 3 through 8 on the math and reading segments of the ITBS with those of all Edgewood public school students. (The school district had administered the test in the fall of 1997, just before the voucher program was announced.) For the most part, the two groups performed comparably.[43] In the words of the confidential report prepared by the Edgewood school district analysts, "few statistically significant differences are to be found" between the test scores of voucher students and those remaining in Edgewood public schools.[44]

Other signs of skimming were also less than overwhelming. According to official Edgewood records, 22 percent of all Edgewood students had limited English proficiency, compared with 17 percent of voucher students. While 20 percent of all Edgewood students participated in bilingual or ESL (English as a second language) programs, 14 percent of voucher students did. Ninety percent of students in the district as a whole were economically disadvantaged; among voucher students, the rate was 77 percent.[45] While the differences were noticeable, they hardly reflected the expectations of most observers.

Robert Aguirre, the administrator of the Edgewood voucher program, was not far off the mark when he observed that the voucher program was not attracting "high-achieving students in an academic sense."[46] The superintendent of San Antonio's Catholic schools noted that in order to meet the needs of the new voucher students, his schools had to add new weekend classes to help some of them with reading and math. "We don't bring in the brightest and smartest students," he said. "We wouldn't have these Saturday programs if that were true."[47]

Other Evaluations

In the Milwaukee and Cleveland voucher programs, other evaluators discovered a similar pattern. The Wisconsin Legislative Audit Bureau found that the ethnic composition of the participants in Milwaukee's expanded school choice program during the 1998–99 school year did not differ significantly from that of students remaining in public schools. Blacks constituted slightly more than 60 percent of both groups, whites approximately 20 percent, and Hispanics 13 percent; the rest were Asians, Native Americans, and other ethnic minorities.[48] A previous evaluation of the smaller Milwaukee program compared the test scores and family background of voucher recipients with those of public school students. Participants in the voucher program had lower average test scores than public school students in general and low-income public school students in particular. Voucher parents in the Milwaukee program were more likely to be African American or Hispanic, less likely to be married, and more likely to have more than one child. They also had lower incomes; however, they were more likely to report that at least one parent had some college education.[49]

In one of the Cleveland evaluations, voucher users were compared with decliners.[50] Users had *lower* annual incomes than decliners by nearly $5,000. The higher usage rate of lower-income families may have been due to the fact that vouchers were offered first to those with the lowest income, giving them more time to find an adequate private school. Also, the voucher itself paid most of the tuition costs in Cleveland. Differences in the education of mothers of users and decliners were too small to be statistically significant. However, African Americans were less likely to use a voucher offered to them than members of other ethnic groups.

Another evaluation of the Cleveland program compared third-grade voucher users with their peers in selected public schools. The analysts reported that "scholarship [voucher] students, like their families, are very similar to their public-school counterparts." According to the results of this investigation, voucher recipients, on average, had lower family incomes and were more likely to be headed by a single mother. However, those third-graders were "slightly higher achieving students" than their counterparts in public schools.[51] They also found that the third-graders who used vouchers were less likely to be from a minority background than were the comparison group of public school students. In addition, mothers of voucher students were somewhat more likely than public school mothers to have completed high school.[52]

In sum, the process of applying for a voucher and then finding a school where it could be used generated modest, albeit inconsistent, selection effects. Generally speaking, young children from low-income families gained entry into a private school regardless of their educational performance, but older children were less readily admitted if their test scores at the time of application were particularly low. In some, but not all, cities students from more stable, better-educated families were more likely to use the vouchers, but the differences, even when apparent, appeared modest. Most surprising, voucher students with learning disabilities were not excluded; on the contrary, parents reported that private schools addressed the needs of those students quite well.

Suspension Rates

Many have wondered whether private schools are more likely to suspend low-income, minority students, especially if they have difficulty adjusting to their new environment.[53] Parents in focus groups, however, indicated just the opposite. One public school mother in Washington, D.C., said that her son was "a hyper child . . . and before they can . . . really sit down and try to help me with him . . . they will suspend him."[54] Another parent, explaining why she was seeking a voucher, noted the problems her son was having in public school: "And he's been suspended. . . . 'Cause he won't stay in the classroom. He disrupts everything. He won't do anything. . . . It's because of how they treat the children. How they speak to the children. There's no respect at all in the school building at all."[55]

To see whether private and public schools treat students from low-income families differently, we asked parents in New York, Dayton, and Washington, D.C., whether their children had been suspended during the past year. A suspension may have simply required students to go to the principal's office, or it may have entailed one or more days' absence from school. Although we did not ask parents to discuss the severity of suspensions, we did obtain information about their frequency.

In general, suspension rates did not vary consistently between public and private schools (see table 3-11). In several comparisons, including those in the Cleveland and Edgewood evaluations, only minor, statistically insignificant differences could be observed. In a few cases, however, larger differences were identified, but they did not all point in the same direction. In Year III in New York, the suspension rate in public schools exceeded that in private schools by 5 percentage points. In the national CSF evaluation, suspension rates were also considerably lower in private than in public schools—5 percent compared with 12 percent, respectively—but in this case the differences were not statistically significant. In Year II in Dayton, suspension rates were 10 percent lower in private than in public schools, once again a sizeable but not a statistically significant difference.

The largest differences were observed among older students in D.C., who in Year I were suspended at a higher rate than their peers in public school.

Table 3-11. *Student Suspension Rates*

Program	Year I			Year II			Year III		
	Private school (percentage)	*Public school (percentage)*	*Impact (percentage difference)*	*Private school (percentage)*	*Public school (percentage)*	*Impact (percentage difference)*	*Private school (percentage)*	*Public school (percentage)*	*Impact (percentage difference)*
New York City	4.0	6.0	−2.0	3.0	2.0	1.0	2.0	7.0	−5.0**
Dayton	13.5	12.5	1.2	8.8	18.9	−10.1	…	…	…
Washington, D.C.									
All students	9.1	5.6	3.5	17.2	6.3	10.9*	18.9	11.4	7.5
Students grades 1–5	4.8	6.5	−1.7	15.9	3.8	12.1**	17.3	10.6	6.7
Students grades 6–8	20.4	2.8	17.6***	19.8	12.1	7.7	26.0	12.7	13.4
National CSF	5.1	11.6	−6.5	…	…	…	…	…	…

*p < .10; **p < .05; ***p < .01; two-tailed test.

According to parents' reports, 20 percent of the D.C. voucher users in grades
6–8 had been suspended, compared with just 3 percent of public school students. Still, this difference disappeared in D.C. in Years II and III, presumably because these older students became better adjusted to their new
schools.

Other information from the D.C. program suggests that older students
confronted serious adjustment problems in the first year after they switched
from public to private schools. For example, younger voucher students (those
in grades 4–5) were slightly but not significantly *more* likely to give their
school an "A" than public school students. But older voucher students, after
one year, were 40 percentage points *less* likely to give their school an "A" than
the older public school students. Also, younger voucher students were much
more likely to say "students are proud to attend my school" than comparable
students who stayed in public schools. Older voucher students, meanwhile,
were *less* likely to give this response than their public school peers. And while
younger voucher students in D.C. private schools were more likely to report
that "students got along with their teachers," older students in public and
private schools gave this response with equal frequency.

By Year III, D.C. private school students, regardless of grade level, were
more likely than public school students to report that teachers "put them
down." In addition, private school students were more likely to say other students "made fun of" them. In New York, by contrast, private school students
reported more positive relationships with teachers and peers than did public
school students. In addition, private school students were more likely to say
they felt proud to attend their school.[56]

School Mobility Rates

Quite apart from suspensions within schools, it remains unclear whether
voucher students will remain in private schools once they have been admitted. Just as a child may migrate from one public school to another, so a wide
variety of factors may encourage families to move their children from one
private school to another or back to a public school. Are mobility rates
among low-income students higher in public or private schools, both within
the school year and from one school year to the next?

There are good reasons to expect higher mobility rates within private
schools. The initial willingness of private schools to accept a wide range of
low-income students could be deceiving; perhaps selection occurs not at the
beginning but later in the educational process. Private schools may admit
young students from low-income families with little regard to their level of

educational achievement or family background, preferring to weed out lower-performing students during the school year. To do that, private schools need not formally expel such students. Often, they need only pressure a student's family to pull its child out of the voucher program or seek out another private school instead—either during the school year or between one school year and the next.

Mobility Rates within the School Year

We asked parents whether their child had changed schools during the past school year. Results in Year I were nearly identical in New York, Dayton, and D.C. School mobility rates within the school year were no higher for voucher recipients than for members of the control group: around 95 percent of both groups stayed in the same school throughout the year.

If a child changed school, we inquired why. The reason most frequently noted by voucher parents in Dayton and Washington concerned the quality of the new school, which a few parents found unacceptable; in New York City, parents most often cited the school's cost. Those concerns, however, affected only a handful of families. Neither response was given by more than 2 percent of voucher recipients.

Very few parents—less than 1 percent—said that they changed schools because their child had been expelled. Even in Washington, D.C., where older students found it more difficult to adjust to their new private school in the first year of the program, less than one-half of 1 percent of all parents gave this response. An evaluation of the Milwaukee program also concluded that although expulsion could be ordered by a private school, in practice "it was seldom used."[57]

Plans for the Coming Year

Not every parent felt that the decision to attend a private school had benefited their child. As one Dayton mother complained: "I wish I would have never put my children there. They will be switching. To me it is just not what the school should be. I thought that it was a good choice, but to me they actually don't really care about the kids, they are just more or less just interested in the scholarship money. That is my opinion. That is how I feel."[58]

To see how general this reaction was, we asked parents in Year I whether they planned to send their child to the same school the following year. Again, we observed comparable mobility rates in the two school sectors. Private school parents, in fact, were less likely to say that their child was changing schools the next year. This finding, however, is somewhat misleading because many public school parents were anticipating a school change because their child was graduating. Most private schools are K–8, whereas many public elementary schools "graduate" their children to middle school or junior high at the end of fourth, fifth, or sixth grade. Once this structural difference between public and private schools was taken into account, only minor differences in the mobility rates of the two groups were observed in the three cities.[59]

If a change in school for the next year was being contemplated, we asked parents why. The answers given most often by parents of students in public schools in the three cities referred to the unacceptable quality of the school or the fact that the family was moving. Although those two factors were mentioned with less frequency, they also topped the list of concerns of parents of voucher students in private schools in New York City and Washington, D.C. Parents of voucher students in Dayton cited the inconvenience of a school's location most often. Hardly any parents of voucher students in any of the cities said that their child had been asked not to return.

We also compared the education and family background of students who left the program at the end of Year I with those of students who remained. The results in Washington, D.C., were typical. Neither initial student test scores nor a student's physical or learning disabilities as reported by parents were significantly related to the likelihood that a student would remain in the voucher program into its second year. Nor were mother's marital status or parents' involvement in school related to the decision to leave the program.

Even though no skimming along educational lines was detected in D.C., economic factors did seem to affect the probability that a family would remain in the voucher program—a selection effect that very likely was due to the fact that vouchers typically covered only about half of the cost of private school tuition. Mothers of students remaining in the program into Year II were more likely to be employed full time and less likely to receive welfare benefits or food stamps. Also, mothers of continuing students were slightly better educated, had somewhat higher residential mobility rates, were slightly more likely to be white, and were more likely to have been born outside the United States.

Cumulative Effects of Baseline Characteristics

While occasionally detectable, skimming at any one point in time was relatively inconsequential—hardly the sort anticipated by critics of school choice. But even though only a small amount of selection may occur at any single point in time, perhaps over time effects accumulate, ultimately generating quite different populations of public and private school students.

To test this possibility, we used two probit models containing sixteen baseline student and family background characteristics to estimate (1) who needed a voucher, when offered; and (2) who among initial users remained in private schools. The models estimated voucher usage in New York City, Dayton, and Washington, D.C., over the first two years of the programs.[60] By including in these models baseline information on sixteen student and family background characteristics, more precise estimates of the overall pattern of skimming that occurred over the first two years were obtained.

Table 3-12 distills the key findings, showing which baseline characteristics—initial test scores, special education needs, family background characteristics, and parents' involvement in child's education—affected the probability that a student would remain in the voucher program. None of the models predicted much of the variance in voucher use. In other words, nearly all the variation in the likelihood that students would use the voucher over a two-year period was left unexplained by all sixteen items taken together.

Across the three cities, little by way of consistency is observed. Within each city, however, interesting patterns arise. To interpret the substantive meaning of the coefficients reported in table 3-12, we calculated how a change in certain key variables, holding all others at their means, affected the likelihood that a student would take a voucher and then remain in private school for two years. In New York City, being on welfare decreased the probability that someone would take a voucher by 8 percentage points and decreased by 7 percentage points the likelihood that users would remain in a private school for two years. African Americans were 15 percentage points more likely to take a voucher but 2 percentage points less likely to remain in a private school for two years. Having a learning disability decreased the probabilities by 14 and 13 percentage points, respectively. Finally, moving from one standard deviation below the mean of religious observance to one standard deviation above increased by 15 percentage points the chances that students would take a voucher offered to them and increased by 4 percentage points the likelihood that users would remain in a private school for two years.

In Dayton, moving from one standard deviation below the mean of mother's education to one standard deviation above the mean increased the probability that a student would take a voucher by 16 percentage points and that users would remain in a private school by 3 percentage points. An equivalent change for residential stability increased the probabilities by 7 and 2 percentage points, respectively. Moving from one standard deviation below the mean on baseline reading test scores to one standard deviation above the mean decreased the probability that a student would take a voucher by less

Table 3-12. *Determinants of Likelihood of Students' Participating in Voucher Program*
Coefficient

Characteristic	New York City	Dayton	Washington, D.C.
	Probability voucher offer accepted		
Family characteristics			
Employed full-time	−0.17	−0.01	0.22
Residential stability	0.19	0.42*	0.14
Mother's education	0.08	0.83***	0.62**
Welfare recipient	−0.27**	−0.05	−0.21
Religious observance	0.79***	−0.01	0.15
Married	−0.20	−0.02	0.03
Family size	−0.00	−1.01	0.18
Parents' involvement	0.22	0.15	−0.15
Student characteristics			
Math test scores	0.004	0.003	0.000
Reading test scores	−0.002	−0.006**	0.004*
Learning disability	−0.40**	−0.02	−0.28
Physical disability	−0.35	−0.38	−0.20
Gifted learner	−0.15	−0.11	−0.12
Non-English speaker	0.05	−0.71	−0.38
African American	0.49***	−0.15	0.06
Other racial minority	0.32*	−0.30	. . .

continued on next page

than 0.2 of a percentage point; the impact on the probability that users would remain in a private school was even smaller. Being African American decreased the probability that students would take a voucher by 6 percentage points, but increased the probability that a student would remain in private school for two years by 15 percentage points. Finally, while being employed full-time did not have any substantive impact on the probability that students in Dayton would take a voucher, it increased the probability that users would remain in private schools by fully 18 percentage points.

In D.C., moving from one standard deviation below the mean of mother's education to one standard deviation above the mean increased the probability that a student would take a voucher by 10 percent, though it had no substantive impact on the probability that voucher users would remain in private school for two years. A two standard deviation swing on baseline reading scores changed the probability that a student offered a voucher would use it

Table 3-12. *Determinants of Likelihood of Students' Participating in Voucher Program (continued)*
Coefficient

Characteristic	New York City	Dayton	Washington, D.C.
	Probability voucher users remain in program two years		
Family characteristics			
Employed full-time	−0.07	0.47*	0.31
Residential stability	0.18	0.11	−0.17
Mother's education	−0.04	0.17	−0.02
Welfare recipient	−0.32**	0.12	−0.29
Religious observance	0.26	−0.14	0.46**
Married	−0.07	−0.24	−0.18
Family size	−0.24	0.58	−1.28***
Parents' involvement	−0.07	−0.55	0.19
Student characteristics			
Math test scores	0.000	0.006	0.000
Reading test scores	−0.000	0.001	0.001
Learning disability	−0.50**	0.22	−0.06
Physical disability	0.01	...	0.60
Gifted learner	0.48**	−0.25	−0.04
Non-English speaker	−0.01	...	0.76
African American	−0.10	0.39*	−0.76**
Other racial minority	0.23**	−0.57	...

*p < .10, two-tailed test; **p < .05; ***p < .01. Probits estimated with robust standard errors, using unweighted data. The first model estimates the impact of covariates on the probability that students took a voucher, given that they were offered one; the second model estimates the probability that students stayed in a private school for two years, given that they initially took a voucher. All variables except test scores are rescaled to fall between 0 and 1. Parents' involvement measures differ slightly from city to city. Missing values for covariates imputed by best-subset regression.

by less than 0.1 of a percentage point; its impact on the probability that users would stay in private school was even smaller. While moving from one standard deviation below the mean of religious observance to one standard deviation above the mean had a negligible impact on the likelihood that students offered vouchers would take them, it increased chances that users would remain in a private school for two years by 8 percentage points. While African Americans were slightly more likely to take vouchers offered to them, they were fully 27 percentage points less likely to remain in a private school for two years. Finally, moving from one standard deviation below the mean of family size to one standard deviation above the mean increased the likelihood that students offered vouchers would use them by 2 percentage points, but decreased the probability that users would remain in private school for two years by 17 percentage points.

Conclusions

Skimming has long been part of the U.S. public school system. The residential marketplace is responsible for much of it. Families that can afford to do so rent apartments and purchase homes in neighborhoods known for the quality of the local public schools. Since the desirability of neighborhood schools is factored into the value of the homes in any given neighborhood, a circular effect is created that perpetuates residential selection as long as current practices of public school assignment persist.[61]

Whether vouchers will accentuate, or ameliorate, the inequalities built into the structure of the U.S. public school system is central to the voucher debate. On the basis of the information currently available, it does not seem that vouchers will substantially increase the selectivity of the American educational system. Voucher programs, as they operate today, do not engage in significant skimming. On the contrary, they increase the number of choices that low-income parents perceive to be available.

In most respects, applicants to voucher programs do not differ dramatically from a cross-section of the eligible low-income population. Of particular note is the fact that applicants to the Children's Scholarship Fund program were just as likely to have children with special education needs as the eligible population. Although the parents of applicants were advantaged in some respects, they also were more likely to be African Americans and to have a child in a segregated school.

Among those who applied, private schools did not appear to be highly selective, especially where younger children were concerned. Initial test scores of those admitted to private school were virtually identical to scores of those not admitted. Even the presence of a learning disability did not present a strong barrier to using a voucher. African Americans and Hispanics were just as likely—and in New York City, more likely—to use a voucher as were whites. Parents' education was weakly and inconsistently associated with taking advantage of voucher opportunities.

After a student entered a private school, only moderate selection effects were observed. Younger students generally did not encounter serious adjustment problems when switching from public to private schools, and for the most part, no difference between younger children's suspension rates in public and private schools emerged. Also, school mobility rates both within the school year and from one year to the next were much the same in public and private schools.

One important exception to an otherwise consistent pattern was evident. In Washington, D.C., where a sufficiently large sample of older students (sixth to eighth graders) was available for study, we observed both private school skimming and adjustment difficulties in Year I. By Year II, however, the adjustment difficulties faded away.

On the whole, these findings earn school vouchers a surprisingly positive grade on the selection line of the report card. Skimming is such a pervasive feature of modern life that one would expect voucher programs to serve a disproportionate number of children of talented, privileged, and well connected people. But several factors mitigate this effect. First, public schools already are highly stratified. Parents with higher incomes already live in parts of metropolitan areas where better schools are available, and the ability to relocate may satisfy their demand for educational choice. In addition, magnet schools and other specialized learning programs give parents with high-performing children further options within the public school system. If the need for more choice is greatest among poor families and below-average to average students, then one would not expect a voucher program to cause much additional skimming.

Admittedly, the evidence available on skimming comes from small-scale interventions in their initial years of operation that focused on low-income families. Perhaps large-scale interventions involving a broader segment of the population operating over the long run will produce a more stratified educational system, one in which the best and brightest students leave the public schools while the less advantaged are left behind. Urban private schools might become more selective as their excess capacity diminishes, even though, for now, they appear to be accepting all comers. To test this hypothesis, one would have to observe large-scale interventions over a sustained period of time. Until such experiments demonstrate that selection is more extensive under a system of open choice than a system of residential choice, arguments against vouchers on the basis of skimming appear to be overstated.

4

Attending Urban Schools

At Welton Academy—the all-boys preparatory school portrayed in the 1985 movie *Dead Poets Society*—bagpipes play while students with names like Knox, Cameron, Neal, and Todd shuffle into the auditorium at the beginning of each semester to recite the 150-year-old institution's motto: "Tradition, honor, discipline, excellence." In the library at Mailor-Callow Prep School—the elite Manhattan private school depicted in the 2000 movie *Finding Forrester*—portraits of "the greats" serve as a continual reminder of the intellectual legacy that its students have inherited. Latin, chemistry, and philosophy instructors stride through marble foyers wearing bow ties, sweater vests, and tweed jackets in John Knowles's *A Separate Peace*. With its cupola, red brick dormitories, arched passageways bearing Latin inscriptions, bells, and clock towers—all set amid elms and ivy, misted by the fog rising over the river—Devon is "the most beautiful school in New England."

Holden Caufield—the protagonist in J. D. Salinger's *The Catcher in the Rye*—passed through both Whooton School and Elkton Hills before getting "the ax" from Pency Prep for not adequately applying himself, as illustrated by the fact that he forgot all of the fencing team's equipment on a subway in New York City. By Holden's account, though, all was copacetic, inasmuch as his boarding schools were stuffed with "phonies" from "wealthy families."

Few, if any, students in the voucher programs we evaluated attended any such school. Institutions like Andover, Exeter, and Sidwell Friends may educate the scions of the nation's wealthiest and best-connected families and inspire coming-of-age stories, but they play no practical role in school voucher programs. For poor families in large metropolitan areas, the disparity between fictional fortresses of wealth and privilege and the private schools their children attend could not be more pronounced. In many ways, public schools appear better equipped than the relatively spartan Catholic, Lutheran, and other Christian schools that most inner-city poor students attend. Yet these private schools have other assets—smaller classes, a more orderly environment, a better system of communication with families, and higher homework expectations for students. In this chapter we use results from the randomized field trials (RFTs) in New York City, Dayton, Ohio, Washington, D.C., and the Children's Scholarship Fund (CSF) programs to compare the private schools attended by voucher students with the public schools attended by students who would have switched to a private school if they had been given a voucher.[1]

Public and Private School Expenditures

When lobbying state legislatures, superintendents and teachers unions insist that money is the key. In the words of Harold O. Levy, the chancellor of New York City's schools: "You do it [education] the old-fashioned way. It's money. Money."[2] In adjudicating lawsuits that request equal school funding across school districts, many state judges have agreed. Districts that are strapped for cash, judges have argued, cannot hope to provide their students with an equal opportunity to succeed in life: "No one can ensure that adequate facilities and educational opportunities will lead to the success of the students in this state. One thing that is apparent, though, is that substandard facilities and inadequate resources and opportunities for any of those students are a sure formula for failure."[3]

Certainly, if additional monies can be spent wisely and effectively, a strong case can be made that the state should bolster educational funding and, to the extent possible, equalize funding among schools. Yet many studies of school expenditures have found little connection between what the state spends on education and how much students learn. How schools allocate existing resources surely has an impact on student achievement, but total resources available to the schools is "at best weakly linked to student performance."[4] A handful of studies show clearly positive effects of expenditures on test scores, but others show negative effects, and the vast majority show no effect at all.[5]

The optimum amount to spend on education is necessarily a matter of judgment. Over the past half-century, public expenditures on education have risen dramatically, even in constant dollars, keeping pace with the growth of the U.S. economy as a whole. In 1995, the United States allotted about 3.5

percent of its gross domestic product to public schools—about the same percentage that it did in 1950.[6] Some may deem that spending rate sufficient; others may think it not enough. Regardless, it vastly exceeds the amount that private schools spend. In the 1993–94 school year, public schools in the United States spent, on average, just over $6,100 per pupil.[7] By comparison, the average private school expenditure per pupil was estimated at $3,380, just over half of the amount spent by public schools.[8] Catholic and Lutheran schools spent $2,378 and $2,251 per pupil, respectively.[9] Among other effects, the differences in aggregate expenditures had important consequences for teachers' salaries: public school teachers earned, on average, one-third more than private school teachers.[10]

Columbia Teachers' College policy analyst Henry Levin correctly notes that public and private expenditures cannot be directly compared because public schools provide a broader array of services than private schools.[11] But with access to the financial records of both public and Catholic schools in three New York City boroughs—the Bronx, Brooklyn, and Manhattan—we were able to conduct a fairer comparison than previous scholars.[12] We deducted from the public school ledger all costs that most private schools do not incur—among others, all monies spent on transportation, special education, school lunches, and other ancillary services. We even excluded the very substantial costs of the educational bureaucracy that manages the operations of the public schools at the city, borough, and district level. All these deductions constituted no less than 40 percent of total public school costs. But even after expenditures for all of these items are subtracted, public schools still spent more than $5,000 per pupil each year, more than twice the $2,400 per pupil spent by Catholic schools, fully 72 percent of which comes from tuition.[13]

Although we were unable to make as precise a comparison elsewhere, available information made it abundantly clear that schools serving voucher students in Washington, D.C., Dayton, and San Antonio also operated with significantly fewer resources than the local public schools. In Washington, tuition at the private schools attended by voucher students averaged $3,113 per year.[14] If we assume that the tuition-to-expenditure ratio in D.C. was the same as in the three New York boroughs, then total per-pupil expenditures for those private schools averaged $3,988 in the 1998–99 school year. Again, considering only those services and programs that both public and private schools cover, adjusted per-pupil expenditures in Washington public schools still totaled more than twice private school expenditures, or $8,185, as estimated from data for the 1995–96 school year.[15]

The same patterns emerged in Dayton and San Antonio. In 1998–99, students in the Dayton voucher program paid, on average, $2,600 in tuition, while the Dayton public school system spent an adjusted average of $5,528 per pupil. In San Antonio, voucher students paid, on average, $1,982 in tuition, less than one-third of the adjusted average per-pupil expenditure of Edgewood public schools, which in 1997–98 amounted to $6,060.

Physical Facilities and Programs

Public and private schools rely on very different sources of funding. Public schools depend primarily on tax revenues collected at the local, state, and national level, and they therefore must appeal to a broad constituency. In many central cities, the amount public schools actually receive depends in good part on the lobbying efforts of interest groups and employee organizations. Most private schools, meanwhile, are heavily dependent on tuition payments and charitable events in which parents are extensively engaged. While religious schools receive some subsidies from their sponsoring church, students' parents provide the vast majority of their revenues. To the extent that different institutions and populations with different resources and expectations fund public and private schools, we can expect to see monies spent on different kinds of educational objectives.

With more money and subject to pressures from constituencies with stakes in specific programs, public schools construct more complex physical facilities and offer a broader range of programs. According to parents' reports in Dayton, Washington, D.C., and New York City, the biggest difference between public and private schools concerned the availability of programs for non-English speakers: 71 percent of public school parents reported such a program at their school, compared with 43 percent of private school parents (table 4-1). Other ways in which private schools fared less well than the public schools were, in descending order of magnitude: the availability of a nurse's office; a special education program; guidance counselors; a cafeteria; a library; programs for advanced learners; a gymnasium; an art program; and computer labs. There was no difference in the reported availability of music programs. Meanwhile, parents of children in private schools were more likely than their public school peers to report the availability of individual tutors and after-school programs.[16]

To see how the shift to a private school affected students from differing ethnic groups, we examined this question wherever sizable numbers of more than one ethnic group participated in the evaluation. Table 4-2 pro-

Table 4-1. *Facilities and Programs in Public and Private Schools*

	Year I		
Facilities and programs	Private (percentage)	Public (percentage)	Impact (percentage difference)
Programs for non-English speakers			
Two-city average	43	71	−28***
New York City	48	77	−29***
Dayton	n.a.	n.a.	n.a.
Washington, D.C.	35	58	−24***
Nurse's office			
Three-city average	75	94	−19***
New York City	80	94	−14***
Dayton	72	98	−25***
Washington, D.C.	57	94	−37***
Special education programs			
Three-city average	67	81	−14***
New York City	62	79	−17***
Dayton	82	88	−7
Washington, D.C.	67	78	−12**
Cafeteria			
Three-city average	86	96	−10***
New York City	90	96	−6**
Dayton	91	97	−6
Washington, D.C.	67	97	−30***
Child Counselors			
Three-city average	77	85	−8***
New York City	76	84	−8**
Dayton	56	79	−23***
Washington, D.C.	86	89	−4
Library			
Three-city average	92	96	−5**
New York City	87	94	−7***
Dayton	97	99	−2
Washington, D.C.	90	96	−6**
Gym			
Three-city average	88	88	0
New York City	92	88	4**
Dayton	85	100	−15***
Washington, D.C.	76	77	−1

continued on next page

Table 4-1. *Facilities and Programs in Public and Private Schools (continued)*

Facilities and programs	Year I		
	Private (percentage)	Public (percentage)	Impact (percentage difference)
Programs for advanced learners			
Two-city average	59	58	1
New York City	64	60	4
Dayton	n.a.	n.a.	n.a.
Washington, D.C.	65	52	13*
Arts program			
Three-city average	82	81	2
New York City	81	76	5
Dayton	87	90	−3
Washington, D.C.	78	81	−3
Computer lab			
Three-city average	86	84	2
New York City	89	83	6**
Dayton	80	71	10
Washington, D.C.	81	89	−8**
Music program			
Three-city average	88	84	4
New York City	83	75	8***
Dayton	100	93	6*
Washington, D.C.	84	84	0
After-school program			
Three-city average	91	85	6**
New York City	92	88	4
Dayton	81	67	14*
Washington, D.C.	89	79	9**
Individual tutors			
Three-city average	70	54	16***
New York City	63	54	9**
Dayton	79	48	31***
Washington, D.C.	75	56	19***

*$p < .10$; **$p < .05$; ***$p < .01$; two-tailed test.

vides an estimate of the impact of the move to the private sector separately for New York City's blacks and Hispanics in Years I, II, and III. Table 4-3 gives the same information for Dayton's blacks and whites in Years I and II. (There were not enough non–African American students in the Washington, D.C., evaluation to allow for inter–ethnic group comparisons.) To calculate these estimates, we combined all the resource items in table 4-1 into indexes that then were scaled to have a standard deviation of 1.0. Impacts can then be measured in effect sizes, standardized units that allow comparisons across different aspects of school life. As mentioned in chapter 2, an effect size of 0.1 generally is thought to be small; an effect size of 0.25 to 0.4 is moderate; 0.5 to 0.8, large; and 1.0 or more, quite remarkable. (Appendix B lists the questions used to construct indexes discussed throughout this chapter.)

In general, when black students switched to a private school, they experienced a greater reduction in school resources than did other ethnic groups in four of five comparisons. In three of these comparisons, intergroup differences in the resource index were statistically significant. In Year I of the Dayton voucher program, resources for African American private school students were 0.76 of a standard deviation less than for the African American control group, a very large impact.[17] In short, especially for African American students, the switch to a private school meant a switch to a school with fewer facilities.

A full assessment of school facilities and programs must take into account their quality as well as their quantity. Thus far, we have considered only the presence or absence of specific resources within the school—a gymnasium, nurse's office, cafeteria, and the like. We have not considered the quality of the facility or whether it was well maintained. However, in another part of the questionnaire, parents were asked whether they were satisfied with the facilities at the school their child attended. A much higher percentage of private school parents said that they were "very satisfied" with the facilities at their child's school than did their public school peers (see chapter 7, table 7-1), an effect that was quite consistent across ethnic groups and cities.

Focus group conversations of public school parents may help explain why private school parents were more satisfied with their more limited facilities. One Washington, D.C., parent noted that her child's public school "doesn't have enough equipment. The copier's broke. So which means the copier's broke . . . and they have one copy for 26 kids."[18] At another D.C. focus group, the following discussion ensued:

First mother: I mean my kids have come home and told me they don't even have toilet paper. . . .That's ridiculous.

Table 4-2. *Impact of Switching to a Private School on Characteristics of Schools Attended by African American and Hispanic Students in New York City*

Characteristic	African Americans (effect size of impact)	(N)	Hispanics (effect size of impact)	(N)	Significance of difference
School facilities					
Year I	−0.24*	529	−0.15	567	—
Year II	−0.49***	468	−0.08	526	**
Year III	−0.57***	455	0.02	511	**
School programs					
Year I	0.22*	527	0.05	564	—
Year II	−0.16	462	−0.04	522	—
Year III	−0.07	452	−0.03	508	—
Class size					
Year I	−0.61***	515	−0.04	540	***
Year II	−0.21	460	0.01	512	
Year III	−0.53***	449	0.20	504	***
School size					
Year I	−0.88***	366	−0.47***	364	**
Year II	−0.82***	353	−0.54***	408	*
Year III	−0.60***	349	−0.55***	391	—
School-parent communication					
Year I	0.71***	532	0.30**	564	***
Year II	0.78***	469	0.43***	528	**
Year III	0.55***	456	0.41**	513	—
Amount of homework					
Year I	0.64***	527	0.49***	565	—
Year II	0.48***	470	0.33**	527	—
Year III	0.62***	457	0.48**	514	—
Dress code					
Year I	1.47***	525	1.30***	559	—
Year II	1.06***	461	0.90***	512	—
Year III	0.97***	454	1.01***	510	—
Hallway monitors					
Year I	−0.62***	516	−0.55***	556	—
Year II	−0.67***	464	−0.10	519	***
Year III	−0.67***	451	−0.14	507	**
School disruptions					
Year I	−0.46***	524	−0.02	564	**
Year II	−0.27**	465	−0.16	523	—
Year III	−0.19	455	0.11	508	—

*$p < .10$, two-tailed test; **$p < .05$; ***$p < .01$. The last column denotes whether the estimated impact for African Americans is significantly different from that for Hispanics. Weighted two-stage least squares regressions performed; treatment status used as instrument. All variables are continuous and have been rescaled to have a standard deviation of 1.0; their impacts, therefore, are estimated in effect sizes.

Table 4-3. *Impact of Switching to a Private School on Characteristics of Schools Attended by African American and White Students in Dayton, Ohio*

Characteristic	African Americans (effect size of impact)	(N)	Whites (effect size of impact)	(N)	Significance of difference
School facilities					
Year I	−0.76***	326	−0.24	115	—
Year II	0.21	243	−1.03***	96	**
School programs					
Year I	0.37**	324	0.44	114	—
Year II	0.66***	242	−0.29	96	**
Class size					
Year I	−0.47**	319	−0.30	112	—
Year II	−0.18	229	0.11	94	—
School size					
Year I	−1.01***	244	−0.80***	97	—
Year II	−0.79***	183	−0.36	80	—
School-parent communication					
Year I	0.63***	327	0.71***	114	—
Year II	0.45**	244	0.35	95	—
Amount of homework					
Year I	0.10	327	0.01	115	—
Year II	0.39	241	−0.40	95	—
Dress code					
Year I	0.59***	323	0.97***	112	—
Year II	0.66***	237	0.25	90	—
Hallway monitors					
Year I	−0.29*	321	−0.53*	112	—
Year II	−0.61**	239	−0.41	92	—
School disruptions					
Year I	−0.69***	323	−0.92***	114	—
Year II	−0.38	244	−1.85***	96	**

*p < .10, two-tailed test; **p < .05; ***p < .01. The last column denotes whether the estimated impact for African Americans is significantly different from that for whites. Weighted two-stage least squares regressions performed; treatment status used as instrument. All variables are continuous and have been rescaled to have a standard deviation of 1.0; their impacts, therefore, are estimated in effect sizes.

Second mother: Oh, yeah, and they can't drink the water. They had to take a case of water to school.

Third mother: My son took two cases of water to school because some of the kids can't really afford to bring them. They have to sit there all day without water.

Fourth mother: One day this week, . . . the coldest day in school, [name of child] didn't have any heat. The kids had to sit in the classroom with coats on.[19]

Their comments were consistent with a variety of news reports at the time indicating that the physical condition of some public schools bordered on dilapidated. For instance, thousands of fire-code violations prompted D.C. school officials to close numerous schools in the 1990s while repair work was completed.[20] Still, not every parent in the public school control group complained about the facilities. One mother who had moved her child to a charter school was quite pleased with the results: "They're pretty good . . . they got elevators. They redid everything. They redid the windows. Heating is good. Cooling, of course, may be a problem in the summer 'cause if the teacher doesn't provide the fan, and it's hot, so it's uncomfortable."[21]

Class Size

Of all school resources, many parents and teachers place the greatest importance on class size. But despite the popularity of smaller classes, researchers have not reached consistent conclusions regarding their efficacy. Two experimental studies illustrate well the range of findings in the research literature. On the one side, a study of class size in Connecticut that took advantage of a natural experimental-like situation (accidental, sharp differences in class size) found little effect of class size on student achievement.[22] But an RFT conducted in Tennessee, the STAR study, found that reduced class size had positive effects. Young children in classes of sixteen students scored about 0.2 of standard deviation higher on standardized tests over a three-year period compared with students in classes of twenty-four students.[23]

But if researchers disagree, parents uniformly prefer smaller classes. Time and again, they complained about the size of public school classes. Said one D.C. parent who moved her child to the suburbs after not getting a voucher, "The classrooms were too big. The teachers were good teachers, mind me . . . them teachers were good teachers. And they're trying their best with these kids. But you cannot teach twenty-six or twenty kids at one time."[24]

Despite their popularity, smaller classes come at a high price. The single largest expense in education is the cost of personnel, and a reduction in class size from twenty-four to sixteen students (the size of the reduction in the Tennessee STAR study) requires a 50 percent increase in the number of teachers. The number of required classrooms also increases, which may necessitate new construction. In California, reducing class size to twenty students or fewer in grades 1 through 3 cost the state $1.5 billion annually. To attract new teachers, many districts have had to increase salaries by as much as 20 percent, adding further to the price tag.[25]

If public and private schools allocated their funds the same way, then private schools, with roughly half as much funding, presumably would place more students in each class. It is therefore surprising to learn that in New York City, Dayton, and Washington, D.C., parents reported *smaller* classes in the private schools. On average, class-size differences amounted to three students—twenty students in private schools, twenty-three in public schools. Results from the evaluation of the national CSF program were very similar—private school parents on average reported twenty students in the classroom, compared with an average of twenty-four reported for public schools. Admittedly, those were only parents' estimates. Nonetheless, they mirror the U.S. Department of Education's estimate that intersector differences amount, on average, to three students, with public schools placing twenty-three students in a class and private schools twenty.[26]

The reduction in class size was greater when African Americans switched to private schools. As shown in tables 4-2 and 4-3, all intergroup differences were in the same direction and two were statistically significant. The biggest reduction in class size for African Americans (observed in Year I of the New York program) was large: 0.61 of a standard deviation, or nearly five students per class. By comparison, class-size reductions were statistically insignificant for both Hispanics in New York and whites in Dayton. In short, one way in which African American students particularly benefited from the switch to a private school was in the greater reduction in class size.

School Size

If most parents and educators think that smaller classes, if affordable, are much to be preferred, no such consensus exists with respect to the optimum size of a school. For decades, experts held to the maxim that bigger was better. In the 1950s, Harvard president James Conant argued that all high schools should have graduating classes of at least 100 students, for only then could they provide a diverse curriculum with demanding courses for college-bound students.[27] To account for dropouts, four-year high schools would require upward of 600 students. And for Conant, this represented the minimum—still bigger schools allowed for an even more diverse curriculum. Following these strictures, schools in many communities attended to the needs of a thousand or more students wandering the halls and picking from the wide selection of subjects and extracurricular activities in their catalogs.[28]

It is easy to see how educators could have become enthralled with big schools. Small ones, like small kids, convey few bragging rights. With a larger talent pool, big schools can more easily mount community-oriented productions that bring credit and public attention to the school, assets that are needed for an institution that must justify itself not only to parents but to taxpayers, voters, and political officials as well. All else equal, the bigger the school, the better its sports, theater, art, and music presentations. Bigger schools have more students who receive external awards and gain admission to selective colleges, bolstering the school's reputation.

Big schools also can serve social purposes. In the 1960s and 1970s, a number of sociologists heralded large schools as a solution to segregation. By catering to wider catchments, schools could encompass diverse neighborhoods, bringing together rich and poor students of a variety of races and ethnicities. Big schools also can more easily provide specialized facilities for disabled students.[29]

Despite the political drift toward bigger schools over the past fifty years, the little red schoolhouse came back into vogue at the end of the twentieth century. When two troubled youth killed a teacher, twelve classmates, and themselves at Columbine High School in Littleton, Colorado, in the spring of 1999, many concluded that shopping-mall high schools alienate students and should be scrapped. In large, anonymous schools, critics contended, regulations substitute for community networks and teachers are forced to spend more time attending to social problems than to classroom instruction. Nevertheless, no RFTs demonstrate that smaller schools perform much better. Although some studies indicate that students learn more in smaller schools, other studies find quite the opposite.[30]

Although research on school size is inconclusive, private school leaders seem to regard smaller schools as more desirable than do public school policymakers. According to U.S. Department of Education data, public elementary schools contain, on average, 547 students, compared with 210 students in private schools.[31] That estimate does not differ substantially from the estimates of parents who participated in the national CSF evaluation. Asked for the approximate number of students in the school their oldest child was attending, parents, on average, indicated that public schools numbered 513 students, compared with 234 students in private schools. In Dayton, New York City, and Washington, D.C., the differences were somewhat smaller, though the overall pattern was the same. Compared with the public schools serving the same population, private schools in the three cities were, on average, 38 percent smaller: private schools had 278 students, compared with 450 students in public schools.[32]

For African Americans in both New York and Dayton, the shift to private schools had a greater impact on the average size of schools than it did for other ethnic groups (again, see tables 4-2 and 4-3). In Year I of the New York program, the switch reduced the average size of the school attended by African Americans by 0.8 of a standard deviation, and in Dayton by more than 1.0 standard deviation, or, in each case, by approximately 185 students. Hispanics and whites who switched to the private sector also left larger schools for smaller ones, but the magnitude of the change was considerably smaller.

Nonetheless, the connection between school size and student learning is not well-established. Nor are most of the other "hard" indicators of school quality, such as teachers' salaries, types of facilities, or range of programs.[33] Given the difficulty of identifying easily quantifiable factors that affect school quality, a number of scholars have searched for softer, more subtle indicators. We turn now to less tangible but perhaps more meaningful differences between public and private schools.

Effective Schools

A number of scholars in the early 1980s conducted case studies that sought to identify the factors that contribute to an effective school. Although researchers do not agree on any one list of critical factors, most concede the importance of a school's mission, its leadership, parents' involvement, teachers' expectations, and student homework. Research by George Madaus, Peter Airasian, and Thomas Kellaghan has been particularly influential. Drawing on others' studies and their own detailed analysis of Irish schools, the authors concluded that effective schools emphasized "homework and study," adding that "pupils expect—and are expected—to do well." Regardless of a student's background, effective schools managed to convey and uphold a commitment "to structure, discipline, homework, and [a] general press to achieve in the school."[34] In another wide-ranging review of the literature on effective public schools, University of Wisconsin professors Stewart Purkey and Marshall Smith found that five "organizational and structural" attributes were especially important—school autonomy from the central office, clear instructional leadership, staff stability, a coherent curriculum, and staff development. In addition, effective schools solicited parents' involvement and support, recognized academic success, provided the maximum feasible amount of learning time, and had the support of the central office of the school district. [35] According to Purkey and Smith, the various factors all complemented one another, structural forces fostering an environment in which the latter processes could effectively yield achievement gains.

Along the same lines, John Chubb and Terry Moe concluded that effective schools have "clear school goals, rigorous academic standards, order and discipline, homework, strong leadership by the principal, teacher participation in decision making, parental support and cooperation, and high expectations for student performance."[36] In their study, Chubb and Moe found that principals at effective schools consistently reported more cooperation, predictability, and informality in their relations with parents. In addition, they reported that superintendents and central office administrators had less oversight regarding curriculum, instructional methods, hiring and firing of personnel, and disciplinary standards. Chubb and Moe found that overall, more than 60 percent of effective schools had an above-average level of administrative autonomy, compared with less than one-third of ineffective schools.

Although a fair measure of consensus exists among scholars on what makes for an effective school, those who have reviewed the literature emphasize slightly different characteristics. Madaus and his colleagues stress the importance of homework and high expectations. Purkey and Smith emphasize parents' involvement, local school autonomy, and a climate in the classroom that maximizes the amount of time engaged in learning. Chubb and Moe add to the list a clear mission and teamwork within the school.

In our research, parents were surveyed about several of those characteristics. They were asked to report on the frequency of communication between school and family, the amount and quality of homework, the degree of order in the classroom, and the methods schools used to maintain discipline.[37] One may wonder whether parents are well-informed enough about school life to give accurate reports, but, as already has been shown, their estimates of school and class size in the public and private sector did not differ materially from estimates provided by the U.S. Department of Education. If parents are as accurate in estimating some of the softer attributes of schools as they are in estimating school and class size, they may be able to tell us whether moving to a private school constituted a switch to a more effective school. Let us first examine a matter about which parents should be well informed, the frequency of communication between school and home.

School-Parent Communications

Private schools may be expected to communicate more extensively with families, if only because it is in their interest to keep their customers. Just as successful stores run responsive customer service departments and compile mailing lists of their regular clientele, so private schools may take extra pains to maintain a strong system of communication with the families they serve. Although individual teachers may make special efforts to reach out to families, public schools, as public institutions ultimately responsible to voters and taxpayers, do not have the same stake in maintaining close connections with parents.

Typical are the words of one mother who complained that officials at her public school did not keep her informed about her son's problems:

> [H]e would fight every day. He was coming home, "Mom, guess what? I got in a fight at lunchtime." Every day. And I told him, "If I hear you say that one more time I am going to ground you. I don't want to hear you say that anymore. You need to stop fighting." But . . . the principal never called me. The teacher never made contact with me. Nothing. To me, more or less, they just didn't care. They just let them do what they wanted.[38]

In contrast, one private school parent described how regular communication between parents and teachers allowed her to monitor her child's academic progress:

> [T]here is a lot of communication, especially on a weekly basis, because they bring home their folders with all their work in it, and it says, like my daughter at the middle school, it says, that she got three papers that has had a D or an F on it. So that I can come over and say, "Hey, how come we got a D on this, or why wasn't it finished or whatever." And then the D, F papers the parents have to sign. So this way you know, on a weekly basis, and you have to sign their folder and send it back with them. So on a weekly basis I am getting feedback as to what they did that week, how they did on it. In the public schools I never saw that.[39]

Some other communications between private schools and families did not concern academic matters or social problems, but rather a need for involvement in and assistance to the school. Said one parent in Dayton: "Everything is at a higher expectation [in private schools]. Even from the parents, they're expecting you . . . to come to the school one week a year and volunteer."

In our surveys, we asked a wide variety of questions about school-parent communication. For the most part, we found that parents of students in private schools reported higher levels of communication with their school than did parents of students in public school (see table 4-4). More parents of students in private schools reported

—that they receive newsletters about what is going on in school (88 percent of private school parents versus 68 percent of the control group);

—that they participate in instruction (68 percent versus 50 percent);

—that they are notified when their child is sent to the office for disruptive behavior (91 percent versus 77 percent);

—that they receive notes about their child from the teacher (93 percent versus 78 percent);

—that they speak to classes about their jobs (44 percent versus 33 percent);

—that they are informed of midterm progress (93 percent versus 84 percent).

In the national CSF evaluation, parents were asked how many times they had spoken with their child's teacher on the telephone the previous year. Those in private schools reported 3.2 such conversations, on average, compared with 2.4 conversations reported by their public school peers. However, private school parents were no more likely to have attended a parent-teacher conference or volunteered at their child's school.[40]

One private school parent who also was a public school teacher explained the differences mainly in terms of the types of families in the two school systems:

> That is the difference between the public school and private school. I teach in a public school. Parent involvement. In private school, they say they want you out, they are there. Public says they want you there, you might have some show up. That is half the battle. Get the parent involved, check the homework, sign this, sign that. [I had a] parent-teacher conference yesterday—one parent. The parents just aren't there.[41]

The communication patterns observed here, however, probably are not due to families per se.[42] Because RFTs were conducted, the two groups of parents at baseline were virtually identical to one another—all that differentiated them was the offer of a voucher. Still, family behaviors may change when a child switches to a private school. As one parent said, "If you're paying for something, you're going to, of course, be more involved."[43]

Not all parents, however, perceive such contacts between school and family as an unalloyed blessing. Consider the words of this focus group mother:

Table 4-4. *Communication Practices at Public and Private Schools*

| | Year I | | |
| | Private school (percentage) | Public school (percentage) | Impact (percentage difference) |
Communication practice			
Parents receive newsletter about school			
Three-city average	88	68	20***
New York City	86	67	19***
Dayton	96	74	22***
Washington, D.C.	91	69	22***
Parents participate in instruction			
Three-city average	68	50	18***
New York City	66	50	16***
Dayton	72	42	30***
Washington, D.C.	69	53	16***
Parents receive notes from teachers			
Three-city average	93	78	14***
New York City	91	79	12***
Dayton	94	76	18***
Washington, D.C.	94	77	16***
Parents notified when child sent to office for first time because of disruptive behavior			
Three-city average	91	77	14***
New York City	89	81	8***
Dayton	91	73	19***
Washington, D.C.	90	63	27***
Parents speak to classes about their jobs			
Three-city average	44	33	11**
New York City	45	33	12***
Dayton	55	40	15
Washington, D.C.	38	31	7
Parents informed about student progress halfway through the grading period			
Three-city average	93	84	9**
New York City	93	83	10***
Dayton	94	95	–0
Washington, D.C.	91	75	17***
Regular parent/teacher conferences held			
Three-city average	95	90	5**
New York City	94	90	4**
Dayton	98	88	10**
Washington, D.C.	96	89	7**
Parent open houses held at school			
Three-city average	95	90	5**
New York City	93	87	6***
Dayton	97	95	2
Washington, D.C.	96	92	5*

$*p < .10$, two-tailed test; $**p < .05$; $***p < .01$.

I'm beginning to wonder about the private school. . . . I don't think they ask you what type of things that you want to do. They basically send letters home and say this is what we do every year . . . this is what you are required to do. They don't give you an option, like with the activity fee that they include in your tuition . . . [Child's name] has only been there two years, and the first year it was like, you pay $200 at a certain time of the year and this is for some type of activity, and every parent is required to pay this $200. OK, it was no problem because it was a fundraiser, but this year they took the $200 and broke it down and added it to your tuition every month.[44]

In all five comparisons reported in tables 4-2 and 4-3, the impact of the switch from a public to a private school on school-parent communication was larger for African Americans than for other ethnic groups. In two cases, the differences in impact for African Americans and other ethnic groups were statistically significant. The impact on school-parent communication for blacks was as high as 0.78 of a standard deviation in Year II of the New York program, again a very large impact. Apparently, black families are treated very differently by public and private school officials. Private schools also communicated more with white and Hispanic families than public schools did, but the differences were not as large as those for African Americans.

Homework

Although most agree that consistent school-parent communication supports the learning process, experts have reached no consensus about the pedagogical value of homework. According to the literature on effective schools, homework is an important ingredient.[45] However, other scholars have argued that heavy homework assignments for children in grades 2–4 produce more "negative student attitudes."[46] Even when a positive relation between achievement and the amount of homework is observed, without conducting an RFT it is not easy to determine whether homework itself actually contributes to learning or whether able, studious, engaged students simply do more of their homework.

According to parents, teachers in private schools assign more homework than do their public school counterparts. Perhaps private school teachers assign more homework because private school parents are more likely to insist that it be done. Alternatively, private schools may feel the need to convince parents that the school is serious and that their tuition money is being spent wisely. In any case, differences between private and public schools were noticeable. Seventy-two percent of private school parents observed that their children did at least an hour of homework every night, compared with 56 percent of public school parents.[47] In addition to assigning more homework, private schools appeared to provide the right level of homework for individual students. Ninety percent of private school parents said that the difficulty of the homework was "appropriate" for their child, compared with 72 percent of public school parents.

In New York City, both African American and Hispanic private school students spent more time on homework (see table 4-2). In all three years the impact of the switch to a private school was larger for African American students, although in no case was the intergroup difference statistically significant. In Dayton, black private school parents reported more homework than their public school peers. In contrast, the switch to a private school had a negative (though statistically insignificant) impact on the amount of homework for white students in Year II of the Dayton program. In short, there is some suggestion in these data that African American students were especially likely to benefit from the homework policies of private schools—if one believes that more homework is desirable.

Focus group conversations certainly suggested that parents thought that way. One parent explained her decision to apply for a voucher as follows: "No homework, no homework. There [at public school], it was always like she would do the same work every time, every week it was the same work. . . . [Now, after changing to the new private school] our thing is that as soon as we get home from school, everybody is to sit around a table and do the homework. There's no watching TV, there's nothing until the homework is done."[48] Another private school mother put it this way:

> *Mother:* My kids never even had homework in the public schools.
> *Moderator:* So [name of parent], you're saying no homework [in] public schools . . .
> *Mother:* No, he didn't even have a concept of how to come home every day and do homework.
> *Moderator:* But now . . . ?
> *Mother:* He has homework every day. I look in his bag. His teacher writes notes. They have a homework book where they have to write their homework in a book. I have to sign the book every day.[49]

One parent even considered homework assignments the key to her child's success at school:

> Last year my son was in the first grade, and . . . I thought it was a lot of homework that he had to do. He brought home . . . six pages . . . of

homework at night, and we have to do them, and I thought, "What is this teacher doing?" And then, he had to do a book report every week at first grade. I said, "First grade?". . . I was confused at the beginning, but I look at it now, it really helped him because she was constantly giving him all this homework, and this year, when he give me his homework to check, . . . he read fast . . . he knew it. So it really helped him. It really helped him a lot.[50]

Students' reports are consistent with their parents'. Forty-five percent of private school students in Dayton and Washington reported that they did at least an hour of homework a night, compared with 39 percent of public school students.[51] In addition, private school students reported that they did more of the homework assigned to them. More than three-quarters of private school students in San Antonio and New York City indicated that they did all of their homework, compared with roughly two-thirds of public school students.[52]

School Climate

Even though the homework policies of public and private schools differed, discipline and order represented a top priority for both. The two sectors, however, employed different strategies to achieve that end. Public schools were more likely to set rules designed to maintain order within the school building. For example, public schools were more likely to require all students to have hall passes and visitors to sign in when entering the building. Eighty-one percent of the public school parents said that hall passes were required, compared with 68 percent of private school parents. Similarly, in two of the three cities a higher proportion of public school parents reported that visitors had to sign in at the main office. As shown in tables 4-2 and 4-3, the differences between public and private schools were larger for African Americans than for other ethnic groups in four of five comparisons. In two comparisons, the differences were statistically significant. For African Americans, the magnitude of the reduction was as high as 0.67 of a standard deviation.

To help maintain discipline and instill school pride, almost all private schools insisted that students wear uniforms. In responses to our surveys, no single difference between public and private schools was as large as the difference in the percentages reporting a school uniform requirement. Ninety-four percent of private school parents said their school had one, versus only 41 percent of their public school peers. As measured in standard deviations, the impacts were especially large for African Americans and Hispanics in New York City—more than 1.0 standard deviation in Years I, II, and III. The contrast in dress codes of public and private schools was nearly as large in Dayton.

In focus groups, private school parents expressed little but praise for school uniforms. In the view of one mother, uniforms alleviate peer pressures: "Since they are all in uniform, a child cannot criticize the other. What do you say? You're wearing the same thing I'm wearing."[53] Said another: "As far as having pressure that you're wearing clothes from such-and-such store—one's wearing clothes from Kmart, the other is wearing clothes from J.C. Penney—that's the pressure they were getting [in public school]. . . . Over here [at the private school] they don't get that."[54]

Both public and private school administrators are concerned about order; but the latter are more successful at maintaining it. A survey undertaken by Educational Testing Service (ETS) found that discipline problems are less serious in private middle schools than in public middle schools. Fourteen percent of public school students, but only 2 to 3 percent of private school students, stated that physical conflicts were a serious or moderate problem. Four percent of public school students reported that racial or cultural conflicts were a serious or moderate problem, compared with less than 1 percent of private school students. While 9 percent of public school students said that they felt unsafe in school, only 4 percent of private school students felt that way.[55]

The differences that we observed were larger, perhaps because we surveyed only students attending inner-city schools. For example, 63 percent of public school parents thought that fighting was a serious problem at their child's school, compared with 32 percent of private school parents (table 4-5). Forty-eight percent of public school parents considered truancy a problem, compared with 26 percent of private school parents. Tardiness was perceived to be a problem by 54 percent of public school parents, versus just one-third of private school parents. Forty-two percent of those with a student in public school, but just 22 percent of private school parents, reported that destruction of property constituted a serious problem. Finally, 39 percent of public school parents said that cheating was a problem, compared with 26 percent of private school parents.

In New York City, the switch to a private school had a disproportionately large impact on the level of disruptions experienced by African American students (see table 4-2). Although the impact of a change in schools did not significantly reduce the disruption level for Hispanics, for African Americans the impact was as much as 0.46 of a standard deviation. In Dayton, Year I impacts for African Americans and whites were to reduce disruptions by 0.69 and 0.92 of a standard deviation, respectively (see table 4-3).

Table 4-5. *Social Problems at Public and Private Schools*

Social problem	Year I		
	Private school (percentage)	Public school (percentage)	Impact (percentage difference)
Fighting			
Three-city average	32	63	–31***
New York City	39	65	–26***
Dayton	16	66	–50***
Washington, D.C.	25	55	–29***
Truancy			
Three-city average	26	48	–22***
New York City	35	50	–15***
Dayton	11	45	–34***
Washington, D.C.	18	44	26***
Tardiness			
Three-city average	33	54	–21***
New York City	38	57	–19***
Dayton	15	51	–36***
Washington, D.C.	34	49	–15***
Destruction of property			
Three-city average	22	42	–20***
New York City	29	44	–15***
Dayton	8	41	–33***
Washington, D.C.	17	37	–20***
Cheating			
Three-city average	26	39	–13***
New York City	33	41	–8**
Dayton	9	43	–34***
Washington, D.C.	23	33	–10**

*$p < .10$, two-tailed test; **$p < .05$; ***$p < .01$. Percentage of parents who say problem at their child's school is "very serious."

Focus group discussions reinforced the impression that private schools maintain considerably more order in the classroom.[56] One of the more telling anecdotes involved a second-grade student:

Last year one of the little boys in my daughter's class was a trouble-maker, was serving after-school detention. And he was just being a little pill. And I looked at him, and I said, "Joshua, you're lucky, when I was in second grade, if I would have had detention, I would have had to have written one thousand times, 'I will behave.'" He looked at me and said, "Well, I wouldn't do it." I said, "Well, my parents were paying $300 a month to send me to school. . . ." And he looked at me and said, "Yeah, if my Mom was paying $300 a month, I would have to do what I was told."[57]

Another parent put the private school advantage this way: "I don't really think it's a [question of] good kids. . . . It was just like something different there when you walk through those doors. Because you're like, like seeing everybody else walking in a straight line. So, after walking crooked you started walking straight too."[58]

In many public schools, reform-minded educators have introduced open classrooms and multiple grades in order to help create a more relaxed learning atmosphere. The innovations seemed to exacerbate the discipline problems in Washington, D.C., public schools, at least in the view of some parents. Said one mother:

I have two boys. Both of them are in the first grade. . . . Last year they were fine because they had a closed classroom. This year, my youngest son, he's not doing too well. . . . The classroom is too big. Discipline is terrible. . . . I've seen the teachers snatch the kids around there, they running all in the hallways, and you can hear what's going on in that classroom all the way over there.[59]

There are, of course, voucher parents who are unsatisfied with the climate of their private school, just as there are public school parents who have a favorable impression of their school's orderliness. On average, however, private school parents reported fewer problems and greater discipline than their public school peers. The source of success may be the different disciplinary methods employed by private schools or differences in the peers that these low-income students encountered in school. At this point, our research cannot distinguish between these possibilities. Nonetheless, it does appear that private schools in urban settings have managed to find ways of using their limited resources to deliver services in a manner that more closely approximates the ideals defined by the literature on effective schools.

Discussion

Public and private schools have different strategies for improving their effectiveness. Public schools have garnered enough political support to spend, on average, about twice as much per pupil as private schools do. They use their extra resources to pay employees higher salaries, to build large complex facilities, and to offer a wide variety of specialized programs and services. Because private school revenues come primarily from tuition, their expenditures fall well short of those of public schools. With fewer dollars to spend, they run smaller, simpler operations with fewer facilities. However, they manage to keep their classes smaller than those in public schools. In addition, they emphasize school-parent communication, homework, and orderly classrooms, none of which is particularly costly.

As suggested by the differential theory of choice set forth in chapter 1, the effects of switching to a private school often were especially large for African American students. Their parents reported sharp disjunctions between public and private schools, more so than did Hispanic parents in New York and white parents in Dayton. The private schools that African American students attended were much smaller, had noticeably smaller classes, gave more homework, and were decidedly less disruptive and less rule based than the public schools attended by African American students. In most of those respects, the private schools attended by students of other ethnic backgrounds also differed from the schools that they would have attended had they remained in public school, but for them the switch constituted a less dramatic change. One cannot infer from our results whether African Americans were coming from particularly poor public schools or enrolling in particularly effective private schools. All that we know is that along some dimensions, the impact on a school's educational climate of going private was greater for African Americans than for other ethnic groups.

As important as these changes are, much of the discussion surrounding school vouchers focuses on their potential for sparking widespread social transformation. Taking a positive view, some commentators have claimed that vouchers will enhance parents' involvement in their child's education, build students' self-esteem, and increase social capital by encouraging closer ties among private school parents. But others worry that vouchers will subject students to harsh discipline and foster racial isolation and political intolerance. We turn now to such secondary, but potentially important, consequences.

5

Social Consequences

Big rocks make big splashes. The exact size of the splash depends also on the speed at which the rock is traveling and the depth of the pond. But one thing is for certain: the impact is greatest at the point where the rock strikes the water—the undulating waves gradually fade away. And so it is with most social interventions. Their clearest impact, no matter the size, occurs in the immediate vicinity, at the point where they touch the lives of their subjects. Still, interventions may also have ripple effects—secondary consequences for related institutions and practices and, possibly, tertiary consequences for more distant concerns.

So far, we have examined the primary effects of school vouchers. School vouchers were designed to give parents a greater choice of schools, and so they did. Further, they were designed to enable students to attend new schools that differed markedly from the ones they attended before. And again, they did. Voucher recipients attended smaller schools with fewer students in the classroom; school-parent communication was more extensive; students had more homework, which was better suited to their individual needs; and the schools experienced less fighting, cheating, property destruction, truancy, and absenteeism.

But did vouchers transform other aspects of children's lives? Many of those involved in the public debate have predicted all kinds of ripple effects, positive and negative. Voucher proponents promise buoyant waves. Parents will become engaged educators and actively involved citizens. Students will learn more, acquire a better self-image, and, by attending faith-based schools, become religiously observant. Critics, in contrast, forecast stormy seas. Students' self-esteem will suffer from the high academic standards and strict disciplinary practices that characterize private schools. Greater racial isolation will result from both parents' preferences and private schools' admissions policies, and as segregation intensifies, so will political intolerance and alienation. Parents will pick schools more for their religious mission than their educational objectives, transforming schools into churches, temples, and mosques.

Most ripple effects will become fully evident only after large-scale voucher interventions have been in operation for many years. For the most part, small-scale pilot programs cannot be expected to produce a profound social transformation. Still, small-scale programs may provide some early indications of how voucher programs change the lives of those who participate in them.

In this chapter we explore indications of potential ripple effects that many observers have forecasted. Although we focus on results obtained from the three randomized field trials (RFTs) conducted in New York City; Dayton, Ohio; and Washington, D.C., we also summarize relevant findings from other studies.[1] Following our introductory analogy, the reader may already have guessed our principal finding: the waves set in motion by the pilot programs were usually small and mostly insignificant.

Parental Involvement

Many observers expect vouchers to do more than simply facilitate the transfer of some students from public schools to private schools. With a greater selection of schools to choose from, it often is said, parents will become more engaged in their child's education and social life. Exhibiting more caution than many commentators, John Brandl, dean of the Humphrey Institute of Public Affairs at the University of Minnesota, surmises "that religious schools sometimes draw out from parents . . . increased attentiveness to children's educational progress."[2] More boldly, Alan Bonsteel argues that vouchers give parents a greater stake in the schools, both religious and secular, that their child attends: "The families are strengthened through their involvement in the decision-making process, either through direct participation in the governance of the school or through the leverage of their right to leave if their needs and desires are not satisfied."[3]

The contrast between private school parents and parents of students in public school is sharp, says Andrew Coulson. Public school parents are required to do little more than dress their children in the morning and point them toward the school bus. They often feel powerless within the educational system, knowing that their attempts to effect positive change too frequently go nowhere. The natural result of the peripheral role assigned to parents by public schools, Coulson argues, is a growing apathy toward schooling.[4] As a solution, Coulson recommends private scholarships that provide partial funding for low-income families—almost exactly the type of program that we evaluated. If Coulson's analysis is correct, one should detect a noticeable change in the level of involvement of parents whose children attended private schools.

We asked parents participating in the three-city RFTs a series of questions about their involvement in their children's education: whether they had worked on a school project with their child, attended school activities with their child, discussed with the child his or her experiences at school, worked with their child on homework, and helped the child with math or reading that was not part of the homework. In the baseline surveys, most applicants for school vouchers reported very high levels of involvement in their children's education.[5] It is quite clear that parents who applied to these small, targeted voucher programs were a highly motivated lot from the beginning.

The vouchers themselves, however, had little additional impact. In some years, in some cities, a few differences were observed (see table 5-1). For example, after two years, private school parents in Washington were significantly *more* likely to discuss school experiences and help their child with math or reading that was not part of their homework. But, after two years, private school parents in Dayton were *less* likely to say that they had worked with their child on a school project or attended school activities with their child. But on average, in the three cities taken together, switching to a private school had little effect on the family's focus on education.

Most other voucher evaluations have reached similar conclusions. Our nationwide survey of the Children's Scholarship Fund found little impact of vouchers on parents' involvement;[6] neither did the evaluation of the Milwaukee voucher program.[7] Although attending a private school increased parents' involvement in San Antonio's Edgewood school district, it had a negative effect in another San Antonio voucher program.[8]

To see whether the private school effects varied by ethnic group, we constructed for each city an index of parents' involvement (as well as similarly constructed indexes of other factors considered in this chapter) from the relevant items in the surveys administered to parents and students. As in chapter 4, we constructed indexes that have a standard deviation of 1.0, thereby measuring impacts as effect sizes. Tables 5-2 and 5-3 report the findings for New York City and Dayton, respectively. Appendix B lists all the survey items used to construct the indexes.

Table 5-1. *Parents' Involvement in Child's Education*

Activity[a]	Year I			Year II		
	Private school (percentage) (1)	Public school (percentage) (2)	Impact (percentage difference) (3)	Private school (percentage) (4)	Public school (percentage) (5)	Impact (percentage difference) (6)
Worked on a school project						
Three-city average	37	42	−5	26	30	−3
New York City	37	40	−3	32	30	2
Dayton	13	21	−8	4	25	−21**
Washington, D.C.	61	67	−6	20	31	−12
Attended school activities with child						
Three-city average	12	11	1	25	25	0
New York City	8	7	1	24	27	−3
Dayton	14	14	0	6	25	−19**
Washington, D.C.	26	24	2	28	21	7
Discussed child's experiences in school						
Three-city average	71	74	−4	81	81	−0
New York City	70	75	−5	81	83	−2
Dayton	72	73	−1	66	80	−14
Washington, D.C.	74	74	0	88	64	23**
Worked on homework						
Three-city average	64	66	−2	60	63	−3
New York City	68	68	0	66	71	−5
Dayton	52	55	−3	33	47	−14
Washington, D.C.	61	67	−6	65	52	14
Helped with math/reading that was not part of homework						
Three-city average	49	51	−2	58	60	−2
New York City	52	54	−2	59	63	−4
Dayton	37	36	1	25	36	−12
Washington, D.C.	51	54	−3	88	64	23**

$*p < .10$; $**p < .05$; $***p < .01$; two-tailed tests. Some figures may not sum due to rounding.

a. Percent of parents participating six or more times in the previous month.

Table 5-2. *Impact of Switching to a Private School on Other Outcomes for African American and Hispanic Students in New York City*

Factor	African Americans (effect size of impact)	(N)	Hispanics (effect size of impact)	(N)	Significance of difference
Parents' involvement in child's education					
Year I	−0.04	531	−0.11	568	—
Year II	−0.06	470	−0.15	529	—
Year III	−0.15	458	−0.40**	514	—
Parents' engagement in school community (social capital)					
Year I	−0.15	518	0.04	553	—
Year II	−0.23*	470	−0.08	529	—
Year III	−0.21	458	−0.03	514	—
Students' self-confidence					
Year I	−0.24*	445	0.06	513	—
Year II	−0.13	524	0.12	614	—
Year III	0.14	480	0.43***	622	—
Students have well-behaved friends					
Year I	−0.01	459[a]	0.18	516	—
Year II	0.11	512	0.03	598	—
Year III	−0.01	477	0.41***	615	*
Students are racially segregated					
Year I	−0.02	517	−0.07	553	—
Year II	−0.06	457	−0.11*	513	—
Year III	−0.06	444	−0.17**	495	—
Students' religious practice					
Year I	0.59***	469	0.47***	533	—
Year II	0.51***	539	0.43***	671	—
Year III	0.53***	512	0.38**	634	—

*$p < .10$, two-tailed test; **$p < .05$; ***$p < .01$. The last column denotes whether the impact for African Americans is significantly different from that for Hispanics. Weighted two-stage least squares regressions performed; treatment status used as instrument. All models control for lottery indicators. Dichotomous variables include suspensions and racial segregation. All other variables are continuous and have been rescaled to have a standard deviation of 1.0; impacts, therefore, are estimated in effect sizes. Items for well-behaved friends, self-confidence, and religious practice are drawn from student surveys; all other items come from parent surveys.

a. The number of observations for student survey items exceeds the number for parent survey items each year because parents were asked only about the oldest child who qualified for a voucher. In addition, because surveys were administered only to students in grades 4 and above, the number of observations for student surveys increased each year as younger students progressed through school.

Table 5-3. *Impact of Switching to a Private School on Other Outcomes for African American and White Students in Dayton, Ohio*

Factor	African Americans (effect size of impact)	(N)	Whites (effect size of impact)	(N)	Significance of difference
Parents' involvement in child's education					
Year I	−0.07	329	0.05	115	—
Year II	−0.06	242	−0.75	96	—
Parents' engagement in school community (social capital)					
Year I	−0.13	329	0.00	115	—
Year II	−0.19	239	0.49	96	—
Students' self-confidence					
Year I	0.07	194[a]	0.12	69	—
Year II	0.19	198	−0.47	78	—
Students have well-behaved friends					
Year I	−0.20	185	0.34	66	—
Year II	−0.16	201	−0.21	80	—
Students are racially segregated					
Year I	0.47**	323	. . .	. . .	—
Year II	−0.02	241	. . .	. . .	—
Students' religious practice					
Year I	0.28	187	0.75*	67	—
Year II	0.20	204	0.25	81	—

$*p < .10$, two-tailed test; $**p < .05$; $***p < .01$. The last column denotes whether the estimated impact for African Americans is statistically significantly different from that for whites. Weighted two-stage least squares regressions performed; treatment status used as instrument. Dichotomous variables include suspensions and racial segregation. All other variables are continuous and have been rescaled to have a standard deviation of 1.0; impacts, therefore, represent effect sizes. Items for well-behaved friends, self-confidence, and religious practice are drawn from student surveys; all other items come from parent surveys.

a. In Dayton, unlike in New York, we asked parents to complete a separate survey for each of their children, not just the oldest child. Thus the number of observations for student survey items is lower than the number of observations for parent surveys. Still, because surveys were administered only to students in grades 4 and above, the number of observations for student surveys increased each year as younger students progressed through school.

With regard to parents' involvement in their child's education, impacts did not vary by ethnic group membership. Almost every impact in New York City and Dayton was insignificant. Only in the third year in New York City was the private school impact significantly negative for Hispanics, perhaps indicating that the family was letting the private school take the responsibility for the child's education. Further, the impacts for African Americans and other ethnic groups did not differ substantially from one another.

These findings contradict much of the conventional wisdom concerning private and public schools. Private school parents are generally thought to be more involved in their children's education, but if that is so, their participation may be due more to their personal characteristics than to the impact of the school per se. When school impacts are more carefully estimated by means of an RFT, vouchers do not—at least in the short run—increase parents' attention to their children's education.

But what about their impact on parents' engagement in the school community? Do vouchers increase the amount of social capital that schools may need to do their work effectively?

Social Capital

James Coleman and his colleagues originally coined the term *social capital* to refer to the resources generated by the more or less accidental interaction among adults in a well-functioning community.[9] As noted in chapter 1, Coleman thought that Catholic schools were effective at least in part because Catholic parents met one another at religious services, bingo parties, and other gatherings. Although those communal occasions had no ostensible educational content, the social capital generated by adult interaction was believed to have important, if indirect, educational consequences. Anthony Bryk and his colleagues also argue that communal relationships, deeply rooted in Catholic traditions, subtly but effectively support the learning process.[10]

The emphasis on Catholic traditions may be overdrawn. It may be, in Joseph Viteritti's words, that the very "process of choosing, in and of itself, produces social capital in a community."[11] When people freely choose to join private groups, they are more likely to work together as a team on behalf of a common cause, fostering a sense of solidarity. The very fact that parents decide to choose their child's school leads them to search out other parents to learn more about what is happening in alternative educational settings.[12] Also, compared with public schools, private schools can more easily distribute telephone numbers and addresses, justified by their need to enlist parents' participation in candy sales, newspaper drives, or school auctions. As a result, opportunities for parents and school employees to interact with one another abound.

Public schools, meanwhile, may have a much more difficult time building a sense of community among families, especially within cities. To maintain privacy and guard against crime, many public schools are not allowed to share lists of families' names and addresses. Public school families in the inner city may attend fewer school activities, because high labor costs sharply limit the amount of time public schools are open to the public. Metal detectors and locked doors often limit access to urban school buildings. All such factors—potential violence, regulatory constraints, labor costs, contractual obligations with employees—may greatly restrict opportunities for community dialogue and the formation of social capital in public settings.

Although the theory seems plausible, it has yet to be proven. Even Coleman's study of public and private schools failed to provide direct evidence that private schools are any better at generating social capital than public schools. (Instead, he merely speculated that social capital was one reason why Catholic school students scored higher on standardized tests than public school students did.) Neighborhood public schools may help stimulate conversations among parents who meet one another at school events, at community meetings held in school buildings, and in the course of shopping or taking walks through the neighborhood. Private school families, in contrast, may live far apart, and that fact may undermine, rather than strengthen, community ties.

To examine the issue, we asked parents a number of questions concerning social capital formation: whether they talked to other parents about their child's school, the number of parent-teacher meetings they had attended, the number of hours they had volunteered at school, and whether they were members of a PTA or similar organization.

Judging from the responses, the impact of vouchers on the formation of social capital was uncertain at best. In Year I, in the three cities, two significant differences between public and private school parents were observed. But in both cases private school parents were *less* involved in either parent-teacher meetings or a parent-teacher organization. In Year II, moreover, fewer private than public school parents said that they talked to other parents about their child's school at least once a week, and in Washington, D.C., membership in a PTA or similar organization was decidedly lower among private school parents. (See table 5-4.) Perhaps parents in private schools are spread more widely across the city, making communication more difficult. Or perhaps conversations among parents become less urgent when they perceive fewer problems at school.

Table 5-4. *Social Capital: Parents' Participation in Child's School*

	Year I			Year II		
City	Private school (1)	Public school (2)	Impact (difference) (3)	Private school (4)	Public school (5)	Impact (difference) (6)
Percent of parents who report talking to other parents about child's school at least once a week						
Three-city average	23%	23%	0	25%	36%	−11*
New York City	28%	28%	0	27%	37%	−11**
Dayton	23%	16%	8	19%	39%	−20*
Washington, D.C.	16%	19%	−3	29%	32%	−3
Number of parent-teacher meetings parent attended in the past year						
Three-city average	2.5	2.6	−0.1	2.4	2.5	−0.1
New York City	2.6	2.7	−0.0	2.4	2.5	−0.1
Dayton	2.1	2.3	−0.2	2.0	2.2	−0.2
Washington, D.C.	2.4	2.6	−0.2*	2.3	2.6	−0.3
Number of hours parent volunteered in child's school in the past month						
Three-city average	1.1	1.0	0.1	0.9	1.0	−0.1
New York City	1.1	1.0	0.1	0.8	0.9	−0.1
Dayton	1.0	1.0	0.0	0.6	1.2	−0.6
Washington, D.C.	1.5	1.4	0.1	1.9	1.3	0.6
Percent of parents who are members of a PTA or similar organization						
Three-city average	15%	21%	−6	14%	18%	−5
New York City	12%	19%	−7**	13%	16%	−3
Dayton	18%	19%	−1	25%	23%	2
Washington, D.C.	37%	41%	−5	21%	53%	−32***

*$p < .10$; **$p < .05$; ***$p < .01$; two-tailed test.

Still, it would be premature to draw the conclusion that vouchers will depress reserves of social capital in big cities. When all the indicators of social capital are considered together, as determined by an index constructed from the items just mentioned, there seems to be little impact on social capital from the voucher program at all, either positive or negative. The only significant negative impact observed was for African American students in New York City in Year II; otherwise, the effects were statistically insignificant (see tables 5-2 and 5-3). In sum, should these pilot programs be indicators of the extent to which school choice programs will generate greater community engagement, then social capital theorists must lower their expectations.

Self-Confidence

Even though vouchers had only minor effects on parents' involvement in either their children's education or the community at large, they still might have had significant effects on students' self-confidence. Market-oriented theorists, for instance, make the case that private schools will boost self-confidence because parents will expect the schools to treat their children well.[13] Some believe that religious schools may be especially effective in that regard. Those who favor faith-based education, for example, say that religious schools enhance a student's sense of self-worth because teachers and administrators attend to each child's spiritual welfare.

Others, however, do not share that view. Both the heinous private boarding school and the Catholic nun's harsh rule have provided fodder for many a gripping novel and engrossing movie—from *David Copperfield* and *Jane Eyre* to *School Ties* and *Scent of a Woman*. Political theorist James Dwyer argues that religious schools "have adverse psychological effects for many students, including diminished self-esteem, extreme anxiety, and pronounced and sometimes life-long anger and resentment."[14] Education professor Peter McLaren says that religious instruction focuses "preponderantly on self-denial, endurance, and on one's individual faults and inadequacies." Because of such instruction, he says, "students experienced a diminished self-image and frequent—and sometimes intolerable—feelings of guilt."[15]

Some parents in focus group conversations expressed concern about the effect of private schools on students' self-esteem. In Edgewood, for example, a parent explained that she had withdrawn her son from the program because she felt that he had endured all sorts of humiliation when he switched to a new private school. She explained her decision in these words:

> [My son] was sent in those nine weeks six times or more to the dean for detention. I mean, I don't mind if he did something wrong and they punished him by [having him] mopping the floor—that's what they did to him. If I have him in that school and that's how they deal with it, that's fine—if it was his fault. But he got different detentions for different things. Some was his fault, some they weren't. The last one he got, it was because he wore black pants. They could wear black, blue, or khaki, so my son had all of them. But he had some black pants that are jeans. They were black jeans, but they didn't have any labels or nothing—just black jeans. I used to see a lot of boys using that and using not a khaki color but an ivory color that wasn't the proper color.

I told [my son], use the black pants for today because I hadn't washed the khaki ones nor the blue ones. I'm pretty sure you can use them, because I've seen a lot of the kids using them. So he used them, and he got in trouble for them—he got detention.[16]

Other parents, however, recounted more positive experiences when they switched their child to a private school. In the words of another Edgewood parent: "But they were like always telling me that my son was bad [at his prior public school]. In this [private] school now he's in, he's a good student. He's very good. He's very polite. He's—I don't know—he's different. He's changed a lot."[17]

A similar point was made by a Dayton parent who did not win a scholarship but paid for a private school nonetheless: "[It] is killing me to pay to keep him in there, but it is such a difference [from when he was in public school]. The difference in the child and his attitude toward school. He comes home and does his work on his own. There is no problem with him. . . . There is such a difference in these private schools and these public schools here."[18]

To estimate more precisely the impact of attending a private school, we asked students in grades 4 and above who were participating in the voucher programs a variety of questions conventionally thought to measure an individual's sense of self-worth. We asked them to indicate whether they agreed strongly, agreed, disagreed, or disagreed strongly with the following statements:

—I feel good about myself.
—If I work really hard, I will do well in school.
—To do well in school, good luck is more important than hard work.
—I am able to do things as well as most other people.
—Every time I try to get ahead, something or somebody stops me.
—I am satisfied with myself.
—I certainly feel useless at times.
—At times I think I am no good at all.
—When I make plans, I am almost certain I can make them work.
—I feel I do not have much to be proud of.

For the most part, no significant differences in the self-esteem of private and public school students were detected in any of the RFTs.[19] However, some exceptions emerged. After two years in Dayton, for example, private school students were significantly more likely than the control group to say, "I feel good about myself," and in Washington, private school students were more likely to say that they were "able to do things as well as most other people."

The positive impact of private schooling on the self-confidence of students seemed to grow over time—at least in New York City. For Hispanics, no significant differences were observed in Years I and II, but the index of self-confidence reveals a positive impact of attending a private school in Year III for this group of students (see table 5-2.) For African Americans in New York, the direction of the shift is similar, in this case from a negative impact on self-confidence in Year I to a positive (though statistically insignificant) impact in Year III (table 5-2). However, in Dayton, the self-confidence of white students deteriorated between Year I and Year II (though in neither year was the impact statistically significant).

On the whole, the impact of school choice on inner-city students' self-confidence appeared to be moderately positive. In some respects, that is remarkable. Given all of the difficulties of adjusting to a new school—finding new friends, abiding by new rules, responding to new expectations—one might expect students' self-confidence, at least initially, to suffer. Instead, the admittedly modest differences that were observed generally point in the opposite direction. On occasional items, in some cities, students attending private schools appeared slightly more confident than their public school peers, and there is some suggestion that in New York City, over the longer run, private schools may have enhanced students' self-confidence.

Student Friendships

When switching from a public to a private school, students may be forced to develop an entirely new set of friendships. According to some observers, that possibility represents the single most important contribution of a school voucher program to the education of central-city students. Public schools are shaped by the neighborhood peer-group culture, which in some urban environments is dominated by street gangs.[20] Only by extracting their children from such settings, the argument runs, can parents expect them to profit from the educational opportunities their schools have to offer.

To see whether school vouchers altered students' social lives, we asked students participating in the Washington, D.C., and Dayton voucher programs in Year II and III to name their four best friends at school. We then asked

—whether their parents knew their friends;

—whether their friends were of a different race;

—whether they received good grades;

—whether they got into trouble with teachers;

—whether they used bad language;

—whether they smoked cigarettes;

—whether they drank alcohol;

—whether they used illegal drugs.

No differences between students in public and private schools were observed in either city, in either year. According to those measures, at least, poor students living in central cities did not find a particularly different set of friends when they switched from public to private schools.

A slightly different set of questions was asked in New York City. Although we detected no effects in Year I, we observed some differences in the type of friendships students cultivated in Year II. Those differences, however, were not all positive. On the one hand, private school students in New York City were more likely to report that their friends received good grades and did not use bad language; on the other hand, they were less likely to say that their parents knew their friends—a sign, perhaps, that the school was not as close to home or that the friends were so new that parents had not yet had occasion to meet them.

When isolating different ethnic groups in New York City and Dayton, we still found little evidence that vouchers contributed positively—or negatively—to students' patterns of friendship. The one exception to this general pattern was observed in Year III in New York City, when a positive impact of private schooling on friendship patterns was observed for Hispanics (see table 5-2).

Taking into account all the information for all students together as well as for students in different ethnic groups, private schooling appears to have had only modest effects on students' friendship patterns. It may be that changes in peer relationships proceed slowly, becoming visible only after many years in one school setting or another. At least in the short term, however, we have no reason to believe that friendship patterns are significantly altered by choice. Again, the ripple effects appear miniscule.

Ethnic Isolation and Conflict

Racial segregation remains one of the country's most serious social problems. Nearly a half-century after the U.S. Supreme Court declared segregated schools unconstitutional, many students still attend schools with predominantly minority student bodies.[21] Indeed, public schools remain just as segregated now as they were in the early 1970s, and in the past decade, racial segregation, especially in the South, appears to have worsened.

Prominent political figures and newspaper commentators have expressed concern that school-choice programs would only aggravate the trend. In accepting a "Friend of Education" award from the National Education Association, Jim Hunt, a former governor of North Carolina, suggested that "vouchers . . . build up private schools, in effect creating a separate and unequal system." Drawing out the implications of his remarks, newspaper accounts suggested that "vouchers could speed up the decline in racial integration in public schools."[22] Some academics have reached similar conclusions. According to education professor David Berliner and his co-authors, "Vouchers add another means to segregate our citizens, this time using public money."[23] After analyzing New Zealand's national school-choice system, Edward Fiske and Helen Ladd went so far as to claim that "the basic forces unleashed by parental choice . . . are likely to push systems toward greater ethnic and socioeconomic polarization under almost any circumstance."[24]

School-choice advocates steadfastly defend vouchers against such criticisms. Far from increasing segregation, says choice advocate Clifford Cobb, vouchers "are likely to increase the level of integration by fostering schools that bring diverse people together by attraction rather than compulsion." Cobb points out that public schools in most cities remain heavily segregated and that "expanding options in independent schools could break down existing racial and ethnic barriers."[25] Others point out that, even in the absence of vouchers, private schools nationwide are 7 percentage points more racially integrated than public schools.[26] Using data drawn from a nationally representative sample of parents, Terry Moe shows that minority parents are especially likely to take advantage of larger voucher programs, further integrating private schools.[27]

To estimate the voucher programs' impact on racial integration and comity, participating parents and students were asked a variety of questions concerning the racial composition of classes, the race of students with whom participating students ate lunch, the number of friends of another race that students had, and the degree of racial conflict in the school. Although neither skeptics' worst fears nor advocates' highest hopes were confirmed, the voucher programs, on the whole, had more positive than negative impacts.

Integration in the Classroom

We asked parents about the percentage of students in their child's classroom that were from a minority background. When results from the three cities were averaged together, no significant effects were observed. Still, we did detect some variation among the three cities (table 5-5). In both Years I and II, the New York vouchers appeared to reduce the likelihood that all of a student's classmates would be from a minority ethnic group. In Dayton, students in private schools were more likely to attend segregated classrooms in Year I, but not in Year II. In Washington, D.C., we did not observe any significant programmatic effects in either year. Comparable findings held for African Americans and Hispanics in New York, while in Dayton African

Table 5-5. *School Racial Integration*

	Year I			Year II		
Degree of racial integration	*Private school (percentage)* (1)	*Public school (percentage)* (2)	*Impact (percentage difference)* (3)	*Private school (percentage)* (4)	*Public school (percentage)* (5)	*Impact (percentage difference)* (6)
Less than 50 percent minority						
Three-city average	20	14	7*	16	13	3
New York City	18	11	7***	13	11	2
Dayton	52	30	22***	60	18	42***
Washington, D.C.	21	20	1	14	27	−13
All minority						
Three-city average	29	30	−1	25	29	−4
New York City	28	37	−9***	30	38	−8**
Dayton	14	5	9***	6	8	−3
Washington, D.C.	40	39	0	44	32	12

*p < .10; **p < .05; ***p < .01; two-tailed tests.

Americans were more segregated in private schools in Year I but not in Year II (tables 5-2 and 5-3).

Inasmuch as results varied across the three cities, findings from the nation-wide CSF program are of particular interest. According to parents' responses, students who used vouchers to attend private schools were nearly 20 percent-age points less likely to attend segregated classes than their public school peers.[28] Positive effects held both for African American students and those from other ethnic backgrounds.[29]

While students in private schools were slightly less likely to attend fully segregated classes, they were slightly more likely to attend classes that were at least 50 percent white. In the three cities, vouchers increased by 10 percent-age points the likelihood that a student would attend a class in which a majority of his or her peers were white. Similarly, in the nationwide CSF pro-gram, private school students were 21 percentage points more likely to attend majority-white classrooms than their cohorts in public schools.[30]

Interracial friendship and comity

By formally admitting students to a school, administrators determine its racial composition. But what about the informal relationships that develop among students? A number of studies have found that informal patterns of association between students of different ethnic backgrounds are more com-

Table 5-6. *Interracial Friendship and Conflict*

	Year I			Year II		
	Private school (percentage)	Public school (percentage)	Impact (percentage difference)	Private school (percentage)	Public school (percentage)	Impact (percentage difference)
City	(1)	(2)	(3)	(4)	(5)	(6)
Percent of students reporting that they eat lunch with students of other racial groups "most" or "all of the time"						
Dayton	n.a.	n.a.	. . .	56%	65%	–8
Washington, D.C.	n.a.	n.a.	. . .	43%	43%	0
CSF	61%	58%	3	. . .	. . .	. . .
Average number of student's four closest friends who are of a different race						
Dayton	n.a.	n.a.	. . .	1.2	0.9	0.3
Washington, D.C.	n.a.	n.a.	. . .	0.9	0.8	0.0
CSF	1.2	1.3	0.1	. . .	. . .	. . .
Percent of parents saying that racial conflict is a serious problem at child's school						
Three-city average	22%	26%	–5	22%	34%	–13**
New York City	31%	38%	–7*	26%	41%	–15***
Dayton	16%	30%	–15*	9%	32%	–23**
Washington, D.C.	18%	14%	5	24%	21%	3
CSF	3%	22%	–19**	. . .	. . .	

$*p < .10; **p < .05; ***p < .01$; two-tailed test.

mon in private schools. A U.S. Department of Education survey of public and private schools, for example, found more interracial friendships among students in private schools than among those in public schools.[31] Another study found that students in San Antonio private schools were more likely to sit next to someone of another racial group at lunch time than students in local public schools.[32]

Those studies were not randomized experiments, however, and their results could have been affected by the type of students attending the two kinds of schools. To see whether a voucher intervention changed informal patterns of association among students from different racial groups, we asked students participating in the Dayton and Washington programs how often they ate lunch with students from other ethnic backgrounds and how many of their friends were of a different race or ethnic group.

On neither item did we detect differences between public and private school students. Vouchers did not increase the likelihood that a student would either befriend or interact with children from other ethnic backgrounds (table 5-6). Neither did we observe any differences on the two items in the evaluation of the nationwide CSF program.[33] Also, in the Edgewood school district in San Antonio, students who remained in public schools were just as likely as private school students to say that they ate lunch with students of other ethnic backgrounds.[34]

If vouchers did not affect friendship patterns, did they have any impact on interracial conflict? In one national survey conducted by the U.S. Department of Education, students, teachers, and administrators all reported less interracial fighting in private schools than public schools.[35] Evidence from the three-city RFTs bears out that finding. On average, private school parents in New York City, Dayton, and Washington were less likely than their public school counterparts to report that racial conflict was a serious problem at their child's school. The differences were 5 percentage points in Year I and 13 percentage points in Year II, the latter being statistically significant. Similarly, in the nationwide CSF program, racial conflict was 19 percentage points lower in private schools than in the public schools attended by the control group.[36]

Although small, those ripple effects appear encouraging. Even though extreme racial segregation was not reduced in the three cities, it did decline significantly in the national CSF voucher program. Also, more students were in majority-white classrooms in both the national and the three-city programs. Although we found little effect of vouchers on interracial friendship patterns, we observed noticeable reductions in the incidence of racial conflict.

Political Tolerance and Civic Participation

Closely related to the controversy over racial isolation and conflict is the debate over political tolerance and civic participation. Henry Levin of Columbia University's Teachers College has argued that as vouchers segregate students by race, they erode the foundations of a democracy. "Effective participation in a democracy," he writes, "requires a willingness to tolerate diversity as well as an acceptance of a common set of values and a shared base of knowledge. . . . But by segregating students, . . . exposure to diversity . . . is seriously undermined."[37] Much the same point was made by education professor Frances Paterson: "As we debate the wisdom of various proposals to privatize all or part of American education, we should consider whether [this] . . . might increase the Balkanization of our society . . . by encouraging young people to develop a value system that is based on an us-versus-them world view."[38]

Providing equally alarming prose on the other side of the issue, Clifford Cobb points out that Horace Mann, often credited as the founder of the public school, "drew his inspiration from ancient Sparta and [nineteenth century] Prussia, rather than from states that valued dissent" and that "the Nazis . . . and Communists all shut down alternative (particularly sectarian) schools that were not controlled by the state."[39]

If at times the language seems more polemical than measured, the underlying concerns remain quite genuine. In a particularly thoughtful discussion, Princeton political theorist Steven Macedo, while acknowledging the educational advantages of school choice, still wonders whether the resulting schools can serve the public good: "The health of our political society requires that we learn how to negotiate cultural boundaries and promote wider sympathies among citizens. Far from being a waste, this is crucial political work. Where will this work be done if not in the common schools?"[40]

Peter Berger and Richard Neuhaus make the case that the preservation of religious identity strengthens the polity as a whole: "The goal of public policy in a pluralistic society is to sustain as many particularities as possible, in the hope that most people will accept, discover, or devise one that fits." If that can be accomplished, "individuals, would be more 'at home' in society, and the political order would be more 'meaningful'. . . . [Otherwise,] the political order becomes detached from the values and realities of individual life. Deprived of its moral foundation, the political order is 'delegitimated.'"[41]

Despite the intensity of the debate among academics, the general public does not think public and private schools differ much in this respect. According to one survey, a majority of adults believe that public and private schools are equally able to "teach democratic values," but among those who make a distinction, private schools are favored over public schools by a two-to-one margin.[42] Research tends to confirm the general public's view of the matter. Most studies show few negative effects of existing private schools on social cohesion or political engagement. Those who attend private schools are more likely to participate in politics, volunteer their service to community groups, and express at least as much tolerance as students attending public schools. Private school students also are more public spirited than their public school peers. According to one national study, students at private schools were more likely to think that it is important to help others and volunteer for community causes. In confidential surveys, public school administrators were less likely than their private school colleagues to say that their school did an outstanding job of promoting citizenship. Similar differences appeared when administrators were asked to rate their school's performance in teaching values and morals and in promoting awareness of social issues. Students educated in private secular and Catholic schools (but not in fundamentalist schools) also were more likely to be tolerant of unpopular groups than public

Table 5-7. *Student Agreement with Selected Statements Indicating Political Tolerance*

Measure of tolerance	Private school (percentage)	Public school (percentage)	Impact (percentage difference)
People whose views students oppose *should "definitely" be able to:*			
Give a speech in students' community			
Washington, D.C. (Year II)	34	18	16*
Washington, D.C. (Year III)	8	28	−20
CSF (Year I)	50	49	1
Live in students' neighborhood			
Washington, D.C. (Year II)	47	27	20**
Washington, D.C. (Year III)	27	35	−8
CSF (Year I)	73	60	13
Run for U.S. president			
Washington, D.C. (Year II)	37	20	18*
Washington, D.C. (Year III)	17	26	−9
CSF (Year I)	49	49	0

*$p < .10$; **$p < .05$; ***$p < .01$; two-tailed test.

school students, and private school students were more likely to say that their school expected them to volunteer.[43]

Once again, however, none of these studies were conducted as RFTs. Since it is possible that families that send their children to private schools are more tolerant and public spirited, it is worth examining in an experimental setting what impact private schooling may have on a student's tolerance of others. We examined this question in Washington, D.C., in Years II and III. Students in grades 4 through 9 were asked whether people whose views they oppose should "definitely" be able to give a speech in their community, live in their neighborhood, and run for president. As shown in table 5-7, in Year II students in private schools were more likely to respond affirmatively to all three questions. However, there were no significant differences in Year III, and the signs themselves pointed in a negative direction in this year. In the nationwide evaluation, a significant positive effect was observed on an index of toleration constructed from the items in table 5-7, though not on any one specific item.[44]

It is too soon to conclude that vouchers increase political tolerance. On the other hand, there is no evidence that voucher programs lead to the balkanization of society.

Religious Considerations

As chapter 2 has detailed, most families that received vouchers used them to attend religious schools. Moreover, most of them selected schools that matched their own religious affiliations. For example, in the CSF program, fully 82 percent of the students attending Protestant schools were themselves Protestant, though we do not know whether the brand of Protestantism was an exact match in all, or even most, of those cases. Of students attending Catholic schools, 59 percent were themselves from Catholic families.

Given the strong connection between the religious affiliations of schools and families, voucher programs may strengthen religious commitment. To assess the related impacts of switching to a private school, we asked parents participating in the voucher programs how often they attended religious services. We also asked students in grades 4 and above whether they participated in church youth groups, whether they had received religious instruction outside of school during the past year, and how often they had attended religious services outside school during the past year.

The impacts differed for parents and students, and not in the direction we expected. On the one hand, the impact on parents was negligible in the three cities, and to our surprise, it often appeared more negative than positive. Despite (because of?) the fact that applicants for vouchers, at baseline, were religiously more observant than the typical American adult, the program itself had no additional impact on parents' church attendance.[45] In Year II in Dayton, church attendance rates among private school parents were actually lower than among public school parents. Perhaps by then parents felt that their private school was attending to the religious needs of their children and that family efforts could be relaxed. In any case, there was no sign that private schools required parents to participate in church life.

On the other hand, vouchers had a positive impact on students' religious observance (table 5-8). Students in private schools were much more likely to report that they had participated in church youth groups "a lot," and the same was true for the frequency of religious instruction outside of school. In all cities the differences pointed in the same direction, although in some cities they were not statistically significant.

Religious impacts were also evident when students were asked how often they attended religious services outside of school during the past year. Whether we considered all students simultaneously or each ethnic group separately, students in private schools reported higher church attendance rates— (see tables 5-2 and 5-3). The same findings emerged in the Edgewood school district. However, significant differences between students in public and private schools were not detected in the nationwide CSF study.

Table 5-8. *Student Reports of Selected Religious Practices*

| | Year I | | | Year II | | |
| | Private school (percentage) | Public school (percentage) | Impact (percentage difference) | Private school (percentage) | Public school (percentage) | Impact (percentage difference) |
Religious practice	(1)	(2)	(3)	(4)	(5)	(6)
Attended religious services in past year						
Three-city average	68	38	29***	56	30	26***
New York City	67	37	30***	59	32	27***
Dayton	68	38	31***	54	23	31**
Washington, D.C.	63	40	23***	46	28	18
Participated in church youth group activities "a lot" in past year						
Three-city average	. . .	. . .	. . .	47	37	9**
New York City	48	31	17***	50	40	10***
Dayton	n.a.	n.a.	. . .	54	44	10
Washington, D.C.	n.a.	n.a.	. . .	42	42	0
Received religious instruction outside school "a lot" in past year						
Three-city average	27	19	8	28	17	11*
New York City	30	20	10***	27	14	13***
Dayton	19	13	6	32	22	10
Washington, D.C.	23	23	0	22	25	−3

*p < .10; **p < .05; ***p < .01; two-tailed tests.

These positive impacts on students' religious practice may have been fully intended by their parents. Even more, parents may have explicitly chosen private schools more for religious than educational reasons, thereby raising important constitutional questions. We now examine the various factors that motivate parents to send their children to private schools.

Motivation for Participating in the Programs

In *The Case against School Choice*, political scientists Kevin Smith and Kenneth Meier argue that academic quality does not figure prominently in parents' thinking about schools. "Geographical proximity and the convenience it represents seem to be the primary" reasons why parents and students use vouchers to attend private schools. "Religious services and the socioeconomic and racial composition of the enrollment seem to be the next most important concern."[46] As they see it, the evidence indicates that "the demands many parents seek to fulfill in the private education sector are for religious services, racial segregation, and the 'right' socioeconomic status of their children's peers."[47] These authors are not alone in their assessment of parents' motivations. The Carnegie Foundation for the Advancement of Teaching has claimed that "when parents do select another school, academic concerns often are not central to the decision."[48]

In contrast, Mark Schneider and his coauthors argue that educational considerations are more important.[49] In their study, they found that parents typically emphasize educational aspects of schools over factors such as students' ethnic background or school location. They state that "our results are congruent with the growing body of work showing that parents consistently emphasize the importance of the academic aspects of schools."[50] Teacher quality and student test scores were the first and second most important considerations in selecting a school.

The findings of Schneider and his colleagues may apply only to middle-class families living in suburban areas; low-income families living in central cities may pay less attention to a school's educational quality. According to one Twentieth Century Fund report, low-income parents are not "natural 'consumers' of education."[51] Similarly, an American Federation of Teachers' report on the Cleveland voucher program suggests that parents sought scholarships not because of "'failing' public schools" but "for religious reasons or because they already had a sibling attending the same school."[52]

If the focus group discussions we held are any indication, such assertions appear to be mistaken. Time and again, parents indicated that when choosing a private school academic considerations were paramount. One Washington mother explained her decision in these terms:

> I'm really not satisfied with [my child's public school] teacher when she attended the third grade. She failed my daughter the first two quarters. I know my daughter has an attitude problem. I know her mouth is kind of smart. . . . And by the teacher not helping me to help her, [it's] just giving her more attitude and pushing her away. . . . I want to hurry up and get her into private school because I don't want her transition to catch her when she gets older. I want her to learn it and know it now before she get any older and it be harder and she like, "I can't do it."[53]

A Dayton mother, after extolling the various benefits of a religious education, was asked directly why she had applied for a scholarship. "[Religion] is not the only reason," she replied. "Like I said, it's more about the education."[54] As another parent put it, "I want my child to get the best education possible without a lot of disciplinary problems in the classroom. That is my biggest concern."[55]

To see whether focus group comments represented most parents' views, all parents participating in the evaluations were asked to indicate the relative importance of a number of different reasons for picking the school they chose for their child. To assess the sensitivity of parents' responses to the exact phrasing of the questions, the questions were posed in different ways in the various evaluations.[56] In Year II of the Dayton and Washington, D.C., programs, parents were asked to select the single most important reason for choosing a school. In Year II in New York City and Year I in Dayton and D.C., parents were asked to list the three most important reasons, without choosing among them.

The constitutional debate over vouchers lingers on the question of whether voucher programs represent *primarily* an educational or religious intervention. By asking parents to indicate the single most important reason for selecting a school, the D.C. and Dayton evaluations provided fresh insight into the matter. On the whole, parents appeared to be motivated by educational concerns. As shown in the first column of table 5-9, 52 percent of the Washington, D.C., parents who used a voucher in Year II said that the "academic quality" of the school was the most important reason for selecting the school. "What is taught in school" and "teacher quality" were chosen by 7 and 3 percent, respectively. School safety and discipline were the primary reasons for another 6 and 5 percent of parents, respectively. Just 8 percent said that religious instruction was the primary consideration.

In Dayton, comparable findings were observed in Year II. Academic quality was chosen by 39 percent of private school parents, what is taught in school by 21 percent, discipline by 9 percent, and religious instruction by 12 percent. Similar results were obtained in San Antonio. Approximately 60 percent of the voucher parents there identified the school's academic quality, what is taught in class, or teacher quality as most important. Only 15 percent ranked a school's religious affiliation as the most important factor.[57]

Responses did not change materially when the question was worded slightly differently. For example, when Washington, D.C., parents who used vouchers were given a chance in Year I to identify the three important reasons for selecting a school, 70 percent noted the school's academic quality (second column of table 5-9). Roughly one-third of the parents cited religious

Table 5-9. *Reasons for Selecting a Private School*[a]

Reason	Cited as the most important reason (percentage)	Cited as one of the three most important reasons (percentage)
Academic quality		
New York City[b]	n.a.	59
Dayton[c]	39	69
Washington, D.C.[c]	52	70
What is taught in school		
New York City	n.a.	27
Dayton	21	23
Washington, D.C.	7	24
Teacher quality		
New York City	n.a.	35
Dayton	2	41
Washington, D.C.	3	35
Discipline		
New York City	n.a.	42
Dayton	9	38
Washington, D.C.	5	37
Religious instruction		
New York City	n.a.	28
Dayton	12	39
Washington, D.C.	8	35
School safety		
New York City	n.a.	36
Dayton	0	34
Washington, D.C.	6	30
Class size		
New York City	n.a.	21
Dayton	0	28
Washington, D.C.	2	29
Children's friendships		
New York City	n.a.	0
Dayton	0	6
Washington, D.C.	0	1
Sports		
New York City	n.a.	0
Dayton	0	1
Washington, D.C.	0	0

a. Figures reflect responses of parents who used a voucher to send their child to a private school.

b. New York figures in column 2 come from Year II surveys.

c. In Dayton and Washington, D.C., figures in column 1 come from Year II surveys; figures in column 2 come from Year I surveys.

instruction as one of the three most important considerations. An equal percentage mentioned school discipline. More than one-quarter of the parents also mentioned class size, teacher quality, and school safety. Less than 2 percent said that the sports program or children's friendships were among the three most important reasons. Comparable findings hold for Dayton in Year I and New York City in Year II.[58]

In Milwaukee, a survey by the Legislative Audit Bureau asked voucher parents to note all their reasons for selecting a private school. The three reasons mentioned most often were that the school maintained higher educational standards, that it had good teachers, and that it was safe and orderly. Provision of religious instruction was the fourth-mentioned reason. Less than 15 percent highlighted the relevance of a school's ethnic composition.[59]

For the most part, parents claimed that educational considerations—academic quality, school discipline, effective teaching, school safety—figured most prominently in their selection of a private school. While still important, religion represented a secondary consideration.

Conclusion

The waves generated by these voucher programs hardly constituted tsunamis that radically altered the social landscape. On the contrary, the few ripple effects that were observed in these voucher programs seem rather benign. Those who expect vouchers to enhance family life may be pleased to learn that students became more religiously observant and somewhat more self-confident. However, they may be disappointed that private schools did not seem to alter student friendship patterns during the early years of the voucher programs, and that parents, as a result of the voucher program, did not become more involved in their child's education. Neither did parents attend church more frequently or communicate more with other parents about school life.

But if some of the highest hopes of voucher advocates appear misplaced, so do the worst fears of voucher critics. Vouchers seemed, if anything, to reduce racial isolation, not strengthen it. They seemed to facilitate racial comity, not undermine it. Rather than fostering political intolerance, private schools may enhance respect for the rights of others. Nor did parents draw upon superfluous criteria when selecting a private school. Few parents said that location, a child's friendships, or sports played a major role in their choice of a school. While some parents cited religious affiliation as an important reason for selecting a school, many more cited academic quality, safety, and disciplinary considerations.

Voucher advocates and skeptics who wish to ignore these findings may claim that the programs are too new or too small to say anything about the likely consequences of a large-scale voucher initiative. We reserve a fuller answer to that question for the closing chapter. At this point, we note only one curiosity: If the societal costs and benefits of vouchers are as large as those who debate the issue have claimed, then in trial runs one ought to see almost immediately at least some sign of their consequences. We did not.

6

The Urban Test Score Gap

Switching to a private school changed the educational experiences of inner-city low-income students in important ways. Compared with their peers in public schools, voucher students were taught in smaller classes located in much smaller schools. They received more homework assignments, faced fewer disruptions, and abided by stricter dress codes. Communication between their school and parents was more extensive. Meanwhile, students in public schools enjoyed more physical resources and academic programs, and they were subject to closer supervision when they moved throughout the school building. Still other aspects of schooling changed hardly at all. Suspension rates, parents' involvement in their child's education, students' self-esteem, students' friendship patterns, and schools' racial composition all remained much the same, regardless of whether a student attended a public or private school.

How do these changes translate into learning? Or, to put it more precisely, do inner-city students who attend private schools score higher on standardized tests than their public school peers?

Standardized Test Performance

Students' performance on standardized tests in reading and math may say very little about the quality of their elementary and middle schools; the multiple-choice questions that constitute those tests surely do not capture all that students learn in school. Although scholars have found that the performance of high-school students on such tests does a fairly good job of predicting their future success in the labor market,[1] few if any studies have shown that the performance of elementary and middle-school students on standardized tests has important downstream consequences.

It also is difficult to know whether changes in test scores from one elementary year to the next are meaningful. Such test score gains (or losses) are known as value-added measures of school effectiveness because they measure the change in the level or value of the test scores from one period to the next. Such measures are subject to a good deal of natural variation, and any effort to draw strong conclusions from annual shifts is problematic. With his colleague, Thomas Kane, an economist at the University of California in Los Angeles, has shown that value-added analyses used to evaluate schools in North Carolina displayed a good deal of random noise that bedeviled those who attempted to make policy on the basis of their results.[2] In their words, "one-time factors . . . lead to temporary fluctuations in test performance. Some of these factors are likely to be unrelated to the educational practices of a school. For instance, a dog barking on the day of the test, a severe flu season, or one particularly disruptive student in class could lead scores to fluctuate."[3] Such distractions are especially likely to cause havoc with research findings whenever sample sizes are small. In their research, Kane and others find that smaller elementary schools experience greater year-to-year test score swings (positive and negative) than larger schools. For this reason, the researchers note, state accountability regimes reward and punish small schools more frequently, not because their students are experiencing actual learning gains or losses, but because the estimates of their achievement levels are less stable.

Education statistician Anthony Bryk makes much the same point when he cautions against drawing conclusions about the impact of a school intervention from "single grade information. . . . Judging a school by looking at only selected grades can be misleading. We would be better off, from a statistical perspective, to average across adjacent grades to develop a more stable estimate of school productivity."[4]

Test score findings from randomized field trials (RFTs), such as those presented in this chapter, are value-added measures. The treatment and control groups were similar at baseline, so any differences observed subsequently provide estimates of the value added by the voucher intervention. Further, to increase the precision of our estimates, all models explicitly controlled for baseline test scores. To minimize random error in these value-added measures, we combined test scores in reading and math in the analyses presented in this chapter because, by so doing, estimates rely upon a larger number of test items, thereby further reducing random fluctuation. We also based our interpretation on results from all students tested, regardless of grade level, because the number of cases for students for each grade was often quite small. Finally, we combined results from all three cities, weighting the results from each city in accord with the statistical precision of each estimate. All of these steps help guard against drawing erroneous conclusions from value-added test score data.

The debate about the relative capacities of public and private schools to boost student test scores dates back to the seminal work of James Coleman and his colleagues. Under the auspices of the U.S. Department of Education, in 1980 and 1982 Coleman's research team directed the High School and Beyond survey, testing a national sample of public and private high-school students in two waves to generate data on the determinants of academic gains between a student's sophomore and senior year. The team found that private school students performed at a higher level than public school students, even after observable family background characteristics were taken into account.[5]

Critics, however, pointed out flaws in the data and the procedures used to evaluate them.[6] In a 1985 issue of *Sociology of Education,* three particularly well-crafted essays reanalyzed and reinterpreted the data;[7] however, their authors disagreed on whether the data revealed significant impacts of private schools on student achievement. Thomas Hoffer, Andrew Greeley, and James Coleman found substantial, positive private school effects on student test performance, while Douglas Wilms found trivial effects, if any. Christopher Jencks mediated the conflict, reaching Solomonic conclusions somewhere in the middle. Debate on the issue has continued along much the same lines ever since. Although few, if any, studies have found that private school students perform less well than public school students, some find no difference at all, while others show positive impacts of private schools on student performance.

Participants in the *Sociology of Education* exchange generally agreed, however, that private schools helped close the education gap between ethnic groups. The Coleman research team found strong positive effects on low-income minority students: Catholic schooling increased minority students' test scores by an estimated 0.15 of a standard deviation annually, nearly three times more than its estimated impact on white students.[8] Jencks showed that Wilms's data, despite their exclusion of dropouts, also contained positive—though not statistically significant—effects of attending Catholic school on African American students' reading scores. Taking all of the evidence from both studies into account, Jencks concluded that "the evidence that Catholic schools are especially helpful for initially disadvantaged students is quite suggestive, though not conclusive."[9]

Subsequent studies have corroborated the early findings. In an analysis of the National Longitudinal Survey of Youth, Derek Neal found that students who attended Catholic schools were more likely to graduate from high school and college and scored higher on standardized tests than those who did not. The effects, Neal noted, were greatest among urban minorities. A Catholic education also had a significant positive effect on blacks' earning potential, but not on that of whites.[10] In separate studies, David Figlio and Joseph Stone as well as William Evans and Robert Schwab reached similar findings with respect to the achievement of African American students.[11] The impact of Catholic schools was particularly large in central cities. Figlio and Stone found, for example, that "the estimated treatment effect [was] more than twice as large for African Americans in big cities [as] for African Americans in general." In a recent reanalysis of these same data, using a new, more sophisticated analytical strategy, Stephen Morgan also identified particularly large Catholic school effects on minority students.[12]

Surveying the literature on school sector effects and private school vouchers, Princeton University economist Cecilia Rouse says that "the overall impact of private schools is mixed, [but] it does appear that Catholic schools generate higher test scores for African-Americans."[13] Similarly, Jeffrey Grogger and Derek Neal concluded that "urban minorities in Catholic schools fare much better than similar students in public schools," while the effects for urban whites and suburban students generally are "at best mixed."[14]

One cannot rule out the possibility, however, that the observed positive effects on African American test scores in these studies were due to selection bias, a problem that arises when members of a population differentiate themselves by freely choosing the treatment condition—in this case, attending a private school. The studies we have cited adjusted for observable family background characteristics, such as mother's education, family income, and other demographic factors. Still, one cannot be sure that the control variables adequately account for an intangible factor—the importance that parents place on education implicit in their willingness to pay for their child's tuition. Some of the analysts used the instrumental variable technique discussed in chapter 2 to adjust for selection bias, while others used propensity scores, but in the absence of information from a randomized field trial (RFT), it remains unclear whether the statistical corrections that were made adequately solved the selection problem.[15]

The best solution to the self-selection problem is the random assignment of students to test and control groups. Until recently, most evaluations of voucher programs were not able to employ a random-assignment research design, and therefore they, too, could not rule out possible selection problems. Privately funded programs in Indianapolis, San Antonio, and Milwaukee admitted students on a first-come, first-served basis. And in the state-funded program in Cleveland, though scholarship winners were initially selected by lottery, all applicants were eventually offered a scholarship, thereby precluding the conduct of an RFT.[16] Private schools in the Milwaukee program did grant admission to voucher recipients randomly, but the intervention, when it was evaluated, was limited to only a few secular schools and data collection was incomplete.[17]

Few of the evaluations of those voucher programs estimated separate impacts for different ethnic groups. In Milwaukee, one researcher estimated positive gains for both Hispanics and African Americans in math, but only for Hispanics in reading. However, those estimates were highly dependent on the characteristics of just three secular schools. Virtually all the Hispanic students in the program attended Bruce Guadalupe Community School, which by all accounts had the strong support of the Hispanic community.[18] African American students, meanwhile, were divided between two schools, Urban Day School and Harambee Community School, which did not have quite the same backing of their communities. The impacts on students in these cases may have been due to the specific characteristics of the very limited number of schools that they attended, making generalization problematic.

The results from the New York City, Dayton, and Washington, D.C., evaluations reported below do not suffer from the same limitations. Because vouchers were awarded by lottery, observed differences between the treatment and control groups can reasonably be attributed to differences in the ways public and private schools operate, not simply to selection mechanisms. Still, the findings reported below largely confirm the scholarly consensus that emerged from earlier panel studies of student achievement in public and private schools. Results from the three-city RFTs show positive impacts on the test performance of African American students but not on the performance of students of other ethnic backgrounds.

Private School Impact on Test Performance

Private school impacts indicate differences between students who used a voucher to switch to private schools and those students in public schools who would have switched to a private school if they had been offered a voucher. Impacts, then, report the effects of the intervention on the change in student performance over time.

Impacts are not the same as the level of a student's performance on a test, which is measured absolutely at any particular moment by counting the number of correct answers to test questions or by comparing specific groups of students with students across the nation. Nor are impacts simply the change in level of performance from one year to the next, generally referred to as gains or losses. Once again, that change can be measured by a raw score, such as the number of questions answered correctly. However, gains and losses usually are measured relative to a national norm. So, for example, if it is said that students' test performances declined, it does not necessarily mean that they answered fewer questions correctly but only that their score fell relative to the national norm, which, as the average child develops and acquires new knowledge and skills, steadily rises from one school year to the next.

The impacts reported in this chapter are the differences in the change that occurred in the private school and the change that would have occurred had students remained in public school, as estimated from the performance of students in the control group. All impacts are calculated in terms of national percentile ranking (NPR) points, which vary between 0 and 100, with a national median of 50.[19] Positive impacts represent gains relative to the national norm. Any such gains would not have occurred had students remained in public school. The same is true for negative impacts, which are losses relative to the national norm that would not have occurred had students remained in public school. All estimates of impacts control separately for students' initial reading and math scores. As mentioned, to produce more stable estimates, we provide estimates that combine reading and math scores. (However, impacts did not differ significantly by subject matter.)

As can be seen in appendix C, performance of the students who attended initial testing sessions was quite low on the baseline math and reading tests administered to them at the time their parents applied for a voucher. Students generally scored between the 20th and 30th percentile, well below the national median of 50 NPR points. Although their scores may have been suppressed by the testing conditions (see discussion below), applicants appear to have come from an educationally disadvantaged population.

Table 6-1 reports the main findings of this chapter, the estimated impacts of attending a private school for students in Year I, Year II, and, in New York and Washington, Year III.[20] The table reveals no overall private school impact of switching to a private school on student test scores in the three cities. Nor does it reveal any private school impact on the test scores of students from other than African American backgrounds (mainly Hispanic students in New York and white students in Dayton). However, the table shows that the switch to a private school had significantly positive impacts on the test scores of African American students.

Table 6-1. *Impact of Switching to a Private School on Test Score Performance*

City	Year I (NPRs)	(N)	Year II (NPRs)	(N)	Year III (NPRs)	(N)
All students						
Three-city average	0.7	2,791	3.7	2,340	0.7	1,937
New York City	1.1	1,449	0.6	1,199	1.4	1,250
Dayton	2.2	409	4.2	382	. . .	
Washington, D.C.	−0.3	933	7.5***	759	−2.1	687
African Americans						
Three-city average	3.9*	1,809	6.3***	1,438	6.6**	1,175
New York City	5.4***	622	4.3**	497	9.2***	519
Dayton	3.3	296	6.5*	273	. . .	
Washington, D.C.	−0.9	891	9.2***	668	−1.9	656
All other ethnic groups						
Three-city average	−1.0	959	−1.4	750	−3.5	760
New York City	−2.2	812	−1.5	612	−3.5ᵃ	729
Dayton	1.0	108	−0.2	96	. . .	
Washington, D.C.	7.4	39	−0.1	42	−1.8	31

*p < .10, two-tailed test; **p < .05; ***p < .01. Weighted two-stage least squares regressions performed; treatment status used as instrument. Impacts expressed in national percentile ranking (NPR) points. In New York City, most non–African Americans in this study are Hispanic; in Dayton, the vast majority are whites. Three-city impacts estimated by weighting each city observation by the inverse of its variance

a The Year III impact for Hispanics in New York is −1.5. The impact for other ethnic groups is −10.3, which is not statistically significant.

Table 6-1 shows that African Americans in all three cities gained, on average, roughly 3.9 NPR points after Year I, 6.3 points after Year II, and 6.6 points after Year III.[21] Results for African American students varied by city. In Year I, the only significant gains were observed in New York City, where African Americans attending a private school scored, on average, 5.4 percentile points higher than members of the control group.[22] In Year II, significant impacts on African American test scores were evident in all three cities, ranging from 4.3 percentile points in New York City, to 6.5 points in Dayton, to 9.2 points in Washington, D.C. The Year III impact of 9.2 points on African American students' test scores in New York City is statistically significant. The −1.9 point impact in Year III in Washington, however, is not.

Figure 6-1 provides information on the estimated levels of test score performance of African American students participating in the evaluation. One needs to be cautious in interpreting levels of student performance relative to the national mean shown in this figure. In these evaluations, students were

Figure 6-1. *African American Students' Test Scores in Public and Private Schools in Three Cities* [a]

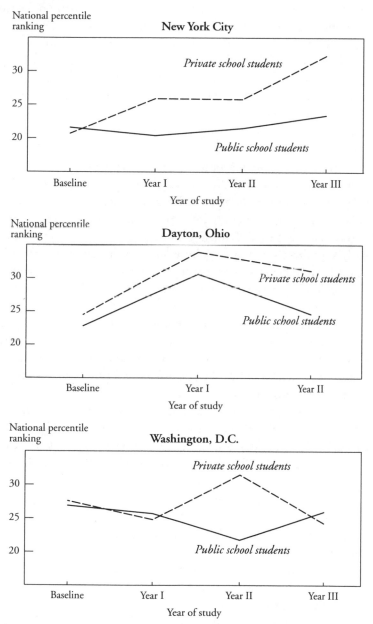

a. Estimated levels on the combined math and reading sections of the Iowa Test of Basic Skills reported for students in private schools and those who would have attended a private school if offered a voucher. Baseline scores are attributed to students based on attendance patterns in Year I. Levels estimated from models used to estimate test-score impacts.

tested outside their normal classroom, usually on a weekend. The administrator of the test, though a school teacher or administrator, was not their regular classroom teacher. Although this procedure ensured that comparisons between the private and public sector were as evenhanded as possible, the more stringent testing conditions may have suppressed the level of performance by all students. Thus, one should not draw the conclusion from the information in figure 6-1 that the participating students, had they been tested in a familiar classroom setting, would have performed as far below the national median of 50 percentile points as they did under these testing conditions.

As long as one focuses not on specific levels but on overall trends in the data, figure 6-1 is quite informative. Consider first the scores in New York City, where the estimates are most precise and the pattern is fairly simple and clear. Relative to the national median, average public school test scores for the African American control group remained nearly constant over all four testing periods. This does not mean that students in the control group were not learning over this four-year period. Rather, it shows that their year-to-year learning rate simply kept them at the same point relative to the national median. For African American students in private schools, however, a substantial gain relative to the national average is observed—by Year III, the difference between public and private students exceeded 9 percentile points.

In Dayton, Ohio, the pattern is slightly different. Both private and public school students improved their scores, relative to the national norm, from baseline to Year I. In Year II, however, the performance of public school students slipped considerably, while the performance of private school students remained noticeably higher.

The most irregular pattern was observed in Washington, D.C. In this city, the scores of the public school control group remained fairly constant between the baseline year and Year I but then dropped noticeably in Year II, only to recover in Year III. The private school pattern is the mirror image of the public school effect. Major gains were registered in Year II, but in Year III scores slipped back to baseline levels.

What accounts for such variations? More specifically, what accounts for the consistent gains of African Americans in private schools in New York City compared to the ups and downs in Washington, D.C.? Although we cannot provide definitive answers, two possibilities come to mind. First, the data from the New York evaluation may provide a more precise—and therefore more stable—estimate of the true impact of a switch to a private school. For one thing, the Year III response rates in New York were 67 percent, somewhat higher than the 60 percent rate in Washington, D.C. More important, by Year III the voucher usage rate in New York City was nearly twice as high as in Washington, D.C. In Year III the vouchers were used by 53 percent of those offered vouchers in New York, compared with just 29 percent of those offered vouchers in Washington, D.C. When take-up rates fall as low as they did in D.C., although estimates of impacts remain unbiased, the data become increasingly noisy, making it all the more difficult to detect effects. (For fuller discussion, see pages 51–53.) This statistical fact alone could account for the greater clarity of the findings in New York.

Are there substantive differences between the New York City and D.C. school systems that could account for both the stable results in New York and the noticeable swings in D.C.? One possibility is the emergence of charter schools in D.C.—but not in New York—over the course of the evaluations. Only one charter school opened in New York City in 1998, and only two others opened in 1999, the last year of the New York evaluation. In D.C., however, charter schools were established in Year I of the evaluation, expanded rapidly in Year II, and constituted a stable presence by Year III. According to D.C. officials, charter schools in 2000–01 (the third year of the D.C. evaluation) enrolled fully 16 percent of all public school students, a percentage larger than in any state in the country. (In Arizona, the locale of the largest statewide charter experiment, about 5 percent of public school students enrolled in charter schools.) Among voucher applicants, interest in charter schools was even higher. Twelve percent of the control group attended a charter school in Year I, 18 percent in Year II, and 24 percent in Year III (see table 2-2 on page 37). At the same time, charter schools were attracting students from private schools, perhaps destabilizing many of these small, struggling schools. Among those offered vouchers, the percentages who did not use them but instead chose to attend a (free) charter school climbed from 3 percent in Year I to 13 percent in Year II to 17 percent in Year III. Clearly, during the course of the evaluation, the arrival of charter schools was altering the school environment for the most choice-minded of D.C. families.

The drop in public school test scores between baseline and Year II could have been due to the instability of the public school environment during this period. After all, D.C. charter schools had hastily opened in Years I and II of the evaluation. Many of them had experienced difficulties during their initial operating year. The recovery in Year III may have been due to the institutionalization and stabilization of the charter schools as well as renewed efforts by traditional D.C. public schools to respond to what was becoming a major challenge to their fiscal well-being. Studies of charter schools in Texas and Michigan have identified such a pattern of performance—initial losses followed by later gains.[23]

Another possibility is that the private schools that serve inner-city students in New York City are of higher quality than those in the District of Columbia. Catholic schools, which constitute the largest share of private schools in both cities, have a longer, richer history in New York City than in D.C. and therefore may deliver a superior education. In New York, Catholic schools were established before the Civil War, emerging out of a concerted struggle between the Catholic community and Protestant-dominated public schools. For generations, a strong, vibrant immigrant community nurtured New York's Catholic schools,[24] and recent studies have found that low-income students in these schools score substantially higher on standardized tests than those in public schools, results that are consistent with ours.[25] By contrast, the Catholic Church has not maintained a comparably strong social, political, or educational presence in the nation's capital. Historically, Washington was a southern city with no industrial base to attract immigrants from European countries with large concentrations of Catholics. The D.C. Catholic schools, as a consequence, may not be as well established as those in New York City, helping to explain why voucher students who attended them did not score higher than their public school peers.

We offer these ideas only as possible explanations of our findings. We cannot definitively show that the expansion of charter schools in Washington or the history of the city's Catholic schools account for the changing estimated impacts of the Washington Scholarship Program. The variation in scores from year to year might just as easily be accounted for by the noisy data set that was available. Still, because Washington's voucher program was operating in a changing environment and could not be precisely evaluated, New York's voucher experiment may provide the clearest insight into the unique impacts of vouchers in urban settings, and especially in cities where charter schools have yet to play a major role.

Assessing the Magnitude of the Impact

How large were these impacts? As discussed in previous chapters, social scientists often answer this question by estimating the size of an impact in terms of standard deviations, generally referred to as effect sizes. An effect size of one full standard deviation is approximately the difference between the nationwide test scores of African American and of white students. By calculating effect sizes, one can determine how much an intervention narrows

Table 6-2. *Aggregate Three-City Impacts of Switching from a Public to a Private School on the Test Scores of African Americans and Other Ethnic Groups*

Measure	African Americans (NPRs)			Other ethnic groups (NPRs)		
	Year I	Year II	Year III	Year I	Year II	Year III
National percentile ranking points	3.9*	6.3***	6.6**	–1.0	–1.4	–3.5
Standard deviation	0.18*	0.28***	0.30**	–0.05	–0.06	–0.16

*p < .10, two-tailed test; **p < .05; ***p < .01. Test scores represent the combined math and reading scores on the Iowa Test of Basic Skills. Impacts expressed in standard deviations are the ratio of the average weighted point estimates over the average unweighted standard deviations for baseline total test scores. Aggregate impacts estimated by weighting each city observation by the inverse of its variance. The Year III impact is from New York City and Washington, D.C., only.

that education gap. As mentioned, no significant private school impact on test scores for non–African American students was observed in any year or city. But as shown in table 6-2, the magnitude of the average impact of switching to a private school on African American test scores, calculated as an effect size and weighting each observation by the precision of the estimate, was 0.18 of a standard deviation in Year I, 0.28 in Year II, and by Year III in Washington and New York City, 0.30.[26] Because whites did not reap any detectible gains from attending a private school, the Year III impact constitutes a 30 percent reduction in the national test score gap between blacks and whites.

The impacts of attending private school on African American students are comparable to those found in the Tennessee STAR study, an evaluation of a class-size reduction intervention that also was conducted through a randomized field trial. According to a recent reanalysis of data from Tennessee, after two years the impact on African American students of reducing class sizes was, on average, 7 to 8 percentile points, only slightly larger than the 6.6-point average impact for black students who switched to a private school.[27]

Another way of assessing the size of the effects of switching from a public to a private school is to compare them to those presented in *Improving Student Achievement*, a RAND study released in August 2000.[28] In Texas and North Carolina, which have introduced rigorous accountability systems that involve statewide testing and are identified as the most successful states in improving school achievement, the study reports what it says are "remarkable" one-year gains in math scores of "as much as 0.06 to 0.07 [of a] standard deviation per year"—or 0.18 to 0.21 of a standard deviation over three years. The Year III effects of the school voucher intervention on African American students observed here are moderately larger than these effects.

Methodological Questions

Although randomized field trials generally are regarded as the gold standard in social science research, they are not without methodological problems. Our solutions to those problems are discussed in full in both chapter 2 and the appendixes, but it is worth mentioning them briefly now. Not all students in the study attended follow-up testing sessions. To adjust for that fact, the data were weighted according to the inverse of the probability that each child, on the basis of his or her baseline profile, would attend testing sessions in Years I, II, and III. In addition, not everyone who was offered a voucher used it, and some students who were not offered a voucher nevertheless attended a private school. To obtain a consistent and unbiased estimate of the effects of attending a private school, two-stage least squares regressions were estimated using the results of the voucher lottery as the instrument.

This instrumental variable analysis obviates the need to control for family background characteristics.[29] To demonstate, we provide in table 6-3 estimates of the impacts of attending a private school on test scores both with and without explicit controls for the mother's educational level, mother's employment status, family size, and whether the family received welfare. The estimated impacts remain essentially the same, whether or not the variables are included. For the cities in the study, on average, the impacts, once background controls were included in the model, were 6.3 percentile points in Year II and 6.7 points in Year III.

Hawthorne Effects

Test score gains may not have been due to attending a private school but to a surge of enthusiasm associated with winning a lottery, something akin to a Hawthorne effect. This phenomenon occurs when, for example, employees respond favorably to minor alterations in their working environment, such as a change in the color of their office walls. Learning that their children could attend a private school may have invigorated parents' interest in their children's education, causing a temporary Hawthorne effect.

Although theoretically possible, for a host of reasons Hawthorne effects probably are not responsible for the positive impacts on African American students' test scores. First, no private school impact on parents' involvement in their child's education was observed (see chapter 5). Second, there is no obvious reason why Hawthorne effects should be observed for blacks but not

Table 6-3. *Estimated Impacts of Switching from a Public to a Private School on African Americans' Combined Test Scores, with and without Controls for Family Background Characteristics*

City	Year II		Year III	
	Original results (NPRs)	Controlling for family background (NPRs)	Original results (NPRs)	Controlling for family background (NPRs)
Three-city average impact	6.3**	6.4**	6.6**	6.7**
New York City	4.3**	4.5**	9.2***	9.1***
Dayton	6.5*	5.9	. . .	. . .
Washington, D.C.	9.2***	9.2*	–1.9	–0.9

*p < .10, two-tailed test; **p < .05; ***p < .01. Weighted two-stage least squares regressions performed; treatment status used as instrument. All models control for baseline test scores, mother's education, employment status, whether the family received welfare, and family size. Missing values for demographic variables imputed by best-subset regression. New York City model also includes lottery indicators. Impacts expressed in terms of national percentile ranking (NPR) points. Average three-city impact is based on effects observed in the three cities weighted by the inverse of the variance of the point estimates.

for other ethnic groups. Third, the impact of attending a private school on test scores does not take the form of an initial upsurge followed by a general decline. On the contrary, the increment is greater, on average, in Year II than in Year I. Only in New York do impacts drop slightly—and insignificantly— between Years I and II, yet in Year III they rebound to reach a high of over 9 percentile points.

Perhaps most important, it is hard to imagine why parents' temporary excitement at winning a lottery would cause students to score higher. Although parents may have been enthusiastic about switching schools, their children—who were being asked to change schools, form new friendships, adjust to new rules and expectations, and acquire new study habits—were less so (see chapter 7). In Washington, D.C., for instance, older students who transferred to private schools indicated resentment over those changes.[30] Although they recovered in Year II, the pattern hardly reflects the workings of a Hawthorne effect.

Finally, the scientific community's once-ardent belief in the placebo effect, a close cousin of the Hawthorne effect, has itself begun to wane. A 2001 study found that the original research identifying the placebo effect never compared the placebo with no intervention at all. What is more, studies that did compare placebos to no intervention found little difference in their impact.[31] After examining more than 100 such studies, the investigators con-

Table 6-4. *Three-City Impacts of Attending a Private School on African Americans' Test Scores, by Grade Level*

Impact	Year I (NPRs)	Total observations	Year II (NPRs)	Total observations	Year III (NPRs)	Total observations
For all grades	3.9*	1,809	6.3***	1,438	6.6**	1,175
By Year I grade level						
Second	8.6*	389	7.1	314	8.3	271
Third	−2.4	400	−0.4	328	3.6	318
Fourth	9.2**	368	3.9	302	2.9	274
Fifth	6.8*	275	8.6**	221	12.4**	202
Sixth	2.6	162	12.7*	140	n.a.[a]	n.a.
Seventh	1.7	140	−0.2	109	...	...
Eighth	−16.8	75	...	...	...	...

*$p < .10$, two-tailed test; **$p < .05$; ***$p < .01$. Impacts expressed in terms of national percentile ranking (NPR) points. "Total observations" refers to the sum of the observations used to generate city-specific impacts, which are then weighted by the inverse of their variances to estimate an overall effect. Impacts in grades 6–8 estimated only in Dayton and Washington.

a. Data for the sixth-grade cohort in Year III are available only from Washington, D.C., and hence are not reported here. See appendix C for grade-level impacts for each city.

cluded that apparent placebo effects seem to be little more than natural fluctuations in the course of a disease, not the psychological impact of taking a pill. People are not so easily fooled by sugar pills, it now appears. Nor, we suspect, can children be fooled into learning.

Grade-Level Effects

It is possible that the observed effects were concentrated in particular grades. Perhaps public and private schools were equally effective for younger children but not for older ones, or vice versa. When the data are disaggregated by grade level and by city, the number of cases available for investigation for each ethnic group becomes too small to support strong conclusions — especially given the measurement error associated with value-added estimates of student performance.[32] However, it is possible to combine the grade-level results from the three cities in each year of the evaluation in order to ascertain whether older or younger African American students benefited more from the voucher intervention.

Table 6-4 reports the average impacts in Years I and II of attending a private school in the three cities; grade-level impacts in Washington and New York City are reported for Year III. Positive impacts were detected in thirteen of the sixteen observations. Five of the sixteen observations are statistically significant; none of the three negative ones is statistically significant. There is no clear evidence that impacts were greater for older students than younger ones, or vice versa. In Year III, the impacts for African American students in Washington and New York City are large and positive in all four grades and statistically significant in one. In sum, grade-level fluctuations in estimated impacts are as likely to be idiosyncratic as systematic.

Effects by Initial Ability Level

Perhaps the observed ethnic differences in the impact of attending a private school on test scores can be better explained by differences in students' initial test scores, observed in the baseline testing session. Students whose initial scores were low may have had more to gain by attending a private school than higher-performing students. Alternatively, it might be that only higher-performing students had the talent needed to benefit from a private school education. If African Americans are concentrated within a particular portion of the test score distribution, then we may have mistakenly attributed heterogeneous test score effects to ethnicity when the critical distinguishing characteristic really was a student's initial ability level.

To examine this possibility, we estimated separate impacts of attending a private school for students in each of the four quartiles of the baseline test score distribution. No clear patterns emerged. None of the impacts in any year approach conventional levels of statistical significance. Attending a private school does not appear to have a differential impact on student educational performance, conditional upon the students' initial test score performance. For example, in Year II the average impact in the three cities for the lowest quartile was 3.7 percentile points, a statistically insignificant impact. The Year II impact for the other three quartiles, in ascending order, was 3.6, 0.2, and 0.6, respectively. In Year III, average impacts (all statistically insignificant) were, from lowest to highest quartile, –0.1, 0.9, –1.9, –.07.

Distributional Outcomes

Many philosophers—from John Rawls to Ronald Dworkin—define social justice at least partially in terms of equality. While they debate the meaning of equality, most contend that "just" public policies help to mitigate inequalities that arise from "family background circumstances or family choices."[33] Publicly funded education undoubtedly is expected to play a role in this endeavor. The distribution of achievement gains, as much as average changes, constitutes an appropriate criterion for evaluating a school choice intervention.

It is not clear whether one should expect the offer of a voucher to increase or decrease inequalities between high- and low-performing students. On one hand, differences in achievement might be expected to grow. Better students who are offered vouchers may gain access to higher-quality private schools, while lower-scoring students may be relegated to less effective private schools or not admitted to a private school at all, leaving them in a public school that their family had wanted to avoid. If so, the net result could widen the gap between high- and low-performing students who were offered vouchers. Concerned about this eventuality, Carol Ascher and her colleagues asked, "What mechanisms ensure that those students [in private school] who need extra time and attention . . . receive this more costly instruction?"[34]

On the other hand, public schools may be less egalitarian than private schools.[35] Residential choice may separate students by ability as well as by race and income. And to the extent that public schools are judged on the basis of average test scores, they may find it in their interest to work more intensively with higher-performing than lower-performing students. Or they may place poor-performing students in special education programs. Commenting on the rising inequality in reading skills among public school students, Kati Haycock, director of the Education Trust, told the *New York Times*, "It would appear that in a deeply misguided response to demands for higher achievement, [public] schools are focusing their efforts and resources on those students most likely to succeed while neglecting the students who most need help."[36] If private schools, by contrast, need to keep all of their paying customers happy, they may give all students comparable amounts of attention, regardless of ability levels.

We conducted two statistical tests to see whether being offered a voucher altered the distribution of students' test scores. In each of the three cities, we calculated the coefficient of variation at baseline and again in Years I, II, and III separately for those who were offered a voucher and those who were not. The coefficient of variation measures the dispersion of test scores relative to the average score.[37] By tracking this statistic over time, it is possible to determine whether the dispersion in test scores increased or decreased among those who were offered a voucher and those who were not. If inequality is being reduced, the coefficient decreases over time. If inequality is increasing, the coefficient increases. As shown in table 6-5, inequalities in both groups declined over time. In New York City, for example, the coefficient for those offered a voucher declined by 0.12 between baseline and Year I, an indication that student achievement levels were becoming more similar. Considering all cities and all years together, a decline in inequality for those offered a voucher was observed in six of eight comparisons; in only one case was a slight increase evident.

Table 6-5. *Change in the Coefficient of Variation in Test Scores for Those Offered Vouchers and for Control Groups*

	Change in coefficients of variation		
Period	New York City	Dayton	Washington, D.C.
Offered vouchers			
Between baseline and			
Year I	−0.12	−0.21	−0.02
Year II	−0.10	0.04	0.04
Year III	−0.14	. . .	−0.01
Control group			
Between baseline and			
Year I	−0.01	−0.15	−0.03
Year II	−0.04	0.10	0.10
Year III	−0.09	. . .	−0.04

Figures represent the difference in coefficients of variations (standard deviation divided by the mean) using weighted data at Years I, II, and III and at baseline.

The pattern of change was similar for the control group: a decline in inequality was observed in five of eight comparisons. In general, both those offered a voucher and those not offered a voucher experienced a reduction in inequality over time. Differences between the two groups of students were small and inconsistent among cities and from one year to the next. Virtually identical results were obtained when examining African Americans and other ethnic groups separately.

The coefficient of variation allows one to compare the overall distribution of test scores relative to the average performance. A second statistical technique, interquantile regression, allows one to estimate the impact of a voucher offer on differences between higher- and lower-performing students. These models ascertain whether the voucher offer widened or narrowed the difference between the performance of those in the top and those in the bottom quartile. If vouchers exacerbated educational inequalities, the estimated impact of vouchers on the difference between the two groups is positive. If they mitigated educational inequalities, the impact is negative.

Estimates of the impact of vouchers on the difference were obtained for each year in each city, giving us eight possible comparisons. As shown in table 6-6, in five instances we observed positive coefficients, indicating an increase in inequality; in three instances we observed negative coefficients, indicating a decrease in inequality. None of the impacts, however, are statistically significant. In no year or city did vouchers significantly alter the difference between the test scores of the highest- and lowest-performing students.

Table 6-6. *Impact of Voucher Offer on Difference between*
Higher- and Lower-Performing Students

City	Year I (NPRs)	Year II (NPRs)	Year III (NPRs)
New York	−0.6	−0.4	2.4
Dayton	2.7	3.2	. . .
Washington, D.C.	2.5	−1.5	0.7

*p < .10, two-tailed test; **p < .05; ***p < .01. Interquantile regressions performed on unweighted data. Bootstrapped standard errors calculated. All models control for baseline test scores; models in New York also control for lottery indicators. Figures represent the impact of a voucher offer on differences between lower- and higher-performing students expressed in national percentile ranking (NPR) points. Lower-performing students are at and below the 25th percentile; higher-performing students are at and above the 75th percentile.

These findings confirm neither the warning that vouchers will inexorably lead to an increasingly stratified student body nor the promise that vouchers will steadily eliminate inequalities between high- and low-performing students. On the contrary, the offer of vouchers did not seem to reshape the distribution of students' test scores. All ability groups were affected in more or less the same way.

Explaining Test Score Impacts

Are there specific attributes of public and private schools that account for the higher test performance among African American students who switched to the private sector? In chapters 4 and 5, we reported that parents identified many differences between public and private schools. Public schools were larger and had more complex facilities, more varied programming, and more careful monitoring of students outside the classroom. Private schools had a more stringent dress code, fewer disciplinary problems, and smaller classes. Their teachers assigned more homework, and the schools communicated more frequently with parents. However, we found few differences between public and private schools in disciplinary suspensions, racial integration, and parents' involvement in their child's education. Do any of those factors, singly or all together, account for the fact that African American students who switched from public to private schools scored higher than their peers in public schools?

Key Explanatory Factors

To identify the characteristics that most likely account for the pattern of test score impacts that we observed, we first determined whether switching to a

Table 6-7. *Impact of Switching from a Public to a Private School on African Americans' Test Scores in New York City, Controlling for Key School Characteristics*

	Year I (NPRs)		Year II (NPRs)		Year III (NPRs)	
	No school controls (1)	School controls (2)	No school controls (3)	School controls (4)	No school controls (5)	School controls (6)
Attend private school	5.4***	5.7***	4.3**	5.2**	9.2***	10.1***
School disruptions	—	–0.3	—	–2.1***	—	–0.8
Communication	—	–0.4	—	–0.9	—	–0.4
School size	—	–0.1	—	1.0	—	0.7
Class size	—	0.3	—	–0.2	—	0.7
Baseline math score	0.4***	0.4***	0.4***	0.4***	0.3***	0.3***
Baseline reading score	0.4***	0.4***	0.3***	0.3***	0.4***	0.4***
Constant	–2.9	–2.2	0.5	3.4	–6.9	–7.9
Number of cases	622	622	497	497	519	519
Adjusted R^2	.52	.51	.45	.43	.45	.45

*$p < .10$, two-tailed test; **$p < .05$; ***$p < .01$. Weighted two-stage least squares regressions performed; treatment status used as instrument. All models control for lottery indicators. Impacts expressed in terms of national percentile ranking (NPR) points. All models control for baseline test scores and lottery indicators. Missing values for school covariates imputed by best-subset regression.

private school resulted in a bigger change in certain aspects of the education of African American students than of students from other ethnic backgrounds. In chapters 4 and 5, we found that in New York vouchers had a disproportionately beneficial effect for African Americans, compared with Hispanics, on class size, school disruptions, school size, and school communications. In Dayton, African Americans who switched from a public to a private school appeared to gain more with respect to school resources and programs than did their white peers.[38] To see whether these school characteristics explain African American student achievement gains in New York and Dayton, we added them to the original test score models. Presumably, if African Americans are posting test score gains because of smaller classes or fewer disruptions in the private schools that they attend, then inclusion of those features in the explanatory model would attenuate the estimated impact of the switch to a private school.

Table 6-7 reports the results for African American students in New York City. The first, third, and fifth columns report the original estimated impact on African American test scores of switching to a private school in New York City in Years I, II, and III. The second, fourth, and sixth columns report the estimated impacts, after controlling for levels of school disruptions, class size, school size, and school-parent communication. The results are strikingly consistent. In none of the three years did those four factors reduce at all the impact of switching to a private school on test scores. In Year I, after taking into account the effect of these school factors, the estimated impact of the switch was 5.7 NPR points; in Year II, the impact was 5.2 points; and in Year III, it was 10.1 points.

The four factors failed to explain the impact of attending a private school, and only one registered any significant direct impact on student test score performance. School size, class size, and school-parent communication were not correlated with achievement gains in any of the three years in New York City. Only school disruptions had a significant impact on student performance, and the effect, though consistently negative in all three years, was statistically significant just in Year II. Neither separately nor combined did the four factors explain why African American students performed better on tests when they attended a private school—despite the fact that African American parents reported major changes in those four areas when their children switched to a private school.[39]

We repeated this exercise in the other two cities in those years when positive test score impacts were observed for African American students (see table 6-8). In Dayton, African Americans had significantly more school resources and school programs when they switched to the private sector. But when those factors were used to estimate Year II test scores, the size of the estimated impact dropped by less than 1 percentile point, from 6.5 NPR points to 5.9 points. (However, the estimated impact then exceeded conventional levels of statistical significance, $p = .11$.) Furthermore, neither school resources nor programs had a significant, positive direct impact on the test scores of African American students.[40]

In Washington, D.C., we sought to explain African American students' test scores in Year II in two different ways, first by using the two factors— resources and programs—that at first seemed important in Dayton, then by using the four factors—school size, class size, school disruptions, and school-parent communication—that at first seemed important in New York. Once again, however, we could not explain the impact of the switch to a private school on test scores. As shown in table 6-8, the original estimated impact was 9.2 NPR points. When resources and programs were included in the model, the private school impact, instead of attenuating, remained at 9.2 percentile points; when class size, school size, school disruptions, and school-

Table 6-8. *Impact of Switching from a Public to a Private School on African Americans' Test Scores in Dayton and Washington, D.C., Controlling for Key School Characteristics*

	Dayton, Year II (NPRs)		Washington, D.C., Year II (NPRs)		
	No school controls (1)	School controls (2)	No school controls (3)	Some school controls (4)	Other school controls (5)
Attend private school	6.5*	5.9	9.2***	9.2***	13.0***
School resources	—	0.9	—	0.3	—
School programs	—	0.7	—	0.5	—
School disruptions	—	—	—	—	–1.4**
Communication	—	—	—	—	0.1
School size	—	—	—	—	2.5**
Class size	—	—	—	—	1.4*
Baseline math scores	0.2***	0.2***	0.4***	0.4***	0.4***
Baseline reading scores	0.4***	0.4***	0.1***	0.1***	0.1***
Constant	10.8***	4.2	6.5***	6.4*	–3.6
Number of cases	273	273	668	668	668
Adjusted R^2	.35	.35	.33	.33	.32

*$p < .10$, two-tailed test; **$p < .05$; ***$p < .01$. Weighted two-stage least squares regressions performed; treatment status used as instrument. All models control for baseline test scores. Impacts expressed in terms of national percentile ranking (NPR) points. Missing values for school covariates imputed by best-subset regression. Models estimated only for those years when significant positive impacts are observed for African Americans.

parent communications were included, the private school impact increased quite substantially, to as much as 13.0 percentile points. As in Year II in New York City, test scores in D.C. in Year II were reduced by school disruptions. Class size and school size also affected test scores, but in a direction opposite what might be expected. All in all, factors thought to be keys to the difference between public and private schools simply did not account for private school impacts on test scores of African American students.

Comprehensive Analysis

Perhaps other factors—or a combination of all factors—determined students' test scores. To see whether a more comprehensive approach could explain the results, a model that included all plausible factors was constructed, one that made use of all the relevant information from the parent surveys. Comprehensive models such as this do not provide precise estimates of the impact of

Table 6-9. *Impact of Switching from a Public to a Private School on African Americans' Test Scores in New York City, Dayton, and Washington, D.C., Comprehensive Model*

	New York (NPRs)		Dayton (NPRs)		Washington, D.C. (NPRs)	
Year	No school controls (1)	School controls (2)	No school controls (3)	School controls (4)	No school controls (5)	School controls (6)
Year I	5.4***	6.3***	—	—	—	—
Year II	4.3**	6.3**	6.5*	4.7	9.2***	13.6***
Year III	9.2***	11.5***	—	—	—	—

*p < .10, two-tailed test; **p < .05; ***p < .01. Weighted least squares regressions performed. Impacts expressed in terms of national percentile ranking (NPR) points. All models control for baseline test scores, lottery indicators, and their associated interactions. In addition, models control for school disruptions, school-parent communication, school size, class size, suspensions, dress codes, hallway monitoring, school resources, homework, segregation, parents' involvement with child, and parents' involvement in the school. Only African Americans are included in the models. Missing values for school covariates imputed by best-subset regression. Models estimated only in those years when and those cities where significant positive impacts are observed for African Americans.

any particular aspect of school life, such as class size or school disruptions, on students' test scores because the true impact of each factor is partially estimated by others. But the approach provides an excellent way of determining whether the total combination of factors explains the private school advantage for African American students.

Measures of the following factors were included in the comprehensive model: school disruptions, school-parent communication, school size, class size, suspension rates, dress codes, hallway monitoring, school resources and programs, homework, racial integration, parents' involvement with child, and parents' involvement in the school. The models then estimated impacts on African American students' test scores in Years I, II, and III in New York City and in Year II in Dayton and Washington, D.C., the years when and cities where significant private school impacts were observed.

Despite the broad array of factors taken into account, the estimated impact of attending a private school remained essentially unchanged. As shown in table 6-9, all but one of the estimated impacts remained significant. In New York City, the estimated private school impact increased slightly—by about 2 percentile points—in all three years. In Dayton, it slipped slightly, by a little more than 1 percentile point, and in that case was no longer statistically significant. In D.C., it increased by 4 percentile points, yielding a substantial, statistically significant 13.6 percentile points. All the elements that

Table 6-10. *Impact of Switching to a Private School on Test Score Performance in New York City for Hispanics Who Speak English as a First or Second Language*

Year	English first language (NPRs)	(N)	English second language (NPRs)	(N)
Year I	−2.6	399	2.3	305
Year II	−1.6	342	3.1	270
Year III	−1.2	350	1.4	287

*$p < .10$, two-tailed test; **$p < .05$; ***$p < .01$. Weighted two-stage least squares regressions performed; treatment status used as instrument. Impacts expressed in national percentile ranking (NPR) points. All models control for baseline test scores and lottery indicators. In no year is the difference in estimated impacts for the two groups of Hispanics statistically significant.

parents identified as distinctive about private schools, when included together in a comprehensive model, could not explain the private school advantage for African American students.[41]

Language Needs

In New York City, no private school impacts were observed for Hispanic students, despite the fact that consistently positive impacts were observed for African Americans. This result might have been due to the language difficulties that many Hispanics face. Parents reported fewer bilingual and English as a second language (ESL) programs in private than in public schools. Perhaps the lack of such programs in private schools offset whatever other advantages they may have offered Hispanic students.

To test this hypothesis, we compared the impact of switching to a private school on the test scores of Hispanic students whose primary language, according to their parents, was English with the impact on the scores of those for whom English was their second language. As shown in table 6-10, the results, if anything, run directly contrary to expectation. In all three years, students for whom English was the second language posted slightly positive impacts, while students for whom English was the primary language posted slightly negative effects. Neither the positive nor negative impacts— nor the slightly larger differences in impacts—were statistically significant.

These findings do not provide much of a basis for judging the ways in which public and private schools deal with students with special language needs. They probably rule out language, however, as an explanation of why African American but not Hispanic students appear to benefit from vouchers.

Table 6-11. *Impact of Switching to a Private School on Test Score Performance in New York City for First- and Multiple-Generation Hispanics*

Year	U.S. born (NPRs)	(N)	Foreign born (NPRs)	(N)
Year I	−0.6	203	−1.5	501
Year II	−0.1	167	−2.5	445
Year III	0.9	180	−2.3	457

*$p < .10$, two-tailed test; **$p < .05$; ***$p < .01$. Weighted two-stage least squares regressions performed; treatment status used as instrument. Inpact expressed in national percentile ranking (NPR) points. All models control for baseline test scores and lottery indicators. In no year is the difference in the estimated impacts for the two groups of Hispanics statistically significant.

First-Generation Compared with Multiple-Generation Hispanics

Many of the Hispanic students in the New York City voucher program were recent immigrants. Whereas the vast majority of African American parents were born in the United States, most Hispanic parents were born in Puerto Rico or the Dominican Republic. It is possible that the test scores we reported conflated important differences between first- and multiple-generation Hispanics, explaining why Hispanics, on average, did not appear to reap achievement gains from switching from public to private schools.[42]

Table 6-11 reports the impacts of switching to a private school separately for Hispanic students whose parents were born in the United States and for those whose parents were born abroad. Unfortunately, little additional insight into our puzzle is gained. In all three years, impacts for Hispanics with foreign-born parents are slightly negative, while those for Hispanics whose parents were born in the United States hover around zero. None of the impacts, however, are statistically significant, nor are any of the differences in impacts for the two groups of Hispanics statistically significant.

Other Explanations

If school size, class size, school disruptions, school-parent communication, racial composition, dress codes, hallway monitoring, school resources, homework, level of parents' involvement in their child's education, and parents' involvement in the school fail to explain why only African Americans show improvement in their test scores when they are offered a voucher, then what does? The question cannot be answered definitively with the information at hand, but we can speculate on the merits of a variety of alternative explanations.

First, it is possible that one or more of the factors listed above was critical but was not accurately measured in the parent surveys. Since parents' perceptions are not as precise as direct observation, it would be inappropriate, without data collected through direct observation, to rule out these school characteristics as possible explanations for the observed impacts on African American students' test scores. Yet we remain impressed by the reliability and validity of parents' reports. Parents' responses to survey questions were quite consistent from one year to the next and from one city to another. Also, whenever parents' reports could be compared with information from other sources, such as U.S. Department of Education surveys, the results were strikingly similar (see chapter 4).[43]

Still, there were some important dimensions of school life on which we had very little information. The most important, perhaps, are the characteristics of the teachers in public and private schools. Recent research has shown that teacher effectiveness can have a large impact on students' test scores.[44] Perhaps, then, the observed private school impacts were due to instructional factors that none of the items in the parent survey measured adequately. The disparity in the quality of public and private school teachers might have been much wider for African American students than for Hispanic students in New York City or for white students in Dayton. Nor did parent surveys ask about curriculums, teaching techniques, or teachers' expectations of their students. Such factors might be the key to understanding why African American students benefited from choice but other students did not.

The observed test score findings also may derive from the quality of the peer group of students from different ethnic backgrounds.[45] If the influence of public school peers was negative for African American students but not for Hispanics in New York City or for whites in Dayton, and if the switch to a private school enhanced the quality of the peer group, then that might help explain the puzzle. However, we found little change in student friendship patterns as reported by students themselves, casting a measure of doubt on this possible explanation.

Finally, a sizable literature suggests that "street culture" pervades all aspects of the lives of inner-city residents.[46] Private schools may effectively mitigate the problems associated with drugs, violence, and gangs. If African American students in central cities confront a disproportionate share of such problems, then private schools may provide an especially valuable haven from a countervailing street culture that threatens possibilities for learning. A religiously affiliated school may be particularly valuable in this regard. Almost all of the private schools in our studies had a religious connection, and students attending these schools became more religiously observant than the control group remaining in public school. Perhaps the emphasis on moral development and regular religious engagement has the positive impact on young people that proponents of faith-based education expect. It may be that a missionary commitment is required to create a positive educational environment in such a challenging setting. Further research is needed to determine whether religion constitutes a vital part of an effective urban school serving an African American community.

We still do not know what makes private schools successful, at least for African American students. Without an answer, it remains unclear how, or even whether, public schools can introduce appropriate reforms that will replicate our findings. Future pilot studies that contain a larger number of subjects, proceed for longer periods of time, and collect a broader array of information may unearth some of the reasons why school choice may help to close the education gap.

Conclusions

It is possible that conditions specific to an individual city or minor fluctuations in testing conditions may have skewed results in one direction or another. But when similar results emerge from evaluations of school voucher programs in multiple years in three different cities, we can conclude with a fair measure of confidence that the observed differences between treatment and control groups reflected the actual impacts of the programs.

In the three evaluations, students of one ethnic group appeared to benefit from school vouchers while all others remained unaffected. After two and three years, African American students in the three cities who switched from public to private schools scored, on average, approximately 6 percentile points higher on the Iowa Tests of Basic Skills than comparable African American students who remained in public schools. We find no evidence, however, that vouchers significantly improved the test scores of students of other ethnic groups, either Hispanics in New York City or whites in Dayton.

The observed effects for African American students are moderately large. African American students who switched to private schools scored, after one year, 0.18 of a standard deviation higher than the students in the control group. After two years, the effect size increased to 0.28 of a standard deviation. After three years, the effect size remained at this level, though impacts differed noticeably in New York City and Washington, D.C.

Given the public preoccupation with test scores, we end this chapter on a note of caution. One must qualify any generalization from the results of these pilot programs to a large-scale voucher program involving all children in a large urban school system. Only a small fraction of low-income students in the three cities were offered vouchers, and those students constituted only a small proportion of all students attending private schools in those cities. To the extent that voucher applicants in these programs differed from the pool of eligible public school students in general, larger programs could conceivably yield quite different outcomes from those we observed. The only way to know for sure is to introduce larger pilot programs and study them carefully for longer periods of time.

7

Satisfaction with Urban Schools

Most Americans appear to have serious reservations about the current state of public education. Eighty percent of all adults interviewed in a 2000 national Gallup poll gave public schools a grade of C or lower. Their assessments change, however, when they are asked about the schools in their community rather than the quality of public education nationwide. Fully 47 percent of those surveyed gave their local schools a grade of A or B. Among parents, approval ratings rose even further—an impressive 70 percent gave the school their oldest child attended an A or B.[1]

This pattern of assessment applies to more than schools. For instance, according to one study, 81 percent of Americans have a favorable view of their local police department, despite the fact that only 59 percent have confidence in the police as an "institution in American society."[2] Americans also are much more critical of Congress as a whole than they are of their own representatives.[3] When people were asked about their impressions of government agencies in general, "71 percent . . . said that their [own] problems were taken care of, but only 30 percent think that government agencies [generally] do well at taking care of problems."[4]

On reflection, such findings are hardly surprising. Public discourse and the media, both of which tend to be more critical than complimentary, tend to inform most people's judgments about national institutions. Candidates for Congress, for instance, have a strong incentive to attack the institution they hope to join.[5] More generally, those engaged in national debates as well as those seeking higher office rarely praise government agencies—unless they themselves are responsible for an agency's operations. Media pundits—"nattering nabobs of negativism," as Vice President Spiro Agnew once called them—also help to paint a bleak picture of public institutions. News coverage generally emphasizes the interesting and important, which often seems synonymous with failure, scandal, and distress. As one textbook puts it, "a government program that works well is not news; one that is mismanaged, corrupt, or a failure is."[6]

Personal experience, meanwhile, tends to inform citizens' assessments of their local institutions—and, not coincidentally, their opinions of them appear more favorable. That is especially true for central-city public schools, a regular target of harsh criticism by outsiders. No less than 87 percent of households with children in central-city schools claimed to be "satisfied with the public elementary school."[7] Even in Washington, D.C., long criticized for the quality of its schools, 79 percent of parents claimed to be satisfied with their schools.[8] Nationally, African Americans are only slightly less likely to be "very satisfied" with their assigned public schools than whites—45 percent versus 47 percent.[9] Terry Moe, after scrutinizing parents' satisfaction with public schools, concluded that "Americans are fairly satisfied with their local schools overall, and this satisfaction is surprisingly widespread across district contexts. . . . In fact, many people in disadvantaged districts appear to be reasonably satisfied with schools that most experts would characterize as seriously inadequate."[10]

On the basis of such findings, some observers have concluded that school vouchers offer schooling options that most Americans simply do not want. Kevin Smith and Kenneth Meier argue that "using evidence taken from public-school parents to show they are massively dissatisfied with their public schools is impossible, because there is none." They go on to say that "education quality" is not an issue because "the vast majority of public opinion polls indicate that this is a demand already met by public schools."[11] Smith and Meier's contention appears all the more persuasive if one agrees, as many economists do, that consumer satisfaction is the best measure of a product's quality.[12] Generally speaking, to accurately determine the quality of an item—be it a suit, car, or lawn chair—one need only survey the people who use it. For just that reason, California's Blue Cross in 2001 used patient satisfaction as a criterion for adjusting physicians' pay rates.

Still, most economists are reticent to draw conclusions about "satisfaction" unless customers demonstrate a willingness to purchase the product. Consumers of public education may regard low-quality service as satisfactory simply because they do not pay for it directly. Actual behaviors, moreover, indicate strong dissatisfaction with central-city schools. Families that can afford to live elsewhere usually move to the suburbs during their child-rearing years, and the better public schools available there appear to be an important reason.[13]

Similarly, recent voucher campaigns suggest that many low-income families prefer private to public schools. When choice programs are announced, many more families apply than vouchers are available—despite the fact that families have to supplement partial vouchers with other funds. The well-advertised national Children's Scholarship Fund (CSF) program received inquiries from families with 1.25 million children for 40,000 scholarships. About one-third of the families offered vouchers were willing to pay the remaining cost of attending a private school, despite the free public school alternative. Still, it would be useful to know whether those who used vouchers to attend private schools remained satisfied with their new schools.

In this chapter, we examine this question in multiple settings. We report results from the randomized field trials (RFTs) conducted in New York City, Dayton, and Washington, D.C., as well as from the national CSF program. We also include information from other sources, including responses from cross-sections of public school parents in Dayton, Cleveland, and the Edgewood school district in San Antonio. Overall, the findings are unambiguous. The effects on parents' initial satisfaction with their child's switch from a public to a private school, as is reported in the next section of this chaper, were large, clear, sustained, and positive. But just as some new cars quickly lose their luster, so too may the appeal of a private education fade with time. To see whether this was the case with these low-income families, we examine parents' responses in Years II and III. Generally speaking, we find only a small decline in satisfaction with private schools. Next, we search for any changes in satisfaction that might have occurred among those who did not win the voucher lottery. That allows us to make sure that the differences between the two groups were not due to declining satisfaction with public schools. Finally, we compare the responses of parents who switched to private schools with those of a cross-section of all parents of students in big-city public schools, once again finding much higher satisfaction in the private sector.

Initial Enthusiasm: Focus Group Reports

Most parents who used vouchers to send their children to private school expressed delight in focus group discussions with the changes they observed. One Washington, D.C., mother compared her experience with public and private schools in these terms:

[Previously,] at the public school . . . they passed him, because [they had the attitude] "I don't want to be bothered. Let's get him on to the next grade." And [now] because he's in this private school, they're giving him the attention that he needs. . . . I had a parent-teacher conference yesterday, and [the teacher] was like, "I understand, and we're going to work with him reading, trying to get him into reading and writing more often."[14]

Grading policies in public schools were a frequent source of complaint. In the words of one mother: "They were giving away grades. . . .When you're giving away grades it looks good for that moment. But down the road, it's going to hit you . . . you can't get into a decent college or whatever. They just gave away grades. They kept quiet about it. . . .They just want to keep their jobs."[15]

One focus group session with public school parents turned to the question of teachers. Parents recognized that teacher quality varied enormously from school to school and from teacher to teacher. One D.C. mother observed that "some are there just to get that paycheck. . . . And some of them are . . . really dedicated."[16] Another couple thought that the teachers in public schools were satisfactory but that the system as a whole was not:

Mother: [In first grade], there was so many students they had to start up another classroom. So they had to wait until they brought another teacher on board. . . . My child was one of the kids that they transitioned into this new classroom. . . . Then when he got to second grade, he had a teacher that I think worked [for] a good week.

Father: Two weeks

Mother: A good two weeks.

Father: They started school late [because of a court suit over inadequate school facilities]. . .

Mother: She was from New York and . . .

Father: After two weeks she quit. And they didn't have another teacher until . . . January.

Mother: I called [Superintendent] Beckton's office and everything.

Father: And what I couldn't understand. . . . It does not take a rocket scientist to say, we have a pool of teachers where we can pull teachers from to send to certain schools if a teacher leaves.[17]

Of course, parents did not unanimously approve of every private school. An Edgewood father indicated that while his oldest child loved his new school, his two younger children were less content because "they didn't like the way the teachers were treating them." As a result, the father withdrew the younger children from the voucher program and sent them back to public school. Asked whether the children were happy back at their old school, the father replied, "Yeah, because they'd been there since kindergarten. . . . Both my kids are in the gifted and talented program."[18] This father was hardly the only parent to express contentment with his child's public school. Said one Washington, D.C., parent, "I don't have a beef with my kids attending [public] school 'cause they're doing good at [an elementary public school]. They're doing fine."[19] Another mother in D.C. noticed some problems but was still basically pleased with her child's experience at public school:

> He went to [an elementary public school] for five years . . . and I always been at school. I think that helped a lot. 'Cause . . . I always had a good rapport with the teachers and the principal. I helped out with the tests and stuff. So I can say public school's been good to me. But now this year, he goes to . . . this was his first year after being in another school for five years. The first week was pretty rough . . . but then . . . he score the highest in his class on the Stanford 9. So, he's fitting in. But then there's two children in the class who needs to go to special ed. . . . It's distracting.[20]

Initial Enthusiasm: Survey Results

Focus group conversations illustrate some parents' evaluations of their children's schools, but they do not provide a solid basis for generalization. Participants were not a perfect random sample of the test and control groups. And given the setting, group dynamics may have generated more praise of private schools—and more criticism of public schools—than was felt by a cross-section of all participants in the voucher programs. We therefore surveyed parents about their child's school. In addition to inquiring which grade, between A and F, their school deserved, we asked parents whether they were "very satisfied," "satisfied," "dissatisfied," or "very dissatisfied" with each of sixteen characteristics of their child's school.

Table 7-1 presents the average percentage of private and public school parents in the three city voucher programs that were very satisfied with each aspect of school life. Few results from our evaluations exhibited such large differences between the two groups. For example, in Year I, 54 percent of the private school parents said that they were satisfied with the academic program of the school, compared to just 15 percent of the public school parents

Table 7-1. *Parents Very Satisfied with Selected School Characteristics,*
Three-City RFTs
Percentage[a]

Characteristic	Year I		Year II	
	Public schools	Private schools	Public schools	Private schools
What is taught	15.0	55.5	14.7	43.6
Teacher skills	17.8	58.3[b]	16.6	42.7[b]
Academic program	14.6	53.8[c]	14.8	37.9[c]
Freedom to observe religious traditions	8.0	47.1	8.1	36.8
School discipline	15.1	52.9	13.8	35.3
Safety	17.9	54.3	16.4	43.6
Student respect for teachers	18.1	54.3	15.6	39.6
Moral values	17.1	51.6[d]	13.5	36.1[d]
Teacher respect for students	17.0	49.9	17.1	31.9
Class size	11.3	42.4	11.8	32.1
Clarity of school goals	14.5	45.2	13.8	34.0
Teacher-parent relations	22.5	53.0[e]	18.3	43.4[e]
Teamwork among school staff	15.2	44.2	12.8	34.0
Parents' involvement	16.3	42.2[f]	15.0	29.8[f]
School facility	12.2	36.6	8.9	27.9
Location	35.6	50.5	32.6	40.0

a. These figures represent the average results for Dayton, New York City, and Washington, D.C. Survey data for teacher respect for students are not available for New York City, nor is school facility data for Washington, D.C.

b. In New York, the survey asks about parents' satisfaction with "teaching."

c. In New York in both years and in Washington in Year II, the survey asks about parents' satisfaction with "academic quality."

d. In New York, the survey asks about parents' satisfaction with "teaching values."

e. In New York, the survey asks about parents' satisfaction with "teacher-parent communication." In Year II of the Washington study, the survey asks about parents' satisfaction with "amount of information from teachers."

f. In Year II of the Washington study, the survey asks about parents' satisfaction with "parental support for the school."

Table 7-2. *Parent Satisfaction, Children's Scholarship Fund National Study*

Satisfaction measure	Private school parents (percentage)	Public school parents (percentage)	Impact (percentage difference)
Parents "very satisfied" with			
Academic quality	68	23	45***
Safety	71	20	51***
Discipline	58	22	36***
Teaching values	69	25	44***
Parents "very proud" of their child's school	70	25	45***
Parents gave their child's school an A	72	16	56***

*p < .10; **p < .05; ***p < .01; two-tailed test.

in the control group, who would have used a voucher had one been offered to them. Similarly, 58 percent said that they were very satisfied with teacher skills in private schools, but only 18 percent of the public school control group gave the same response. The consistency of the results listed in table 7-1 may be due in part to the fact that the satisfaction items were clustered together on the survey. Nonetheless, parents did draw some distinctions among various aspects of school life. The smallest differences in satisfaction levels had to do with the location of the school. Here, the two groups differed by only 15 percentage points, while a 40 percentage point difference emerged when they were asked about the academic program, what is taught, teacher skills, and freedom to observe religious traditions.

The grades that parents gave their schools were consistent with these findings. On average, 40 percent of private school parents in the three cities gave their school an A, compared with just 14 percent of the control group. The average grade given by private school parents was a B+, compared with a C+ for public school parents.

The effects of switching to a private school in the nationwide RFT of the CSF program resemble those detected in the three city RFTs (table 7-2). More than 70 percent of the private school parents gave their school a grade of A, compared with just 16 percent of the control group. Sixty-eight percent of private school parents were very satisfied with the academic quality of the school, versus 23 percent of the control group. Differences in satisfaction with safety were even larger—71 percent of private school parents appeared very satisfied, opposed to just 20 percent of those in public schools. Similarly, private school parents were much more satisfied with school discipline and the teaching of values at school.

Table 7-3. *Impact of Attending a Private School on Level of Parent Satisfaction*
Effect size

City	Year I	Year II	Year III
All parents			
New York City	1.01***	1.05***	0.94***
Dayton	1.14***	0.59***	. . .
Washington, D.C.	0.66***	0.48***	0.50*
Average impact	0.92***	0.89***	0.85***
African American parents			
New York City	1.18***	1.00***	0.91***
Dayton	1.20***	0.62***	. . .
Washington, D.C.	0.68***	0.47***	0.50*
Average impact	0.97***	0.79***	0.85***
Other parents			
New York City (Hispanics)	0.99**	1.12**	0.99**
Dayton (whites)	0.90*	0.43	. . .

$^*p < .10$; $^{**}p < .05$; $^{***}p < .01$; two-tailed test. Weighted two-stage least squares regressions conducted; treatment status used as instrument. The dependent variable in each city represents an index of satisfaction constructed from the individual satisfaction items listed in table 7-1. Each index has been rescaled to have a standard deviation of 1.0; impacts, therefore, represent effect sizes. Average impact represents the average of the three cities' impacts, each weighted by the inverse of its respective variance.

By aggregating responses to all of the individual items, it is possible to obtain an overall estimate of the effect of attending a private school on parent satisfaction levels. The index takes into account the full range of responses—from "very satisfied" to "very dissatisfied"—on all of the satisfaction items listed in table 7-1. We rescaled the index to have a standard deviation of 1.0. Impacts, therefore, represent effect sizes, the same metric that was used in previous chapters to assess other private school impacts. As mentioned, an effect size of 0.1 is generally thought to be slight, 0.2 moderate, 0.5 large, and 1.0 quite remarkable.

As shown in table 7-3, in Year I, the average impact of attending a private school on the satisfaction of the parents participating in the three city voucher programs was very large: 0.92 of a standard deviation. The impact on those participating in the national CSF program was almost identical—0.95 of a standard deviation. That impact is much higher than the test score impacts discussed in the previous chapter, and it eclipses impacts typically observed in education interventions. Although effects were large in all cities, some differences were evident. The impact of the switch to private schools was largest in Dayton (1.14), slightly less in New York (1.01), and lowest in Washington, D.C. (0.66).

For African Americans participating in the three city voucher programs, the impact of attending a private school on initial enthusiasm was only slightly higher—0.97 standard deviations—than for all parents combined. Similar results were obtained for urban black participants in the national CSF evaluation.[21]

As might be expected, students in the three city programs were less enthusiastic about the change in schools than their parents were. On average, students participating in the three city programs who used their vouchers gave their schools a B+, while students in the control group gave their schools a B–. Students participating in the national CSF program did not differ significantly in their evaluation of public and private schools—both groups gave their schools only a B. Private-school impacts on student reports increased over time. By the third year in New York, 65 percent of private-school students said students get along with the teachers, as compared with 49 percent of public-school students. Private-school students were also more likely to report that students are proud to attend their school. Similarly, they were less likely to feel put down by teachers.

Sustained Satisfaction

Did parents' initial enchantment with a private education steadily fade? As time passes, a variety of forces may undermine voucher recipients' initial enthusiasm. One is cognitive dissonance. Just as new car buyers may exaggerate their enthusiasm in front of friends and family in an attempt to justify the sums they have just spent, so too may voucher recipients feign contentment in an effort to dispel any lingering doubts that they may harbor about disrupting their child's education. However, as the need to justify their choice dissipates, parents may be more willing to criticize their adopted schools. If true, then the observed impacts should gradually disappear. The basis for parents' evaluations may change as well. When asked in Year I about their level of satisfaction, parents may reflect on the differences between the current private and the previous public school. A year or two later, however, the criteria used to judge a school may change—expectations may rise and parents may become increasingly discriminating. Further, as parents become more acquainted with a school's operations and personnel, they have more opportunities to discover its faults and failings. It should not be surprising, therefore, if parents express less satisfaction the longer their child attends a particular school.

Some focus group comments hint that levels of satisfaction may attenuate over time (see chapter 3, page 77). For other parents who participated in focus group sessions, however, the sacrifices required to send their child to a private school over the years was clearly worth it. Said one Dayton mother about the trade-offs involved in obtaining a satisfactory education for her children:

> I like the Christian setting. I like all that being emphasized and the private schooling. It is a consumeristic market, and you can go in and [be listened to as] parents because you are paying the bucks. So I pay for the education double. I am a homeowner, so I pay the taxes and then I pay for my education. So I drive crummy cars. I tell people that I drive crummy cars so that my children can have an education.[22]

To see whether such Year II focus group comments were characteristic of parents as a whole, we again surveyed all those participating in the RFTs about their assessment of their public and private schools. In general, we found that parents with children in private schools continued to express significantly higher levels of satisfaction than parents in the control group. There were, however, slight indications of diminished ardor. The honeymooners, it appeared, had settled into happy, if not quite so passionate, marriages.

In table 7-3, the average size of the effect in the three city RFTS slips ever so slightly from 0.92 to 0.89 to 0.85 from Year I to Year II to Year III. Impacts in New York City and Washington remained steady over the three years. In Dayton, however, impacts on satisfaction fell noticeably—from 1.14 standard deviations to just 0.59 from Year I to Year II.[23]

Levels of satisfaction of black parents in Dayton in Year II remained higher than those of white parents. Whereas the effect size of switching to a private school for African American parents remained large (0.62 of a standard deviations), that for mainly white parents fell to 0.43 of a standard deviation, a statistically insignificant effect. The longer-term impact on satisfaction of the voucher program in Dayton seems to have remained higher for black than for white parents.

Satisfaction of Those Who Did Not Win a Voucher

It is possible that large differences in satisfaction were due not so much to heightened satisfaction among private school parents as to general discontent with public schools among those who had applied for a voucher but did not receive one. Martin Carnoy has suggested that vouchers may have had some kind of reverse placebo effect on those participating in the RFTs.[24] In his view, the process of applying for a voucher and being turned away may have only reinforced parents' discontent with their children's public schools.

Carnoy's hypothesis depends on strong assumptions about the impact of losing a lottery on opinion and behavior over the following year. The hypothesis can be tested because information on parent satisfaction was collected just before the lotteries were conducted. We compared the level of school satisfaction expressed in the baseline survey by parents who were not offered vouchers with the level these parents reported in Years I, II, and III. If the hypothesis is correct, then satisfaction of public school parents in the control group can be expected to plummet in Year I, then perhaps recover in Years II and III.

Table 7-4 reports the average level of satisfaction of members of the control group. The scale ranges from 1 to 4, with 1 being "very dissatisfied" and 4 "very satisfied." We found little support for Carnoy's suggestion. Those not receiving the voucher (the control group) consistently indicated slightly *more* satisfaction with their public school after the lotteries were held than before. The observed positive impact on parental satisfaction does not appear to be an artifact of changing views among the control group.

Comparison of Voucher Users with All Central-City Parents

Simply by having applied for a voucher, participants in the voucher programs registered a certain measure of discontent with their local public schools. Presumably, vouchers appealed to them because they considered their public schools unsatisfactory in some respect. It is not surprising, then, that families that found a place in a private school expressed more enthusiasm than those who remained in public schools. Observed impacts on measures of satisfaction may have been due to an especially low opinion of public schools shared by all voucher applicants instead of to stellar assessments of private schools by parents who used a voucher. To see whether this is the case, one needs to assess the satisfaction level of a cross-section of all families whose children attend public schools.

The question is especially significant if one seeks to generalize to larger-scale voucher interventions. Unless the satisfaction level of voucher applicants resembles that of central-city public school parents in general, then the demand for vouchers is likely to be limited to the most discontented. But if the enthusiasm of voucher users surpasses that of a cross-section of public school parents, then one might expect the demand for vouchers to continue to grow.

Table 7-4. *Index of Public School Satisfaction, Public School Parents in the Control Group*

City	Baseline	Year I	Year II	Year III
All control-group parents				
New York City	2.7	2.8	2.7	2.8
Dayton	2.6	2.7	2.8	. . .
Washington, D.C.	2.8	2.9	2.9	2.9
Average level	2.7	2.8	2.8	2.8
All control-group African American parents				
New York City	2.6	2.7	2.7	2.8
Dayton	2.7	2.7	2.8	. . .
Washington, D.C.	2.8	2.9	2.9	2.9
Average level	2.7	2.7	2.8	2.8

Each index of satisfaction is constructed from the individual satisfaction items listed in table 7-1. Individual items are scored from 1 ("very dissatisfied") to 4 ("very satisfied"). Average level represents the average of the three cities' levels, each weighted by the inverse of their respective variances.

Previous Research

A number of studies have found parents with children in private school to be more satisfied than those with children in public school. A 1999 survey by the U.S. Department of Education found that 78 percent of private school parents were "very satisfied" with their schools, compared to 62 percent of parents who "chose" their public school and 48 percent of parents who were assigned a public school.[25] Similarly, earlier studies found that those who switched to a private school expressed a measure of enthusiasm that was unmatched by the typical public school parent. In a Cleveland evaluation conducted by the University of Indiana School of Education, Kim Metcalf and his colleagues found consistently higher levels of parent satisfaction among voucher recipients than among public school parents. According to their study, differences in satisfaction levels were greatest in academics and school orderliness.[26] In Milwaukee, John Witte and his colleagues found that "in all three years, choice parents were more satisfied with choice schools than they had been with their prior public schools and more satisfied than [Milwaukee public school] parents with their schools. . . . Attitudes were more positive on every item, with 'discipline in the school' showing the greatest increase in satisfaction."[27] Studies of an Indianapolis program and an early voucher program in San Antonio that predates the Horizon program in the Edgewood school district also found that families that used vouchers to

Table 7-5. *Parent Satisfaction, Dayton Study*

Satisfaction measure[a]	Private school parents (percentage)	Random sample of Dayton public school parents (percentage)
Parents "very satisfied" with		
Academic program	51	19
Safety	46	16
Parents' involvement	40	20
Class size	37	11
Parents gave their child's school an A	47	25

a. Data to conduct significance test were unavailable.

attend private school were happier with their schools than families that remained in the public schools.[28] As we shall see, our findings are consistent with these earlier results.

Dayton

In August 1998, Paragon Opinion Research asked a cross-section of Dayton public school parents some of the same questions put to parents in the Dayton voucher evaluation.[29] By comparing their responses with those of voucher recipients after one and two years, it was possible to assess whether families using vouchers were more pleased with their school than was the average Dayton public school parent.

As shown in table 7-5, the results were straightforward. Private school parents were much more enthusiastic about their schools than were public school parents citywide. While 47 percent of the private school parents gave their school an A in Year I, only 25 percent of Dayton public school parents offered such a positive assessment. Paragon also examined parents' satisfaction with specific dimensions of public school life. Once again, private school parents were consistently more pleased than public school parents. At the end of the scholarship program's first year, 51 percent of the private school parents said that they were very satisfied with the academic program, compared with 19 percent of Dayton public school parents. Similar results were obtained for school safety, class size, and parents' involvement.

Cleveland

In 1998, our research team surveyed both voucher recipients and a cross-section of public school parents in Cleveland. As shown in table 7-6, voucher recipients were much more enthusiastic about their school than was the

Table 7-6. *Parents Very Satisfied with Selected School Characteristics, Cleveland*
Percentage

Characteristic	Scholarship recipients (1998)	Public school parents (1998)
Academic program	47***	29
Safety	49***	31
School discipline	48***	25
Parents' involvement	38**	29
Class size	37***	15
School facility	33***	20
Teaching moral values	55***	30
Teacher skills	49**	39
Location	43	43
Student respect for teachers	45***	25

*p < .10; **p < .05; ***p < .01; two-tailed test.

cross-section of public school parents. Nearly half of the parents with children in private schools reported being very satisfied with the academic program of the school, while less than 30 percent of public school parents did so. Half of the private school parents were very satisfied with school safety, compared with just over 30 percent of public school parents . Similar results were obtained for discipline, teacher skills, teaching of moral values, and class size.

Edgewood

The Edgewood evaluation provided an especially good opportunity to compare voucher parents with a cross-section of all public school parents. Recall that virtually every public school family living in the Edgewood school district was offered a voucher. Those who opted to remain in the public sector presumably did so in part because they were content with their current school. They therefore present a hard test of the hypothesis that voucher users are more satisfied with their schools than the typical public school family.

Yet across a host of dimensions, private school parents appeared significantly more satisfied than their public school counterparts. As shown in table 7-7, 61 percent of Horizon parents were very satisfied with their school's academic quality, versus only 35 percent of public school parents. Similarly, 63 percent of Horizon parents were very satisfied with the teaching at their child's school, as opposed to 47 percent of Edgewood public school parents.[30]

Table 7-7. *Parents Very Satisfied with Selected School Characteristics, Edgewood*
Percentage

Characteristic	Horizon schools	Edgewood public schools
Freedom to observe religious traditions	63***	19
Teaching moral values	62***	38
Academic quality	61***	35
Student respect for teachers	60***	39
Discipline	62***	39
School safety	60***	38
Class size	43***	19
Parents' support for school	50***	30
What is taught in school	60***	44
Teaching	63***	47
Parent-teacher communication	58*	46
Clarity of school goals	53**	40
How much school involves parents	43**	31
School facilities	39**	28
Location of school	53	45
Sports program	25	22

*$p < .10$; **$p < .05$; ***$p < .01$; two-tailed test.

In focus group conversations in Edgewood, parents explained why they were more satisfied with private than public schools. Said one father:

My son . . . he's in the fifth-grade right now. In the public school, he . . . didn't want to go to school, he didn't like school and stuff like that. And I'd tell him you got too many more years to go, you know. Now . . . I'll just ask [my two children] . . . how do you like your school now—do you like this one better or the other one better? And they don't hesitate, they tell me this one that they're going to right now.[31]

Another father expressed his enthusiasm for his children's new school this way:

[At the public school] the student asks the teacher, what can I do or I don't understand this. Okay [says the teacher], just go to your book, just read your book. I don't think that's appropriate. . . . My son was going to [a public middle school] and my daughter to [a public elementary school]. They didn't learn anything while they were there. Every time when they came home, they would have questions on their

Table 7-8. *Satisfaction, Children's Scholarship Fund National Study*

Satisfaction measure[a]	Scholarship recipients who attended private schools (percentage)	Low-income central-city families in public schools nationwide (percentage)
Parents "very satisfied" with		
Academic quality	68	47
Safety	71	48
Discipline	58	43
Teaching values	69	42
Parents "very proud" of their		
child's school	70	31
Average grade parents gave their		
child's school	A–	B–

a. Data to conduct significance test were unavailable.

homework. . . . Now that they're going to [a private school], they do their homework; when they get stuck, they'll call me over, and say, listen, can you help, but [in the public school] they couldn't even get started on their homework. They didn't teach you how to get started or at least how to go about it.[32]

An Edgewood mother who used a voucher to send her child to a local private school made much the same point in more colorful terms:

Let's say I have a dog. I take it to the trainer. This trainer will bring back the dog, and the dog comes back like an idiot, doesn't do nothing. Now I take that same dog to another trainer. And the dog comes back and does all these tricks that I want him to do. Who are you going to blame? . . . Use your common sense. Who are you going to blame, the dog or the trainer?[33]

Nationwide CSF Evaluation

Finally, we compared Children's Scholarship Fund voucher users nationwide with a national random sample of low-income central-city families with children in public school. No less than 52 percent of those who used CSF vouchers said that their private school deserved an A, compared with only 26 percent of the public school parents. On average, voucher parents gave their schools an A–, while the national urban sample gave their schools a B– (see table 7-8). While 68 percent of the CSF voucher parents were very satisfied with the academic quality of their schools, only 47 percent of the public school parents were. Similarly, 58 percent of voucher recipients were very satisfied with school discipline, as opposed to only 43 percent of the public school parents. Sixty-nine percent of private school parents, compared with only 42 percent of public school parents, were very satisfied with the teaching of values.

Taken as a whole, the results from Dayton, Cleveland, Edgewood, and the national CSF program are clear cut. Those who used vouchers expressed an enthusiasm for their new private school unmatched by the typical public school parent. As a RAND research report concludes, "the findings on parental satisfaction in voucher programs have been strongly and uniformly positive."[34]

Conclusions

Assessments of parents' satisfaction generated large and robust findings. Among voucher applicants, private school parents were much more satisfied than public school parents. Not only was this true initially, but for the most part it persisted over time. And the enthusiasm expressed by voucher recipients exceeded that of the typical urban public school parent. It is a safe bet that targeted voucher programs initiated in cities besides New York City, Dayton, and Washington, D.C., will enhance parents' assessments of the schools that their children attend.

Does that mean that a large-scale voucher program would generate comparable results? Might not new problems arise when increasing numbers of parents use vouchers to attend private schools? Or, because constitutional questions preclude further consideration of publicly funded voucher programs, are those questions essentially moot? To those vital issues we now turn our attention.

8

Vouchers and Urban Schools

Our evaluations of the national Children's Scholarship Fund voucher program and the programs in New York City, Dayton, Washington, D.C., and San Antonio have revealed a generally consistent set of findings— many positive, many neutral, a few negative. Private schools were smaller than public ones. They also had simpler facilities; for example, they were less likely to have a nurse's office, a gymnasium, or a cafeteria. Their resources were more limited, their expenditures were lower, and their teachers were paid less. Yet, on average, private schools tended to have smaller classes and their educational climate seemed more conducive to learning. Private school students on average experienced less fighting, cheating, disruptive student behavior, property destruction, racial conflict, truancy, and absenteeism. Compared with their peers in public schools, private school students were expected to do more homework; to their parents, the homework they were assigned seemed more appropriate. Private schools also maintained closer communication with families. The test scores of African American students attending private schools rose, thereby helping to close the education gap.

Most dramatically, private school parents were much more satisfied with their children's schools than were similarly situated public school parents. Private school parents were much more likely to give their child's school an "A" than were public school parents, and when asked about specific dimensions of school life, such as academic quality, safety, discipline, teaching, or communication with families, private school parents repeatedly reported much higher levels of satisfaction. Enthusiasm was particularly high one year into

185

the voucher program, but even after two and three years, private school parents reported a substantially higher level of appreciation of their school. Not only were they more pleased than the parents in the control group, they were noticeably more satisfied than public school parents generally, whether or not they had applied for a voucher.

Not only were these consequences of school choice beneficial, but also few adverse side effects were detected. Participants in the voucher programs were not highly selected along either academic or social criteria, as many had feared. No ethnic group suffered a deterioration in test scores, and inequalities in test scores did not increase as a result of the voucher intervention. Still, we did not detect important benefits anticipated by some voucher enthusiasts. For example, we found little, if any, effect of vouchers on parents' involvement in their child's education, student friendship patterns, racial integration, political tolerance, or formation of social capital. While the program enhanced the frequency of religious observance among students, it appears to have had a slightly negative impact on that of their parents.

Evaluations of small pilot programs such as those we have undertaken generally raise as many questions as they answer. What explains the findings? Do positive results justify larger-scale interventions? What are the cost implications of expanded voucher interventions? What will be lost in the process of change? At what pace will change proceed? In summarizing the main results from the evaluation and considering their relevance to the constitutional debate, this chapter reflects on their meaning and implications for public policy. We consider the appropriate amount of a school voucher, potential stratification within a larger-scale voucher intervention, conditions under which new schools might form, the impact on the fiscal stability of traditional public schools, and the relative merits of alternative voucher interventions.

The Education Gap

Voucher interventions that serve African American students seem particularly promising. For one thing, the impact of switching to a private school had a very large impact on the level of school satisfaction expressed by African American parents. African American students who switched from public to private schools also experienced a disproportionately large drop in school disruptions, class size, and school size. In addition, vouchers enhanced school communication with African American families more noticeably than with others. Especially noteworthy was the positive impact on African American test scores, despite the fact that the test scores of students of other ethnic backgrounds were not affected by the voucher intervention. The findings are consistent with other scholarly findings: attending a private school, compared with attending a public school, boosts African American students' test scores, educational attainment, likelihood of pursuing an advanced degree, and future earnings. Even studies that find little comparable benefits for whites typically find that private schools help African Americans. The importance of such findings for the education of African American students has been underappreciated, perhaps because it was thought that they might be due to some selection effect occurring only among African Americans or because no theoretical framework existed to explain why positive effects would be especially concentrated within a single ethnic group. With these new data from randomized field trials confirming prior observational studies, the positive impact of private schools on African American students' educational performance can no longer be dismissed as the product of some mysterious selection effect.

But if selection effects do not explain the results, what does? On this subject, more work needs to be done. But the findings are consistent with a differential theory of school choice. African Americans, more than other groups, live in the poorest, least attractive, and most dangerous communities within metropolitan regions. Because students are assigned to schools on the basis of where they live, public schools inherit all of the racial inequalities that plague housing markets. Precisely because African Americans suffer most under a system of public education based on residency, they stand to benefit the most from the new education opportunities that vouchers afford.

Just exactly how greater choice translates into achievement gains for African American students remains unknown. We were not able to explain the positive impacts of vouchers on African American test scores by any single factor, such as smaller class size, smaller school size, better disciplinary climate, or better school-parent communication. Nor were we able to isolate any combination of those or other factors that might explain the effect. Our inability to identify the exact mechanisms at work, however, is hardly unusual—or surprising. Education is too complex, subtle, and lengthy a process to lend itself to any simple set of explanations. Were it otherwise, the education gap would have been closed by now.

From Pilot to Large-Scale Interventions

If the nation were to undertake larger-scale voucher interventions, the process of change would resemble that often followed in the field of medicine. Prescription drugs and medical procedures typically are subjected to careful studies before being widely disseminated. First, medical products are tested on nonhuman subjects. If the results are promising, their effects on small groups of volunteers are carefully examined in what are known as Phase I and Phase II studies. If the results remain encouraging, major randomized field trials (RFTs), Phase III studies, are undertaken. According to guidelines established by the National Institutes of Health, in Phase III RFTs, researchers carefully monitor between 1,000 and 3,000 subjects to confirm a treatment's effectiveness, monitor its side effects, compare it with other common treatments, and obtain information about its safety.

RFTs involving pills usually take the form of a double-blind trial, in which neither the doctor nor the subject knows whether a subject is receiving the pill or the placebo. When the RFT involves some kind of surgery or various other medical interventions, the researchers obviously do not have the luxury of conducting a blind trial. Regardless, after due deliberation, the U.S. Food and Drug Administration allows a product or procedure to be marketed if positive effects are observed and treatment benefits outweigh adverse side effects. The researchers then conduct final Phase IV studies, in which they monitor the longer-term effects of the treatment on the broader population.

The best evidence currently available on school choice comes from the Phase III–like studies examined in this volume. To date, no one has conducted a Phase IV RFT on the long-term effects of school vouchers, although numerous observational studies have shown positive effects of private schools on the educational achievement of black American students, even when they find no such effects for white Americans. Yet neither those studies nor ours are able to identify the exact educational processes that produced these differential effects. To make further headway, a Phase IV study of school vouchers may be necessary. By carefully monitoring a larger group of students participating in a larger, urban voucher intervention for an extended period of time, we may gain further insight into the various educational impacts of vouchers.

The design of a large-scale intervention should be based on knowledge gained from early experiments. What, then, can policy experts learn from our evaluations? Do these programs tell us anything about the constitutionality of vouchers, appropriate mechanisms to minimize social stratification, the desirable monetary value of vouchers, the rate at which vouchers should be introduced, or the locations where they should first be tried? We consider each in turn.

The Constitutionality of Vouchers

Before vouchers can be disseminated widely, the question of their constitutionality needs to be resolved. Should the Supreme Court deem school vouchers unconstitutional, the government will not provide them, no matter what their benefits to individuals. How then might the Court rule in this matter?

The First Amendment stipulates that the government may not "establish a religion" or "prohibit the free exercise thereof." Do government-funded programs that allow parents to use vouchers to attend religious schools violate those provisions? We cannot scrutinize all of the lengthy, circuitous jurisprudence on this topic.[1] Here we note only that the recent evolution of case law suggests that empirical evidence on the educational impact of voucher programs may prove to be constitutionally significant.

In 1997, the Court, in *Agostini* v. *Felton,* found federal grants to religious schools for services to disadvantaged students to be constitutional.[2] Since the services were secular in nature and their provision was separated from the schools' religious activities, the Court ruled that they did not present an unconstitutional entanglement of church and state. One might surmise that if it is constitutional to give public dollars directly to religious schools, then funds given to families, which flow to religious schools only by virtue of parents' personal choices, would also pass constitutional muster. Yet *Agostini* did not explicitly overrule a 1973 Supreme Court decision, *Committee for Public Education and Religious Liberty* v. *Nyquist,* which declared unconstitutional a New York statute permitting reimbursement of religious school tuition. In that decision, the Court ruled that such grants established incentives to attend religious schools and by doing so violated the First Amendment.[3]

Some legal analysts argue that *Agostini* and other court decisions have so undermined *Nyquist* that it no longer represents controlling legal doctrine. In recent decisions, for example, the Court has upheld the constitutionality of funding a public program through which deaf children attend religious schools, using student fees at a state school to subsidize religious publications, and permitting a student religious group to gather after school in public school buildings.[4] But even though all of those activities would seem to entangle church and state more directly than a voucher program that gives parents choices among religious and secular schools, in one way or another each may be distinguished from the *Nyquist* decision. The assistance to deaf children was said to be neutral, without substantive religious content. The student editors of the religious publications would be denied their right to free speech if they were not given the same access to public resources as other voluntary student associations. Justices applied much the same reasoning in the case involving after-school meetings by a prayer group. None of these decisions either explicitly overturned *Nyquist* or made it absolutely clear whether a government voucher can be used to cover the nonreligious educational services of a religious school.

But perhaps *Nyquist* itself need not be explicitly overturned for the Court to uphold school vouchers. The majority in *Nyquist* distinguished between a law that directed aid to parents whose children were attending religious schools and a law that provided aid to all applicants, whether they attended secular or religious schools. For precisely this reason, the justices in *Nyquist* exonerated the G.I. Bill, which provided aid to students attending both religious and secular colleges. If it can be argued that a voucher program is part and parcel of a state's overall provision of educational opportunities, then the program can be found constitutional without overturning *Nyquist* on the grounds that all students qualify for aid, no matter what school they attend.

The Supreme Court had an opportunity to clarify such ambiguities when plaintiffs appealed a Wisconsin state supreme court decision that upheld the constitutionality of the Milwaukee voucher program. However, the Court chose not to grant *certiorari,* leaving the state ruling intact. That decision may indicate that the Supreme Court agreed with the lower court's ruling, but in the absence of a full consideration of the case on its merits, voucher constitutionality remains in doubt. The legal waters were further muddied when the Supreme Court also left intact lower-court rulings that the Maine and Vermont school choice programs involving religious schools were unconstitutional.[5] The facts in the New England cases differ from those in Wisconsin, so each of these Court decisions not to review the lower courts' decisions can, in principle, be reconciled with the others. But the issue, as of the writing of this book, seemed to be coming to a head. In 2001, the state of Ohio appealed a lower federal court ruling that found the Cleveland voucher program unconstitutional, despite its close resemblance to the Milwaukee program that had passed constitutional muster. Had the Court refused to review the Cleveland decision, it would have allowed two apparently inconsistent lower court decisions to stand. For that reason, perhaps, the Supreme Court agreed to review the Cleveland case.

The Court appears to be divided on the merits of the case, and analysts are well advised to avoid firm predictions about the eventual outcome. Some justices have made their views quite clear in concurring or dissenting opinions on related cases. Clarence Thomas, Antonin Scalia, and William Rehnquist apparently believe that vouchers are constitutional, while Ruth Bader Ginsberg, John Paul Stevens, and David Souter are probably opposed. But the remaining justices, most notably Sandra Day O'Connor, have stated their views in such a carefully circumscribed manner that they retain the flexibility to decide the matter in any number of ways.

In this context, the information in this book may have legal ramifications. Both sides in the constitutional debate readily admit that a government cannot fund a program whose mission is primarily religious. Only if the program's purpose—in principle and actual practice—is primarily educational can government funds flow, directly or indirectly, to religious institutions. In *Agostini* v. *Felton*, for example, the Court took great pains to stress the fact that federal dollars were to be used for strictly educational purposes.

Our research does indicate that vouchers alter students' religious practices. When given a choice, the vast majority of parents send their children to religious schools. When they do so, they generally select one that matches their own religious faith. Also, when selecting a private school, a significant minority of parents is motivated primarily by religious considerations, and private school students report that they participate in more religious services and receive more religious instruction than their public school peers. So it is disingenuous to argue that religion plays no part in school voucher programs. Still, few parents said that they were denied admission to a school because of their religious affiliation, and many students attended schools with a religious affiliation that differed from their own. Moreover, the primary purpose of the voucher programs, as implemented, appears to be more educational than religious. For one thing, the great majority of parents chose their new school more for educational than for religious reasons. Moreover, the educational character of the new private school differed markedly from that of local public schools. As emphasized earlier, parents reported smaller schools, smaller classes, a better educational climate, more homework, and more communication with teachers and school administrators. Parents expressed large gains in satisfaction with the academic program, the quality of the teachers, and many other aspects of school life. The test scores of African American students rose, and no negative educational impacts were observed for other ethnic groups. At the same time, we detected no increase in racial segregation or decrease in political tolerance, outcomes that might occur were the mission of private schools contrary to public purposes.

Nothing reported in previous chapters will change the minds of those who believe that any government funds that flow to religious institutions, directly or indirectly, do so in violation of the First Amendment. Nor will these findings convert those who believe that the government may support the activities of religious organizations, if secular alternatives are also provided. But for those members of the Court who believe that vouchers, in practice, must be *primarily educational*, the evidence now available may be dispositive.

Still, urban school vouchers can pass constitutional muster without being desirable. What are the likely social consequences of a large-scale voucher intervention? Would it further stratify the country's educational system? Would it alter the nature of private schooling? Would it destabilize urban public schools? If urban vouchers are to be introduced, what is the best way to do so?

Selection and Stratification

Central to the school choice debate is the concern that vouchers would contribute further to the already highly stratified system of public education in the United States. If only the best and brightest students choose to move, then vouchers would leave traditional public schools with the least capable students. Our research provides little evidence that such a result is likely. The demographic characteristics of applicants did not differ substantially from those of the eligible population. Although applicants were slightly more advantaged in terms of education and family stability, their children were just as likely to need special education. They also were more likely to be African Americans whose children attended segregated schools.

Families changed from public to private schools for many different reasons. Some highly motivated parents had a talented, productive child who they believed would excel in a private setting. But others had difficult children and hoped that the smaller classes and orderly climate in private schools would prove helpful. Still others sought change for religious reasons, or because they themselves went to a private school, or because they worried about school safety. Because motives were diverse, the degree of self-selection along ability or social lines was kept to a minimum.

Nor were private schools highly selective, especially when admitting younger children. The initial test scores of those admitted to private school were virtually identical to scores of those not admitted. Even having a learning disability did not prove to be a sharp barrier to receiving and making use of a voucher. African Americans and Hispanics were just as likely—and in New York, more likely—to use a voucher as whites. Parents' education and income were only weakly and inconsistently associated with taking advantage of voucher opportunities.

Younger students generally did not encounter serious adjustment problems when switching from public to private schools. No difference between younger children's disciplinary suspension rates in public and private schools were observed. Also, school mobility rates both within the school year and from one year to the next were much the same in public and private schools.

Private schools, however, were more discriminating when admitting students into grades 6 through 8, and older students initially encountered more adjustment problems when switching to a private school.

What kinds of selection effects are likely to emerge in larger voucher programs? It is quite possible that early applicants to a large-scale program would resemble the applicants studied here. Early assessments of the enlarged voucher program in Milwaukee suggest that the private schools there did not discriminate among applicants according to their test scores or ethnic background.[6] Similarly, studies indicate that charter schools cater to a cross-section of students in their communities.[7] Still, the Milwaukee voucher program offered vouchers only to low-income families, and many charter schools are established specifically to serve the disadvantaged.

Urban voucher programs that are not limited to low-income families may not prove to be selective either. Advantaged families with higher incomes have already opted out of large, central-city schools. In 1997–98, whites constituted only 22 percent of the students in the fifty-seven large, mostly central-city school districts that were members of the Council of the Great City Schools, an organization that represents big-city school systems. Nearly 60 percent of all students were eligible for the free-lunch program.[8] Many of the 22 percent of higher-income whites remaining in these cities found niches within the public school system—exam schools, magnet schools, neighborhood schools serving only those within attendance boundaries—that offered desirable alternatives. Certainly, some higher-income families would take advantage of a school voucher program, but there is not much evidence to suggest that they would use it with greater frequency than low-income families with few choices besides the local public school.

Still, should increasing numbers of voucher students apply to private schools, admissions policies could become more restrictive. While private schools may not choose rich over poor, they may well select the more capable and motivated students within low-income populations. If the demand for vouchers increases and the supply of private schools remains constant, the private sector may become less accessible to all groups. The space available in private schools, however, is not necessarily fixed. As more students apply to voucher programs, new schools may arise to meet demand and opportunities to skim off the best and brightest public school students may dissipate. Rather than forcing students to compete for a handful of available seats in existing private schools, a large-scale voucher program may usher in all kinds of new schooling options. Such an outcome, of course, depends in part on the amount of the voucher offered. New schools will open in poor communities only if government policies make it financially rewarding for them to do so.

Voucher Amount

A well-designed voucher initiative must level the playing field for all schools serving an urban community. Voucher schools should receive the same amount per pupil in current dollars as charter schools and traditional public schools. Supplemental dollars should be made available for those with special needs. In addition, the capital costs of the various schools should be funded by the government. Only then will all schools be assured of the same level of public support. Only then will there be incentives to form new schools. And only then will selection effects be kept to a minimum.

Existing Voucher Programs

Most publicly funded voucher programs today are so small that they do little to enrich the existing educational market. In 2001, the Florida voucher plan gave families, at most, only $3,500 toward the cost of a private education. Cleveland's vouchers were even less, set at a maximum of $2,500 per student. Only Milwaukee's program offered relatively large vouchers, $5,326 per student—and even that amount lagged well behind the $9,036 that the school board allocated in 1999 for each student in public school.

Small, poorly funded voucher programs will never give private schools the resources they need to upgrade their facilities, pay their teachers an appropriate salary, or make full use of their educational potential. Even worse, they provide little incentive to those who might otherwise create new, innovative schools. Even Milwaukee's voucher program has attracted to the city only a handful of educational entrepreneurs. Indeed, one of the city's most successful secular voucher schools, Bruce Guadalupe, recently became a charter school in an effort to reap more state funding than it was receiving under the voucher program.

Privately funded programs offer even smaller vouchers. Depending on family income and cost of tuition, students generally received vouchers worth approximately $1,500 a year. Surprisingly, those modest vouchers covered about half of the cost of tuition, mainly because most private schools operate on shoestring budgets. In the national CSF program, nearly 30 percent of voucher recipients paid, in addition to their scholarship, less than $1,000 for their private school and another 40 percent paid between $1,000 and $2,000; only 6 percent said that they paid more than $4,000. Nor could those schools rely on endowments or charitable contributions to provide luxury services at low prices. As discussed in chapter 4, average per-pupil expenditures in private schools were roughly half those in public schools.

To the educated sophisticate, the offerings available at such private schools must appear limited indeed. Although parents reported smaller classes and more intimate environments, they also reported fewer amenities and less extensive programming than their peers in public schools. Private school teachers, meanwhile, were poorly paid. Average salaries in private schools were less than 70 percent of average public school salaries. Because private schools offer lower salaries, they are less likely to hire teachers who are certified and who have master's degrees. Although they are more likely to hire teachers from selective colleges, retaining such teachers at relatively low salaries in inner-city schools is a daunting task even for well-established private schools with a cadre of supportive alumni.

Starting a new school is extremely challenging, expensive, and fraught with uncertainty. At current levels of funding, vouchers do not encourage either profit or nonprofit groups to risk the capital required to launch a new school. Even existing private schools do not have much incentive to add classrooms, hire additional staff, or construct better ancillary facilities to attract more students. The transformation of urban education cannot be based on small, struggling private schools with inadequate facilities and underpaid teachers. Such schools can provide a point of departure for the growth of a voucher program; alone, however, they will not close the education gap.

Charter Schools

The charter school movement underscores the importance of funding in developing new schools. Charter schools constituted a sizeable growth industry in public education during the 1990s. By 2000, nearly 1,700 charter schools in thirty-four states and the District of Columbia served more than 400,000 students.[9]

Like private schools, charter schools are privately owned and operate free of many of the regulations that govern traditional public schools. However, the government provides charter schools with per-pupil funding often comparable to the amount given public schools. Still, most capital costs are borne by the charter schools themselves, which must obtain from private sources the money required to purchase land and buildings and supply initial operating capital. In New York, each charter school is entitled to per-pupil payments of $6,630 from the state, a sizeable amount but still much less than the amount allocated to traditional public schools in New York City.[10]

In 1998, one of New York City's most promising charter schools, Bronx Preparatory, opened its doors to 100 African American and Hispanic fifth-

and sixth-graders in classrooms rented from a local Catholic church. Although by 2001 students were performing well on standardized tests, the school still had a long way to go before it could acquire the amenities taken for granted at most public schools. For example, the school held its physical education classes in local public parks. To accommodate anticipated growth to 800 students in grades 5 through 12, the school was planning to construct a new building on a vacant site. Achieving that goal will require gifts of up to $15 million. Hoping for two to three gifts of $1 million each, four to six of $500,000, and several additional $100,000 gifts, school administrators remain optimistic. Inasmuch as the school has posted successful test scores—and has strong support from Wall Street philanthropists—their plans are not unrealistic.[11] But how many charter schools can assemble such assets? If charter and private schools are to play a more significant role in urban education, their resource base needs to be augmented substantially.

The Duration of Voucher Programs

In addition to the amount of the voucher, the duration of the voucher program will critically influence the cost-benefit analysis of would-be investors in poor communities. Most privately funded voucher programs operating today promise financial support for only three to four years. Even the ten-year commitment made to students in the Edgewood school district was insufficient to stimulate the formation of more than one new school. Such a tepid market response is understandable when funding depends on charitable contributions—private resources can stretch only so far.

Publicly funded voucher programs have not proved to be any more enduring. Powerful political opposition and challenges to their constitutionality have given them a constricted, experimental quality that discourages new educational investment. Florida's program was designed to disappear as soon as F public schools became D or better public schools, and virtually all of them achieved that modest goal within a year. Consequently, Florida's voucher program never got off the ground. In Cleveland, funding has limited the program to fewer than 4,000 students. What is more, the program has continually operated under a legal cloud. Even Milwaukee's program, currently the largest, best funded, and constitutionally most secure, still lacks broad political support. The Wisconsin state senate, which the Democratic party took over in 2001, cut the monetary value of the vouchers and placed additional restrictions on the program. Although the assembly, controlled by Republicans, restored the cuts and the program survived intact, the controversy revealed the program's precarious political footing.

In the short term, vouchers may yield some educational benefits to the low-income families that use them. But sweeping, systemic change will not materialize as long as small numbers of vouchers, worth small amounts of money, are offered to families for short periods of time. The claims of vouchers' strongest advocates as well as those of the most ardent opponents, both of whom forecast all kinds of transformations, will be put to the test only if and when the politics of voucher programs stabilizes, support grows, and increasing numbers of educational entrepreneurs open new private schools. But if those developments were to occur, would they induce such rapid change that the entire structure of public education would be imperiled?

Transition Rates

In *Exit, Voice, and Loyalty*, Albert Hirschman pointed out that if competition is to effectively reform the practices of existing institutions in a marketplace, "voice" and "loyalty" must complement "exit."[12] If customers switch to a new product too quickly, companies may go under before they can respond to the competition. In the fall of 2001, Enron, an energy conglomerate, failed when its customers, lacking loyalty to this relatively new entity, lost faith in its financial integrity upon revelation of its questionable accounting practices. By contrast, companies with long-standing reputations are usually given enough time by loyal customers to adjust to changing market realities. For this reason, American automobile companies, enjoying strong brand loyalty from many of their customers, were able to improve their products and services and thereby survive intense competition from Japanese companies.

Hirschman himself wondered whether school vouchers might lead to a rapid exit from public schools, especially by families most able to demand improvements in the school system. In Hirschman's view, "'Exit' may occasion some impulse toward an improvement in the public schools; but here again this impulse is far less significant than the loss to the public schools of those members—customers who would be most motivated and determined to put up a fight against the deterioration if they did not have the alternative of the private schools."[13] Without any empirical evidence, Hirschman's discussion was unavoidably speculative. Now that choice-like arrangements have been in place for several years, however, it is possible to estimate the probable rate at which families would use vouchers to exit public schools.

Many have fooled themselves into thinking that rapid change is imminent. Voucher advocates, to promote the cause, advertise the widespread interest in the idea among low-income families. Opponents reinforce the impression, suggesting that vouchers will quickly drain public schools of their best families and fiscal resources. The media have fanned the flames, running, for example, front-page stories with such banner headlines as "Minorities Flock to Cause of Vouchers for Schools" and "Young Blacks Turn to School Vouchers as Civil Rights Issue."[14]

Yet loyalty to public schools runs wide and deep in American society. According to one national survey, 64 percent of parents with children in public schools claim that "public schools deserve our support even if they are performing poorly" and 43 percent agree that they "believe in public education, and [that they] wouldn't feel right putting [their] kids in private or parochial school."[15] Quite apart from widespread loyalty to public schools, parents are unlikely to disrupt their child's education unless they feel compelled to do so. Students resist change, complex school admission procedures discourage applicants, and parents worry that new schools will offer few improvements over the schools their children currently attend.

Much has been made of the fact that more than 1.2 million students applied for a CSF scholarship. But that number constitutes only about 8 percent of the eligible population in public and private schools across the nation.[16] Only about half of those who initially inquired followed through with a more detailed application—and only about one-third of those offered a scholarship actually used it. If one can generalize from the pattern among those offered vouchers, somewhere between 1 and 2 percent of the eligible population nationwide would have initially used a CSF voucher if they had been offered one.

The CSF experience provides an estimate of the minimum demand for vouchers within central cities. For a variety of reasons, a publicly funded urban voucher program would attract a considerably higher percentage of voucher users than did the CSF program. For starters, the CSF program was available to all low-income parents across the nation, and the demand for vouchers is much stronger in central cities, where traditional public schools are found wanting. Also, CSF did not attract widespread media attention, as a government intervention would. Instead, it relied on paid advertising—although it did receive a boost when Oprah Winfrey endorsed the program on her popular television show. In addition, the CSF program was a one-time event, announced just months prior to the beginning of the new school year, putting parents on short notice to find an appropriate private school. A publicly funded program would presumably be available on a continuing basis. The CSF voucher covered at most half of the cost of tuition for only three years, and parents were not given any assurance that their children's long-term education needs would be covered. Inasmuch as parents said that cost was a primary consideration affecting their decision to participate, demand likely would have been larger had the voucher been more substantial. Finally, applicants could apply only for a chance at winning a voucher. Had they been guaranteed a voucher, more families would have taken advantage of the opportunity.

Other programs yield higher estimates of the demand for vouchers. In Edgewood, vouchers covered full tuition costs at most private schools for the remainder of the child's elementary and secondary education. With its more handsome financial support, the program attracted, after three years, about 1,300 of the some 12,700 students in the district, or more than 10 percent of the eligible population. In Florida during the 2000–01 school year, 664 students qualified for vouchers because they had attended one of two failing public schools within the Excambia school district. Of those students, fifty-two, or 8 percent of the eligible population, used a voucher to attend one of five private schools, and another 13 percent switched to a nonfailing public school.

The Milwaukee case may be the most instructive. By law, 15 percent of the city's public school population, approximately 16,000 students, may participate in the city's voucher program. All students eligible for the free-lunch program (64 percent of students in the city in 1997–98) qualify for a voucher, which can be redeemed at either secular or religious schools. The amount of the voucher in 2001 exceeded $5,000, enough to cover tuition at most private schools. By 2001 the program had operated for three years, while a smaller antecedent program dated from 1990. The participation rate in the fall of 2001 was somewhat more than 10,000 students—around 16 percent of the city's eligible population, though still short of the 16,000 students permitted by law.

Charter schools provide another source of information about the likely turnover rates in public and private schools following the implementation of a large-scale voucher program. In Arizona, new schools can obtain a charter quite easily, making rapid school expansion possible when demand is strong and capital resources are plentiful. Charter schools receive per-pupil funding that approximates that of public schools in their vicinity.[17] Test scores in Arizona's public schools lag well below the national average, making the state particularly attractive for institutional innovation. Still, as of 2001, five years after the enactment of charter legislation, only 6.5 percent of the students statewide were attending charter schools.

Charter school participation rates are substantially higher in Washington, D.C. As in Arizona, few restrictions were placed on the formation of new charter schools, which were quite well funded from the beginning, although the per-pupil amount still lagged behind that for D.C. public schools.[18] By 2001, five years after the enactment of charter legislation, the District had thirty-one charter schools enrolling nearly 8,000 students, more than 11 percent of the total public school enrollment.

Those examples suggest that a large-scale, adequately financed urban voucher program may initially attract between 10 and 15 percent of public school students, sufficient demand to send a clear competitive signal to public schools but not enough to constitute a dramatic exodus of students that would leave public schools destitute and with no opportunity to respond.[19] The numbers, of course, say little about long-term trends, especially if vouchers are large and their political support secure. Over time, choice programs in central cities may stimulate the formation of new schools, the expansion of existing private schools, and major modifications in the design of public schools. But change will come slowly. School reform, should it occur at all, is likely to proceed incrementally, as do most other political and social changes in the United States

Fiscal Realities

Vouchers, by themselves, do not change the amount spent on public education, only the way it is distributed. Still, a common refrain among critics is that vouchers will destroy the financial backing of public schools. "Vouchers would drain money and abandon public schools under the guise of reform," asserts Gregory Nash, president of the New York state teachers union, adding that they "would divert money away from funding reforms with proven results."[20] Adds New Jersey congressman Donald Payne, "As we take dollars continuously out of the public school system, we're going to leave many, many children behind."[21] If their arguments are correct, then vouchers must have in practice fiscal consequences that are not required in principle.

School Finance

To understand the likely fiscal impact of vouchers, a basic review of school finance is helpful. In 1996–97, 48 percent of public school costs were covered by state governments, 43 percent by local districts, 6 percent by the federal government, and 2 percent by various fees and miscellaneous revenues. Exact figures vary from state to state. North Carolina, for instance, supplied 65 percent of the funding for public schools, while California covered 60 percent; New York, 40 percent; Illinois, 27 percent; and New Hampshire, just 7 percent. For the most part, the percentage paid by local governments varied inversely with those percentages.

Enrollment patterns have different implications for state and local revenues. If a school district depends entirely on local funding, enrollment changes are immaterial—the amount schools receive from residential and business property taxes does not vary with the number of pupils being educated. Even if the school-age population changes, the revenue stream remains constant unless property values or tax rates change. In fact, declining enrollments can actually help school systems that rely principally on local taxes because they secure the same amount of money to educate fewer students.

With state funding, the picture changes. For more than a century, almost all states have allocated most of their money to school districts on a per-pupil basis—apparently in the belief that the cost of schooling varies directly with the number of students being taught. To be sure, certain kinds of students (low-income, special education, and so forth) may receive additional funding, and some districts receive other forms of lump-sum payments. For the most part, however, school districts can expect the amount of state aid to vary with the number of students they enroll.

Fluctuations in student enrollments are not uncommon. Over the past few decades, changing birth rates have had marked consequences for public school enrollments across the nation. In 1971, nearly 51.3 million students were enrolled in elementary and secondary schools. A dozen years later, just under 45 million students attended public schools, a decline of more than 12 percent. By 1996, enrollments soared back to their 1971 levels. Enrollments within specific school districts can fluctuate even more dramatically. As young families move into a community, rapid expansion occurs first in elementary schools, then in secondary schools. Should the district build new facilities to meet demand, it may find itself overextended when students graduate from high school. As enrollments decline, so does the amount of aid provided by the state, and a period of painful downsizing ensues.

During the 1990s, a number of urban districts had to adjust to severe swings in enrollment. Between the school years ending in 1988 and 1998, Dayton and Washington, D.C., suffered enrollment losses of 15 and 11 percent, respectively. Other urban districts, meanwhile, struggled to accommodate rapid growth. The baby bust of the 1970s has given way to a second baby boom that, together with rising immigration rates, has led to rising enrollments in big cities. Between 1988 and 1998, enrollments increased by 13 percent in the fifty-seven central-city school systems that form the Great City Schools Council—and New York City's grew by 14 percent.

A Drain on Public Schools?

Because of the way that state aid formulas work, any school district that loses students, for whatever reason, receives less aid from the state. When a family moves from one district to another, the first loses aid while the second gains.

Likewise, when a family decides to send its child to a private school, the local public school receives less state funding.

Given that most voucher programs remove students from public schools, do they automatically drain vast sums of money from public schools? Not necessarily. When enrollments rise, local revenues remain constant, while state aid climbs proportionately. If enrollments fall, state aid drops proportionately, while local revenues again remain constant. Although public schools lose state funding, they retain all of their local funding, and they have fewer students to teach. The net fiscal impact, therefore, need not cripple public schools. Indeed, it may actually prove salutary.

Some simple math makes the point. Assume that a district receives 45 percent of its funding from the local government, another 45 percent from the state, and 10 percent from the federal government. Next, assume that a voucher program is introduced and that 20 percent of public school students switch to private schools. The public schools automatically lose the state and federal aid that follows those students. Because the district retains all of its local funding while having fewer students to teach, however, per-pupil expenditures actually *increase* by roughly 11 percent.

Should local taxpayers decide to scale back funding when public school enrollments drop, large-scale voucher programs may indirectly bring about declines in per-pupil spending. Further, even if per-pupil expenditures hold constant, falling enrollments may mean a shift of resources from instruction to building maintenance, especially if school boards choose not to close buildings at the same rate that enrollments fall.

But consider the history of the Milwaukee choice program, which began in 1990. The city's public schools are more dependent on state and federal sources than the typical school district: in 2000, the district received 74 percent of its revenues from the state, 10 percent from the federal government, and 16 percent from local revenues.[22] But despite its reliance on state funding, the financial picture of the Milwaukee public school system improved markedly during the decade of the voucher program's operation. Between 1990 and 1999, public school enrollments grew by 8 percent; expenditures rose (in real dollars) by nearly 30 percent, from $675 million to $873 million; and per-pupil expenditures climbed by 22 percent, from $7,559 to $9,036.[23] Given those statistics, it is hard to claim that school choice necessarily depletes the fiscal resources of public schools.

Vouchers nonetheless may adversely affect public school finances if voucher families, charter families, and traditional public school families are pitted against one another. If all voucher and charter funding comes from state sources, while traditional public schools remain heavily dependent on local property taxes, voucher families might join forces with disgruntled tax-payers to oppose higher local funding for traditional public schools. To fore-stall such an alliance, equitable financial arrangements are advisable. Except for special education students, voucher and charter schools should receive the same proportion of their per-pupil funding from the state and the locality that traditional public schools do. Voucher, charter, and traditional public schools then would all benefit proportionately from any increase in local edu-cation funding—and all would suffer proportionately if local funding were reduced.

Rising Public Cost of Education

Although well-designed financial arrangements can assuage concerns about draining funds from public schools, voucher advocates cannot ignore other more urgent questions. If the state were to offer vouchers, would those with children already in private school be the first to apply? And if they did, would that significantly increase the educational costs borne by the taxpayer?

One might argue, as a matter of equity, that both public and private school students should qualify for government assistance. Asking families both to support public schools through their taxes and to pay private school tuition without any offsetting tax deductions or credits strikes some as quite unfair. Indeed, because it places an undue financial burden on families that prefer that their child attend a religious school, some have argued that it contravenes the equal protection, free exercise, and free speech clauses of the Constitution. The issue was litigated in Vermont, where a voucher-like arrangement allowed parents to choose secular but not religious private schools. The Ver-mont Supreme Court, however, was not persuaded. [24]

Whatever the merits of the constitutional argument, offering vouchers to students already enrolled in private schools would undoubtedly increase tax-payer costs, unless efficiency gains were realized. In 2000, about 11 percent of students nationwide attended private schools. Were vouchers equal to per-pupil expenditures offered to all students, taxpayer costs would increase nationwide by 11 percent, or approximately $43 billion dollars.[25]

Though substantial, such increases in public educational expenditures have recent precedent. Between 1983 and 1996, when enrollments in public schools increased by more than 13 percent, per-pupil expenditures in real 1997 dollars increased from $2,307 per pupil in 1981–82 to $5,923 dollars in 1996–97, an increase of no less than 45 percent. Overall, annual public education expenditures, in constant 1999 dollars, rose by no less than $125 billion between 1983 and 1996, climbing from approximately $235 billion in 1983 to $360 billion in 1996 and to $390 billion in 1999.[26] By comparison, the tax burden associated with absorbing the private school sector over a similar period would be only one-third as much.

In short, the cost of even a universal voucher program does not exceed the country's fiscal capacity. Even during the 1980s and early 1990s, when a Republican administration in Washington generally opposed expansion of public service, educational expenditures increased by three times the amount it would take to implement a voucher program that absorbed the entire private sector (an unlikely eventuality). Smaller, more gradual movements toward vouchers would, of course, be much less fiscally demanding.

Still, fiscal realities pose serious problems for voucher advocates. Within the public sector, any transition from one form of organization to another imposes highly visible and politically risky short-term costs. Recent efforts to privatize Social Security, for example, have run aground for precisely that reason. Any generation that begins to save for its own retirement through market investments must not only save more than previous generations but also pay for the retirement of its elders. As Social Security reformers are discovering, no generation seems eager to bear that double burden.

School voucher advocates face a similar difficulty. Although the long-term costs of absorbing private schools into the publicly funded education system may pale in comparison to past increases in public school expenditures, in the short run voucher plans will encounter fewer political obstacles if their initial fiscal impact is kept to a minimum. But finding a design that is both fiscally viable and operationally sound has proven challenging. The remainder of this chapter considers the political and policy merits of a variety of often-proposed voucher programs.

Urban Voucher Programs

Would the impacts of a larger-scale voucher program resemble those we have reported in this volume? The answer depends on the design of the intervention. Is it limited to low-income families, or can anyone apply? What is the monetary value of the voucher? Will families with different incomes and educational needs receive different amounts? May students use vouchers to attend religious schools? What requirements must schools meet to participate in the program? Must a private school, unless it is over-enrolled, accept everyone who applies? If it over-enrolled, does it have to select students by lottery? Are the results of student assessments revealed to the general public?

Voucher programs may have different results depending on how they are structured. Rather than considering all permutations, we have made certain assumptions that seem to us to be either educationally crucial or politically necessary if a sizeable voucher program is ever to be enacted into law. We assume no constitutional barriers to participation by religious schools, because no large-scale voucher program could be initiated without the involvement of those institutions. We assume that schools admit all students for whom they have an appropriate educational program, regardless of race or nationality. We assume that governments may require information from schools about the quality of the educational services they provide, including student performance on standardized tests. We assume that special education dollars follow the student, regardless of the choice of school. We assume a level fiscal playing field, as described above. Within this general framework, three quite different types of voucher programs—vouchers for students at failing schools, low-income vouchers, and central-city vouchers—stand a fighting chance in the current political climate.

Vouchers for Students at Failing Schools

In 1998, the state of Florida enacted a voucher program that targets students attending "failing" public schools. The A+ Education Plan uses test scores on the Florida Comprehensive Assessment Test, attendance rates, dropout rates, school discipline data, and a variety of other performance indicators to grade public schools on a scale from A to F. If a public school receives an F in two of four years, students at that school are awarded vouchers that can be redeemed at a private school or another nonfailing public school. In 1999, fifty-two students from two such schools used vouchers worth up to $4,000 to attend private school; seventy-eight students used vouchers to attend a different public school. In 2000, some observers expected as many as 40,000 vouchers to be awarded, given the number of failing public schools identified the year before. Instead, amazingly, every one of those schools received a passing grade and the state did not offer one additional voucher. The same thing happened again in 2001.

Politically, this kind of voucher program is quite attractive. For starters, this approach targets students who benefit least from their public schools. In addition, it offers important financial incentives for failing public schools to improve—unless they are willing to lose students and the funding that goes with them.

The Florida program seems to have had positive educational effects as well. According to one reporter, "administrators [in at least one county] say the state grading system spurred real changes in the lowest-graded schools, including smaller class sizes, intensive professional development in reading, writing, and math for teachers, and increased involvement by parents."[27] In an assessment of the program, Manhattan Institute senior fellow Jay Greene took advantage of a quasi-experimental condition that occurred as part of the Florida program. Greene compared schools that received an F+ in 1999 with schools that received a D–. He assumed that very little of substance differentiated the two groups, except for the fact that F+ schools were "under the voucher gun," so to speak, while the D– schools were not. He found that test scores climbed more in the F+ than the D– schools.[28] Yet Duke policy analyst Helen Ladd argues that similar improvements could have been achieved simply by implementing an accountability system that grades schools but does not award vouchers.[29]

However such controversies are resolved, the one indisputable lesson to be learned from the Florida pilot program concerns not the exact cause of the public school response but the fragility of any voucher intervention conditioned on public school test scores. Any test of school performance must, for political reasons, be set at a level that will allow most schools to pass the bar. And the formula will have to be designed in a way that does not penalize schools with disproportionate numbers of special education and disadvantaged students. To avoid discrimination against such schools, tests will focus on gains (and losses) in student test scores from one year to the next. Yet many observers have expressed concern that such gains can be achieved by teaching to the test, excluding low-scoring students from the test (by encouraging absenteeism or assigning students to special education programs), and by sheer random fluctuation from one year to the next.[30] When vouchers are tied to ever-changing test scores, the voucher intervention will lack the size and durability needed to stimulate a significant private-sector response. In all probability, the definition of failing will keep the number of such schools to a minimum. And if changes in public-school test scores could eliminate state financial support, neither nonprofit schools nor profit-making companies will be willing to risk the commitment of large-scale resources to the construction of schools, recruitment of personnel, and development of education programs. As attractive as the failing school model appears at first glance, it simply cannot provide a solid basis for voucher-based reform.

Low-Income Vouchers

Rather than tying voucher arrangements to the test scores of public school students, a state might instead consider offering vouchers to all low-income families within the state, regardless of where they live. Such a voucher program has several clear advantages over a failing-school program. First, it takes account of the reality that a school may be good for one student but not for another. Second, it focuses the voucher on a population that cannot easily afford private schooling on its own. Third, the job of identifying eligible applicants is relatively straightforward. Rather than employing a complicated evaluation scheme that is susceptible to all kinds of political and bureaucratic machinations, the program targets a relatively well-defined group of families. And finally, because vouchers are not distributed only when public schools fail, the program is considerably more stable, allaying some of the concerns of would-be private school entrepreneurs.

This kind of program, however, does have one serious shortcoming. If income-based eligibility standards are set, schools that recruit a disproportionate number of families with vouchers may become socioeconomically, and perhaps ethnically, homogeneous. And such schools risk becoming charity houses. Their political strength would be limited and their ability to obtain adequate per-pupil funding thereby jeopardized.

Moreover, a low-income program reaches all school districts within a state, even districts where families are quite satisfied with their local public schools. As the overwhelming defeats of statewide voucher initiatives in California and Michigan in 2000 made clear, voucher proposals, if they are to succeed politically, must target areas where discontent with public schools runs deepest.

Citywide Vouchers

We recommend that instead of devising statewide programs serving a low-income population, states offer vouchers to all families, regardless of income, who live within a central-city district. Such a program has the advantage of treating all citizens alike, stripping the welfare or charity label from vouchers, and, perhaps, providing the best use of choice as a means for closing the education gap. It is, of course, no magic bullet. Urban schools will not be transformed overnight. Although their potential for altering central-city education should not be ignored, vouchers should not be pursued to the exclusion of all other educational reforms. As the Milwaukee case suggests, central-city voucher programs can reach growing numbers of students without adversely affecting the financial integrity of the city's public schools. In fact, there is evidence that public schools in Milwaukee have responded positively to the voucher program.[31]

The Milwaukee model can be improved on, however. The amount of the voucher should equal public school per-pupil expenditures in order to create an even playing field for all schools. Only then will successful private schools be encouraged to expand and new schools to form. The program should be opened to all families so that voucher schools do not become dumping grounds for the poorest, most challenged students within a district. So far, there is little evidence that such a design would transform vouchers into a middle-class entitlement. And if the intervention should help retain some middle-class families within the central city, that may only ameliorate the socioeconomic disparity between city and suburb.

We do not recommend that all states immediately establish voucher programs in all central cities—only a few states need to take the lead. Fortunately, we do not need to insist on the point. The complexities of the U.S. system of government ensure that all innovations must traverse a complex political path before they can be adopted. Even if vouchers are debated in every state legislature, programs will, for the foreseeable future, emerge intact from only a few. Such gradualism has its advantages. New forms of school choice are best introduced incrementally, with careful attention paid to potential pitfalls. Yet the evidence now available provides sufficient basis for experimenting with larger programs. Vouchers, unlike the established system of school choice by residential neighborhood, offer hope that the education gap may eventually be bridged.

A

Response Rates

To promote high response rates, voucher program operators either required or strongly urged recipients to participate in testing sessions if they wished to have their voucher renewed for the next school year. In addition, evaluation teams offered financial incentives and new opportunities to win a voucher to encourage members of the control group and members of the treatment group who remained in public schools to return for follow-up testing.[1] Still, substantial numbers of students were not tested at the end of Years I, II, and III.

Response rates after each year are presented in table 2-3. Roughly 60 percent of the treatment and control samples returned for testing after Year I in Dayton and Washington, D.C.; after Years II and III, 50 percent and 60 percent returned, respectively. In New York City, the response rates were somewhat higher: 82 percent for Year I, 66 percent for Year II, and 67 percent for Year III. Response rates were similar for treatment and control groups in all three cities.[2]

Comparisons of baseline test scores and background characteristics reveal only minor differences between respondents and nonrespondents in all three cities. Table A-1 presents, for example, baseline data on respondents and nonrespondents in the treatment and control groups after Year II in the three cities. Some differences in race, welfare, and religious orientation were detected, but they point in different directions in different cities and do not appear to systematically produce a more advantaged group of respondents in the treatment group nor a particularly disadvantaged control group. In all

Table A-1. *Characteristics of Respondents and Nonrespondents in Treatment and Control Groups in Year II*[a]

	Treatment		Control	
	Attended	*Did not attend*	*Attended*	*Did not attend*
New York City				
African American (percent)	42.4	48.3	41.4	47.2
Welfare recipients (percent)	46.8	35.5	40.6	37.3
Catholic (percent)	54.7	46.4	53.7	43.2
Protestant (percent)	34.3	39.4	35.0	38.8
Overall test scores (average)	20.1	19.5	22.8	22.6
Family size (average)	2.6	2.6	2.4	2.9
Residential mobility (average)	3.7	3.6	3.7	3.7
Church attendance (average)	3.6	3.3	3.4	3.5
Mother's education (average)	2.4	2.4	2.4	2.5
Dayton				
African American (percent)	74.0	65.2	71.9	69.3
Welfare recipients (percent)	16.7	13.8	16.2	16.7
Catholic (percent)	5.8	14.0	13.4	18.1
Protestant (percent)	65.2	58.1	64.6	56.9
Overall test scores (average)	26.3	26.3	27.2	26.2
Family size (average)	3.9	3.6	3.0	3.1
Residential mobility (average)	3.4	3.3	3.3	3.6
Church attendance (average)	3.4	3.3	3.6	3.7
Mother's education (average)	5.6	5.4	5.3	5.6
Washington, D.C.				
African American (percent)	90.4	92.1	90.9	92.1
Welfare recipients (percent)	38.0	34.1	32.1	30.3
Catholic (percent)	15.5	12.6	16.0	13.8
Protestant (percent)	72.7	69.9	65.6	70.6
Overall test scores (average)	26.5	26.4	26.9	26.7
Family size (average)	3.1	3.1	3.3	3.0
Residential mobility (average)	3.4	3.5	3.5	3.4
Church attendance (average)	3.7	3.5	3.7	3.7
Mother's education (average)	5.4	5.0	5.3	5.2

a. Averages refer to the unweighted mean scores of responses on the parent surveys. Mother's education was scaled slightly differently in New York City than in Dayton and Washington, D.C., making intercity comparisons on that item inappropriate.

three cities, intergroup differences in test scores, religious identification, residential mobility rates, church attendance, and family size were essentially nonexistent.

To adjust for the bias associated with nonresponse, in each year and city we generated weights for parents and students in the treatment and control groups. Because those invited to participate in the follow-up studies had provided information about their family characteristics at baseline, it was possible to calculate the probability that each participant in the baseline survey would attend a follow-up session. To do so, we estimated simple logit regressions that used a set of variables assembled from baseline surveys to predict the likelihood that each student would attend a follow-up session. Covariates included mother's education, employment status, marital status, and religious affiliation; family size; whether the family received welfare benefits; whether the student was African American; the student's baseline math score; whether the student had a learning disability; and whether the student had experienced disciplinary problems.[3]

To allow for as much flexibility as possible, separate logit models were estimated for treatment and control group members. For illustrative purposes, table A-2 reports the results in Washington after Year II. Similar results were obtained for other cities and other years.[4] For the most part, the family and student characteristics had a similar impact on response rates for both treatment and control group members. Catholics were less likely to attend follow-up sessions, as were mothers who were employed full-time or were married. Larger families were more likely to attend follow-up sessions, as were African American families and families of students with disciplinary problems. Mother's education, welfare benefits, and math scores had a small or insignificant impact for both treatment and control group members. The most striking difference between the two models concerned students with learning disabilities. While learning disabled students in the treatment group were significantly more likely to attend follow-up sessions, such students in the control group were significantly less likely to attend follow-up sessions.

The models generated a set of predicted values that represent the probability that individuals, given their baseline characteristics, would attend the follow-up session. The weights are simply the inverse of these predicted values, that is,

$$W_j = \frac{1}{F(X\beta)},$$

where $F(\ )$ is the model's normal cumulative distribution function. The range of possible values for W_j was then capped so that the highest weight was four

Table A-2. *Logit Estimates Used to Construct Weights for Treatment and Control Groups in Washington, D.C., in Year II*

	Treatment group	Control group
Family characteristics		
Catholic	−0.5*	−0.8***
Family size	0.2**	0.2**
Employment status	−0.6**	−0.1
Married	−0.6***	−0.3
Mother's education	0.0	−0.1**
Welfare	−0.3	0.2
African American	0.8***	0.6***
Student characteristics		
Learning disabled	0.7**	−1.0**
Disciplinary problems	0.7**	0.7**
Math scores	−0.0	−0.0**
Summary statistics		
Constant	−1.1**	−0.6
Pseudo R^2	.07	.07
Log likelihood	−353.11	−479.83
Number of cases	580	866

*$p < .10$, two-tailed test; **$p < .05$; ***$p < .01$. The dependent variable is coded 1 if the student attended the Year II follow-up session in Washington, D.C., and 0 otherwise. The treatment group consists of all students who were offered a voucher and participated in the baseline study; the control group consists of all students who were not offered a voucher.

times the value of the lowest. (This restriction affected only a handful of observations.) The weights then were rescaled so that the sum of the weights equaled the sum of the total number of actual observations.

To generate the weights we could use only observable characteristics as recorded in parent surveys. To the extent that there were unmeasured or unobservable characteristics that encouraged some families, but not others, to attend follow-up sessions, the weights may not have eliminated the bias associated with nonresponse. However, in order for response bias to explain our findings, three conditions would have to hold. First, respondents would need to differ from nonrespondents on an unmeasured factor that influenced test performance. Second, the difference would have to be larger for one group (treatment or control) than for the other. Third, the difference would have to hold for black students but not for students of other ethnic groups. While we cannot rule out the possibility that all three conditions existed in our study, we find it unlikely enough to be reasonably confident that response bias did not artificially generate the results we report.

It is possible that change in academic performance over time rather than baseline characteristics affected the likelihood that different subgroups within the treatment and control groups would attend subsequent testing sessions. If treatment group families that did not benefit from vouchers dropped out of the study while control group families that were suffering most in public schools continued to attend follow-up sessions consistently, then observed impacts may be somewhat inflated.

Three questions deserve consideration. Did gains in test scores from baseline to Year I (II) decrease the probability that members of the control group would attend the Year II (III) testing session? Did gains increase the probability that members of the treatment group would attend the Year II (III) testing session? Were the differences in observed impacts on response rates for the treatment and control groups statistically significant?

Table A-3 estimates a series of logistic regressions that answer these questions. The dependent variable identifies whether a student attended the Year II (III) follow-up session. The covariates include baseline math and reading test scores, the change in the total test score from baseline to Year I (II), and the change interacted with treatment status. Separate models were run for African Americans and members of other ethnic groups. At the bottom of each column we report the probability that we can reject the following three null hypotheses: (1) changes in test scores have a statistically insignificant effect on attendance at subsequent testing sessions for the control group; (2) the effect for the treatment group is statistically insignificant; and (3) the differences in observed effects for the two groups are not statistically significant.

On the whole, the signs of the coefficients are in the expected direction. Gains in test scores from baseline to Years I and II increased the probability that members of the treatment group attended the subsequent testing session and decreased the probability for members of the control group. The only models that generated statistically significant impacts, however, were for African Americans in New York after three years and for African Americans in Dayton after two years. None of the observed impacts for Hispanics were statistically significant in any year or city.

The model that predicts Year III attendance for African Americans in New York City generated the largest effects. Holding all variables at their means, the model predicted that 83 percent of the students who attended the Year II session would attend the Year III session. An increase of 10 NPR points from baseline to Year II translated into a 3 percentage point drop in the probability that a control group member would attend the Year III testing session and a

Table A-3. *Effect of Change in Test Scores from Baseline to Years I and II on the Likelihood That Students Attend Subsequent Testing Sessions*

| | New York City | | | | Washington, D.C. | Dayton | |
| | *Year II attendance* | | *Year III attendance* | | *Year II attendance* | *Year II attendance* | |
	African Americans	Hispanics	African Americans	Hispanics	African Americans	African Americans	Whites
Y1–Baseline	−0.005	−0.001	...	...	0.002	−0.012	0.001
Y2–Baseline	...	...	−0.023*	−0.004	...	...	...
(Y1–B)*offered voucher	0.0037	0.006	...	...	0.002	0.023*	−0.004
(Y2–B)*offered voucher	...	...	0.031*	0.004	...	...	...
Baseline math score	−0.003	0.012*	0.007	0.002	−0.001	0.001	−0.003
Baseline reading score	0.007	−0.004	0.006	−0.008	−0.001	0.003	0.004
Summary statistics							
Log likelihood	−355.81	−355.68	−212.40	−191.13	−580.55	−189.52	−70.39
Pseudo R^2	0.00	0.01	0.02	0.00	0.00	0.01	0.00
Number of cases	623	709	497	612	891	298	108
P for H_0; $B_1 = 0$	0.63	0.91	0.09	0.76	0.79	0.21	0.94
P for H_0; $B_1 + B_2 = 0$	0.90	0.57	0.50	0.96	0.50	0.28	0.79
P for H_0; $B_2 = 0$	0.77	0.46	0.07	0.78	0.79	0.07	0.79

*$p < .10$, two-tailed test; **$p < .05$; ***$p < .01$. Logit regression models performed on unweighted data. Y1–Baseline refers to the change in the total math and reading test scores from baseline to Year I; Y2–Baseline refers to change from baseline to Year II. (Y1–B)*offered voucher is an interaction term between one variable that is the difference between Year I and baseline test scores and another variable that indicates whether a student was offered a voucher. The dependent variable is coded 1 if the student attended either the second- or third-year follow-up session.

1 percentage point increase in the probability that a member of the treatment group would attend the Year III follow-up session. Unless weighting adjusted for these differences, this response pattern may have marginally contributed to the positive estimate of voucher impacts on test scores.

In New York City, eighty-two African American students who had attended the Year II testing session failed to show up in Year III. The data presented above suggest that those individuals consisted disproportionately of control group members whose scores decreased from baseline to Year II and treatment group members whose scores increased, possibly inflating the estimated impact of attending a private school. To further explore their influence on estimated impacts, we imputed Year III test scores for those individuals based on their treatment status, baseline test scores, test score changes between baseline and Year II, and the Year III weights. While the observed impacts do drop in magnitude, they remain statistically significant. When we examined only those African American students who attended the Year III follow-up session, the estimated impact of being offered a voucher (which is different from the impact of actually attending a private school, as discussed in chapter 2) at Year III was 5.4 NPR points, with 515 observations and a *t*-statistic of 3.7.[5] When we looked at the same population but then imputed Year III test scores for those students who showed up in Year II but not in Year III, the size of the estimated impact of being offered a voucher dropped to 4.6 NPR points, with a *t*-statistic of 3.0.[6]

Another way of estimating the effects of response rates on outcomes is to distinguish between earlier and later respondents. Not all participants came to the first testing session to which they were invited. Given that we know the dates when students came in for testing, we can generate exact estimates of the impact of attending a private school for smaller response rates. In Year I in New York City, for instance, we had an 82 percent response rate. By successively dropping the portion of students who attended later testing sessions, we can readily calculate the impacts for lower response rates.

If observed positive impacts derive from imperfect response rates, we should expect the estimated impact of attending a private school to increase as response rates decline. Presumably, those students who benefit most from treatment should come earlier to the testing sessions, along with those students in the control group who were performing most poorly in public schools. Impacts of attending a private school, then, should be quite large for lower response rates. The differences between the two groups, however, should attenuate (and may actually switch signs) as response rates increase.

Table A-4 reports the estimated impact of attending a private school for African American students for variable response rates. In each row, the first

Table A-4. *Estimated Impact of Attending a Private School for African Americans in New York City for Variable Response Rates*

Impact	Percentage of respondents attending follow-up sessions						
	82	70	66 [a]	60	50	40	30
Year I	5.4***	5.3***	5.0***	4.8***	4.2***	4.4**	5.7***
Year II	...	...	4.3**	3.2*	4.4**	2.7	3.6
Year III	...	...	9.2***	8.3***	7.1***	6.9**	4.2

*p < .10, two-tailed test; **p < .05; ***p < .01. Weighted two-stage least squares regressions performed; treatment status used as instrument. Differential response rates calculated by including in the analysis only the relevant percentage of students who initially attended testing sessions.

a. Total response rate in Year III was 67 percent.

column represents the estimated impact for the full sample of African American students who attended testing sessions. Subsequent columns provide estimates of impacts for lower response rates, based on when students came in for testing.

As can be seen in table A-4, the New York City estimates remained remarkably stable for different response rates. Had we stopped testing students in Year I after the first 30 percent of the sample showed up, we would have recovered almost exactly the same findings that we did after another 52 percent participated—the point estimate for the first 30 percent of students to be tested was 5.7 percentile points, and it was 5.4 for the full sample. In New York City in Years II and III, rather than increasing as response rates declined, the estimated impacts decreased. Moving from a 30 percent response rate to a 66 percent rate, the estimated test score impact of attending a private school increased by roughly 1 NPR point and became statistically significant. From these findings, at least, there is little to suggest that we would have observed significantly different impacts had we managed to test a greater number of students in the treatment and control groups. Observed impacts remained quite steady over the course of testing sessions conducted each year.

B

Construction of
Survey Indexes

Depending on the year in which the surveys were administered, indexes were constructed from all, or a subset, of the items that follow.

School disruptions: "How serious are the following problems at this child's school? Very serious, somewhat serious, or not serious?"
  Kids destroying property; kids being late for schools; kids missing classes; fighting; cheating; racial conflict; guns or other weapons; drugs or alcohol.

Dress codes: "Are students required to wear a uniform?" "Are certain forms of dress forbidden?"

Hallway monitoring: "Are visitors required to sign in at main office?" "Are hall passes required to leave class?"

School resources: "At the school this child attends, which of the following programs or facilities are available to students?"
  A computer lab; a library; a gym; a cafeteria; guidance counselors; a nurses' office.

School programs: "At the school this child attends, which of the following programs or facilities are available to students?"
  Special programs for non-English speakers; individual tutors; special programs for students with learning problems; special programs for advanced learners; a music program; an arts program; an after-school program.

School-parent communication: "Do the following practices exist in this child's school?"

> Parents informed about student grades halfway through the grading period; parents notified when student sent to the office the first time for disruptive behavior; parents speak to classes about their jobs; parents participate in instruction; parent open-house or back-to-school night held at school; regular parent-teacher conferences held; parents receive notes about this student from this child's teachers; parents receive a newsletter about what is going on in this child's school/classroom.

Amount of homework: "Approximately how much homework is assigned on an average day?"

Class size: "Approximately how many students are in this child's class?"

School size: "Approximately how large is the school this child attends?"

Suspensions: "During this past year, was this child ever suspended for disciplinary reasons?"

Racial segregation: "What proportion of students in this child's classroom is minority?"

Parents' involvement in child's education: "In the past month, how often did you do the following?"

> Help this child with his or her homework; help this child with reading or math that was not part of his or her homework; talk with this child about his or her experiences at school; attend school activities; work on school projects.

Parents' involvement with child's school: "How many parent-teacher conferences did you attend this school year?" "How many hours have you volunteered in this child's school this past month?" "Are you a member of a PTA or other similar organization (Parents' Council, for example)?"

Religious practices (student survey): "During the past year, have you participated in church youth groups or religious services?" "Do you go to classes outside of school for religious instruction?"

Well-behaved friends (student survey): "How many of your friends like school?" "How many get good grades?" "How many get into trouble with teachers?" "How many use bad language?" "How many smoke cigarettes?" "How many drink beer or alcohol?" "How many use illegal drugs?"

Self-confidence (student survey): "Do you agree or disagree with the following statements about yourself?"

I feel good about myself; If I work really hard, I will do well in school; To do well in school, good luck is more important than hard work; I am able to do things as well as most other people; Every time I try to get ahead, something or somebody stops me; I am satisfied with myself; I certainly feel useless at times; At times I think I am no good at all; When I make plans, I am almost certain I can make them work; I feel I do not have much to be proud of.

C

*Test Scores of Applicants
to Voucher Programs*

T he following table provides the average test scores and standard deviations for those who participated in the evaluation at baseline, Year I, Year II, and Year III. Raw scores have been converted to national percentile ranking points, which range between zero and 100 and have a median of 50.

Table C-1. *Descriptive Statistics for Baseline Test Scores*

Test scores[a]	Mean (NPRs)	Standard deviation (NPRs)	N
	All Students		
New York City			
Baseline math	18.5	20.8	1,852
Baseline reading	25.0	23.1	1,852
Year I total achievement	25.0	20.6	1,456
Year II total achievement	25.3	20.2	1,199
Year III total achievement	27.5	20.5	1,250
Dayton			
Baseline math	25.0	25.8	725
Baseline reading	28.1	27.3	725
Year I total achievement	35.3	23.5	409
Year II total achievement	30.2	23.1	382
Washington, D.C.			
Baseline math	23.2	21.7	1,582
Baseline reading	30.1	27.0	1,582
Year I total achievement	25.3	19.3	933
Year II total achievement	22.4	19.3	725
Year III total achievement	26.4	20.5	687
	African Americans		
New York City			
Baseline math	16.7	18.7	806
Baseline reading	26.3	23.3	806
Year I total achievement	25.0	20.6	624
Year II total achievement	21.5	18.0	497
Year III total achievement	23.4	18.8	519
Dayton[b]			
Baseline math	21.0	22.9	473
Baseline reading	25.4	25.2	473
Year I total achievement	32.0	21.1	296
Year II total achievement	27.1	20.1	273
Washington, D.C.[b]			
Baseline math	22.7	21.3	1,477
Baseline reading	29.8	26.8	1,477
Year I total achievement	24.8	18.9	891
Year II total achievement	21.5	18.6	668
Year III total achievement	25.9	20.1	656

a. Students' baseline math, reading, and total achievement scores on the Iowa Test of Basic Skills expressed in national percentile ranking (NPR) points. Baseline summary statistics provided for only those students who qualified for follow-up testing evaluations. Baseline total scores are not used in the analysis and are included here only for purposes of comparison.

b. Students in Dayton and Washington, D.C., are included in test score analysis through grade 8. Thus, changes in the number of observations do not directly translate into changes in response rates.

D

The Noisy Data Problem

C hapter 6 presents the average test score impacts of attending a private school for African American students in three cities by grade level. This appendix reports the same findings for each city separately (see table D-1). Impacts vary quite widely by category within each city and by year. The vast majority of impacts are statistically insignificant, and no decipherable pattern suggests that impacts vary systematically by grade level.

One of two factors explains these variations. First, there may be something substantively important (and distinctive) about each year, city, and grade level that generates these impacts. If true, the differences we observe from city to city and year to year reflect the authentic influence of a host of important contextual variables. More likely, though, the variations reflect random error built into statistical models that are estimated with small sample sizes. The estimated grade-level impacts in table D-1 rely upon as few as thirty-two observations.

Ideally, one would like to break apart the data into finer and finer categories in order to precisely identify who benefits from vouchers and who does not. Doing so, however, comes at a cost. With smaller and smaller numbers of observations in each grouping, it becomes increasingly difficult to detect effects, even when they may exist. It is precisely for this reason that statisticians discourage drawing substantive conclusions from models based on data from small samples.

Economists Thomas Kane and Douglas Staiger, for instance, criticize state accountability systems that evaluate individual schools (and teachers within

Table D-1. Impact of Attending a Private School on African American Students' Test Scores, Disaggregated by Grade Level

Year I grade level	New York City			Washington, D.C.			Dayton	
	Year I	Year II	Year III	Year I	Year II	Year III	Year I	Year II
Second	12.5***	2.3	7.7	-1.6	10.2*	10.6	5.1	19.7**
	[152]	[118]	[127]	[183]	[142]	[144]	[54]	[54]
Third	-2.6	-2.5	4.4	-8.3	8.1	0.2	9.7	-1.9
	[179]	[153]	[156]	[176]	[137]	[162]	[45]	[38]
Fourth	7.4**	1.2	8.2*	18.3***	3.5	-20.4*	7.7	14.5
	[167]	[122]	[130]	[147]	[125]	[144]	[54]	[55]
Fifth	8.9***	9.8***	11.7***	3.2	9.7	16.6	-13.8	-1.8
	[124]	[104]	[106]	[114]	[86]	[96]	[37]	[31]
Sixth	...	...	...	-6.6	11.5**	-0.4	11.2*	17.1*
				[125]	[99]	[110]	[37]	[41]
Seventh	...	...	...	-8.3	4.0	...	9.3	-5.7
				[103]	[76]		[37]	[33]
Eighth	...	...	...	-16.7	...	...	-17.1	...
				[43]			[32]	

*p < .10, two-tailed test; **p < .05; ***p < .01. Weighted two-stage least squares regressions performed; treatment status used as instrument. Number of observations included in brackets. Test scores expressed in terms of national percentile ranking points.

those schools) on the basis of test score changes from one year to the next. "With the average elementary school containing only 68 students per grade level, the amount of variation due to the idiosyncrasies of the particular sample of students being tested is often large relative to the total amount of variation observed between schools."[1] The implication? Accountability systems that track small samples of students from year to year have a high probability of sanctioning and rewarding the wrong schools and teachers. Large swings in test scores experienced by small schools (and smaller classes within those schools) are just as likely to arise from random noise as from actual learning trends.

Education statistician Anthony Bryk and his colleagues similarly recommend that "an accountability system [not] use only single grade information." For precisely the reasons Kane and Staiger identify, Bryk and others argue that drawing substantive conclusions about the efficacy of school interventions from small-sample estimates is extremely problematic. To generate more robust findings in their assessment of Chicago public elementary schools, Bryk and others average across adjacent grades.[2] An evaluation of school vouchers and any other intervention also should avoid parsing findings in ways that the data cannot support.

Notes

Chapter One

1. Louis Hartz, *The Liberal Tradition in America* (Harcourt, Brace & World, 1955).

2. John Rawls, *A Theory of Justice* (Belknap, Harvard University Press, 1971), p. 60.

3. Ibid., p. 83.

4. U.S. Bureau of the Census, *Statistical Abstract of the United States 1999* (U.S. Dept. of Commerce, 1999), table 1372, p. 847.

5. As quoted in David McCullough, *John Adams* (Simon and Schuster, 2001), p. 223.

6. "The Northwest Ordinance," in Henry S. Commager, ed., *Documents of American History*, 6th ed. (New York: Appleton-Century-Crofts, 1958), p. 131.

7. Gary Orfield and John T. Yun, *Resegregation in American Schools* (Civil Rights Project, Harvard University, June 1999), table 9.

8. National Center for Education Statistics, *Digest of Education Statistics 1999*, NCES 2000-031 (U.S. Dept. of Education, Office of Educational Research and Improvement, 2000), table 172, p. 190.

9. Ibid., table 8, p. 17.

10. Ibid. For evidence that graduation rates in the 1990s are overstated, see Jay P. Greene, *Graduation Rates in the United States* (Manhattan Institute for Policy Research, 2001).

11. Orfield and Yun, *Resegregation in American Schools.*

12. *Milliken* v. *Bradley I,* 418 U.S. 717 (1974); *Milliken* v. *Bradley II,* 433 U.S. 267 (1977).

13. Orfield and Yun, *Resegregation in American Schools.*

14. Christopher Jencks and Meredith Phillips, "The Black-White Test Score Gap:

An Introduction," in Jencks and Phillips, *The Black-White Test Score Gap* (Brookings, 1998), p. 5–6.

15. Meredith Philips, James Crouse, and John Ralph, "Does the Black-White Test Score Gap Widen after Children Enter School?" in Jencks and Phillips, *The Black-White Test Score Gap*, p. 232. In 2001, the National Center for Education Statistics released a report that found that "*across*-sample findings suggest an overall narrowing of the black-white reading gap between grades 2 and 12" but that "*within*-sample findings would . . . suggest a widening of the black-white reading gap as children progressed through elementary school and little change subsequently." Generally speaking, within-sample findings are more reliable than across-sample findings. National Center for Education Statistics, *Educational Achievement and Black-White Inequality*, NCES 2001-061 (U.S. Department of Education, Office of Educational Research and Improvement, June 2001), p. 41.

16. "Land Ordinance of 1785," in Commager, *Documents of American History*, p. 124.

17. Benjamin Rush, "Plan for the Establishment of Public Schools," in Frederick Rudolph, ed., *Essays on Education in the Early Republic* (Harvard University Press, 1965), p. 6.

18. Thomas Paine, *Rights of Man* (1792), as quoted in David Kirkpatrick, *Choice in Schooling: A Case for Tuition Vouchers* (Loyola University Press, 1990), p. 34.

19. Carl F. Kaestle, *Pillars of the Republic: Common Schools and American Society, 1780-1860* (Hill and Wang, 1983), p. 11.

20. As quoted in Charles L. Glenn Jr., *The Myth of the Common School* (University of Massachusetts Press, 1987), p. 84.

21. Ibid., p. 83.

22. National Center for Education Statistics, *Digest of Education Statistics 2000*, NCES 2001-034 (U.S. Dept. of Education, Office of Educational Research and Improvement, 2001), table 8, p. 7.

23. Ibid., table 398, p. 452.

24. Ibid., table 12, p. 21.

25. For public-school expenditures, see ibid., table 170, p. 192. For private-school expenditures, see National Center for Education Statistics, "Estimates of Expenditures for Private K–12 Schools," Working Paper 95-17 (U.S. Department of Education, Office of Educational Research and Improvement, 1995), p. xiv–xv. The private school figure is adjusted for the Consumer Price Index between 1991 (the last year for which credible estimates of private-school expenditures are available) and 1998 (the last year for which public-school expenditure data are available). A more detailed comparison between the expenditures of urban public and private schools is presented in chapter 4.

26. Michael Garet and others, "The Determinants of Per-Pupil Expenditures in Private Elementary and Secondary Schools: An Exploratory Analysis," Working Paper 97-07 (U.S. Dept. of Education, National Center for Education Statistics, March 1997), table 3, p. 11; *Digest of Education Statistics 2000*, table 74, p. 83. Our estimate of private school salaries assumes that they increased at the same rate as the

cost of living between 1990–91 (the last year for which credible data are available) and 1998–99, the latest year for which public school teacher salaries are available.

27. The Supreme Court intervened, finding in the Constitution the right of families to secure a private education. *Myers* v. *Nebraska,* 262 U.S. 390 (1923); *Pierce* v. *Society of Sisters,* 268 U.S. 510 (1925).

28. Terry M. Moe, *Schools, Vouchers, and the American Public* (Brookings, 2001).

29. John Dewey, *Democracy and Education* (Macmillan, 1916), p. 20–22, 28, 92–96.

30. George S. Counts, *Dare the School Build A New Social Order?* (New York: Arno Press, 1969).

31. The facts in the next three paragraphs are taken from *Digest of Education Statistics 2000,* tables 39, 53, 65, 69, and 90.

32. Both numbers are calculated in 1996 dollars.

33. Despite unionization, teacher pay has barely kept pace with salaries and wages in other sectors of the economy. In fact, teacher pay, as compared to other professions, has actually slipped since unionization. Teacher unions have been more successful at establishing standardized pay scales, grievance procedures to protect workers from discharge, and contracts that limit board and administrative discretion. Eric A. Hanushek and Steven G. Rivkin, "Understanding the Twentieth Century Growth in U.S. School Spending," *Journal of Human Resources,* vol. 32, no. 1 (1997), pp. 35–68; Darius Lakdawalla, "The Declining Quality of Teachers," Working Paper 8263 (Cambridge, Mass.: National Bureau of Economic Research, April 2001); F. Howard Nelson and Jewell C. Gould, "Teacher Salaries, Expenditures and Federal Revenue in School Districts Serving the Nation's Largest Cities 1990–1991 to 2000–2001" (Washington: American Federation of Teachers, 2001), available at (www.aft.org/reports/download/urban_salary.pdf [December 20, 2001]).

34. Paul E. Peterson and Bryan Hassel, eds., *Learning from School Choice* (Brookings, 1998); Paul E. Peterson and David E. Campbell, eds., *Charters, Vouchers, and Public Education* (Brookings, 2001).

35. Bruce Fuller, Richard Elmore, and Gary Orfield, eds., *Who Chooses? Who Loses? Culture, Institutions, and the Unequal Effects of School Choice* (Teachers College Press, 1996), p. 26.

36. Dennis P. Doyle and Marsha Levine, "Magnet Schools: Choice and Quality in Public Education," *Phi Delta Kappa,* vol. 66, no. 4 (1984), pp. 265–70; Rolf K. Blank, Roger E. Levine, and Lauri Steel, "After 15 Years: Magnet Schools in Urban Education," in Fuller, Elmore, and Orfield, *Who Chooses? Who Loses?* pp. 154–72.

37. R. Kenneth Godwin, Frank R. Kemerer, and Valerie J. Martinez, "Comparing Public Choice and Private Voucher Programs in San Antonio," in Peterson and Hassel, *Learning from School Choice,* pp. 275–306; Corrie M. Yu and William L. Taylor, "Difficult Choices: Do Magnet Schools Serve Children in Need?" (Washington: Citizens' Commission on Civil Rights, 1997).

38. California Department of Education, as cited in Fuller, Elmore, and Orfield, *Who Chooses? Who Loses?* pp. 30, 38–39; Carnegie Foundation for the Advancement of Teaching, *School Choice: A Special Report* (Princeton, N.J., 1992).

39. Adam Gamoran, "Student Achievement in Public Magnet, Public Comprehensive, and Private City High Schools," *Educational Evaluation and Policy Analysis*, vol. 18, no. 1 (1996), pp. 1–18; Robert L. Crain, Amy Heebner and Yiu-Pong Si, "The Effectiveness of New York City's Career Magnet Schools: An Evaluation of Ninth-Grade Performance Using an Experimental Design" (Berkeley, Calif.: National Center for Research in Vocational Education, 1992).

40. Mark Schneider, Paul Teske, and Melissa Marschall, *Choosing Schools: Consumer Choice and the Quality of American Schools* (Princeton University Press, 2000).

41. Joseph Viteritti, *Choosing Equality: School Choice, the Constitution, and Civil Society* (Brookings, 1999), pp. 62–63.

42. Fuller, Elmore, and Orfield, *Who Chooses? Who Loses?* p. 33.

43. David J. Armor and Brett M. Peiser, *Competition in Education: A Case Study in Inter-District Choice* (Boston: Pioneer Institute for Public Policy Research, 1997).

44. Compiled from information available in 2001 from the Center for Education Reform, Washington, D.C. See also Bryan C. Hassel, *The Charter School Challenge* (Brookings, 1999), p. 1.

45. On Arizona, see Robert Maranto and others, " Real World School Choice: Arizona Charter Schools," in Robert Maranto and others, *School Choice in the Real World: Lessons from Arizona Charter Schools* (Boulder, Colo.: Westview, 1999), p. 7.

46. U.S. Department of Education, Office of Educational Research and Improvement, *A Study of Charter Schools: First-Year Report* (Washington, 1997); Gregg Vanourek and others, "Charter Schools as Seen by Students, Teachers, and Parents," in Peterson and Hassel, *Learning from School Choice,* pp. 187–212.

47. Caroline Minter Hoxby, "Changing the Profession: How Choice Would Affect Teachers," *Education Matters*, vol. 1 (spring 2001), pp. 57–64.

48. Minnesota Department of Children, Families, and Learning, "Take Credit for Learning," 1997 (www.children.state.mn.us/tax/credits.html).

49. Rob Robinson, senior tax analyst, Arizona Department of Revenue, telephone interview, October 21, 1999.

50. John Stuart Mill, "On Liberty," in George R. La Noue, ed., *Educational Vouchers: Concepts and Controversies* (Teachers College Press, 1972), p. 3–4.

51. Milton Friedman, "The Role of Government in Education," in Robert Solo, ed., *Economics and the Public Interest* (Rutgers University Press, 1955), p. 127.

52. See, for example, *Poindexter* v. *Louisiana,* 275 F. Supp. 833 (1967), as reprinted in LaNoue, *Educational Vouchers.*

53. Christopher Jencks, *Education Vouchers: A Report on Financing Education by Payments to Parents* (Cambridge, Mass.: Center for the Study of Public Policy, 1970).

54. Gary R. Bridge and Julie Blackman, *A Study of Alternatives in American Education,* vol. 4: *Family Choice in Education* (RAND Corporation, 1978); Richard Elmore, "Choice as an Instrument of Public Policy: Evidence from Education and Health Care," in William Clune and John Witte, eds., *Choice and Control in American Education*, vol. 1: *The Theory of Choice and Control in American Education* (Falmer, 1990), p. 285–318.

55. John Chubb and Terry Moe, *Politics, Markets, and America's Schools* (Brookings, 1990).

56. John Dewey, *School and Society*, 2d ed. (University of Chicago Press, 1915), p. 7.

57. As quoted in William Raspberry, "Solidly for Vouchers," *Washington Post*, August 6, 2001, p. 15.

58. Albert Hirschman, *Exit, Voice, and Loyalty* (Harvard University Press, 1970).

59. For a skillful blending of the two theories, see John E. Brandl, *Money and Good Intentions Are Not Enough, or, Why a Liberal Democrat Thinks States Need Both Competition and Community* (Brookings, 1998); also, see John E. Brandl, "Governance and Educational Quality," in Peterson and Hassel, *Learning from School Choice*, pp. 55–81.

60. James S. Coleman, Thomas Hoffer, and Sally Kilgore, *High School Achievement: Public, Catholic, and Private Schools Compared* (Basic Books, 1982); James S. Coleman and Thomas Hoffer, *Public and Private High Schools: The Impact of Communities* (Basic Books, 1987).

61. This point was made originally, and most famously, by Jane Jacobs, *The Death and Life of Great American Cities* (Vintage Press, 1981).

62. Elinor Ostrom, "Crossing the Great Divide: Coproduction, Synergy, and Development," in Peter Evans, ed., *State-Society Synergy: Government and Social Capital in Development* (University of California Press, 1997), pp. 85–118; Elinor Ostrom and James Walker, "Neither Markets nor States: Linking Transformation Processes in Collective Action Arenas," in Dennis C. Mueller, ed., *Perspectives on Public Choice: A Handbook* (Cambridge University Press, 1997), pp. 35–72.

63. Robert Putnam, *Bowling Alone: The Collapse and Revival of American Community* (Simon and Schuster, 2000). For critiques, see Theda Skocpol and Morris P. Fiorina, eds., *Civic Engagement in American Democracy* (Brookings, 1999).

64. Coleman, Hoffer, and Kilgore, *High School Achievement*; Coleman and Hoffer, *Public and Private High Schools*.

65. Amy Stuart Wells, "The Sociology of School Choice," in Edith Rasell and Richard Rothstein, eds., *School Choice: Examining the Evidence* (Washington: Economic Policy Institute, 1993), p. 40.

66. Thomas J. Kane and Douglas O. Staiger, "Randomly Accountable," *Education Next*, vol. 2 (Spring 2002), pp. 56–61.

67. Sharon Gewirtz, Stephen Ball, and Richard Bowe, *Markets, Choice, and Equity in Education* (Buckingham, U.K.: Open University Press, 1995).

68. Ludwig Mises, *Human Action: A Treatise on Economics* (Chicago: Henry Regnery, 1966 [first published 1949]); Frederick A. von Hayek, "The Present State of the Debate," in Frederick A. von Hayek, ed., *Collectivist Economic Planning* (Clifton, N.J.: A. M. Kelley, 1975 [first published 1935]); John M. Marshall, "Private Incentives and Public Information," *American Economic Review*, 64, no. 3 (1974), pp. 373–90.

69. Hans Thorelli and Jack Engledow, "Information Seekers and Information Systems: A Policy Perspective," *Journal of Marketing*, vol. 44 (January 1980), pp. 9–26.; Lawrence F. Feick and Linda L. Price, "The Market Maven: A Diffuser of Marketplace Information," *Journal of Marketing*, vol. 51 (January 1987), pp. 83–97.

70. Mark Schneider and others, "Shopping for Schools: In the Land of the Blind, the One-Eyed Parent May Be Enough," *American Journal of Political Science,* vol. 42 (July 1998), p. 782.

71. Carnegie Foundation for the Advancement of Teaching, *School Choice,* p. 13.

72. Carol Ascher, Norm Fruchter, and Robert Berne, *Hard Lessons: Public Schools and Privatization* (Twentieth Century Fund Press, 1996), p. 40–41.

73. Nicholas Lemann, "A False Panacea," *Atlantic Monthly* (January 1991), p. 104, as quoted in Abigail Thernstrom, *School Choice in Massachusetts* (Boston: Pioneer Institute for Public Policy Research, 1991), p. 40.

74. Richard Kahlenberg, *All Together Now: Creating Middle-Class Schools through Public School Choice* (Brookings, 2000), p. 4.

75. Harry Brighouse, *School Choice and Social Justice* (Oxford University Press, 2000), p. 169.

76. Edward Fiske and Helen Ladd, *When Schools Compete: A Cautionary Tale* (Brookings, 2000), p. 209.

77. Mark Harrison, "Choice Lite: Learning from the New Zealand Experiment," *Education Matters,* vol. 1 (Summer 2001), pp. 84–86.

78. Laura F. Rothstein, "School Choice and Students with Disabilities," in Stephen D. Sugarman and Frank R. Kemerer, eds., *School Choice and Social Controversy* (Brookings, 1999), p. 357.

79. Brighouse, *School Choice and Social Justice,* p. 170.

80. Gewirtz, Ball, and Bowe, *Markets, Choice, and Equity in Education,* pp. 141–42.

81. Richard Herrnstein and Charles Murray, *The Bell Curve* (Free Press, 1994); Richard Rothstein, *The Way We Were? The Myths and Realities of America's Student Achievement* (Twentieth Century Fund Press, 1998.)

82. Michael Kelly, "Dangerous Minds," *New Republic,* December 30, 1996, p. 6.

83. David Berliner, speech before the New Mexico legislature, as quoted in Educational Intelligence Agency communiqué, May 10, 1999 (http://members.aol.com/educintel/eia).

84. Paul Hill, Lawrence Pierce, and James Guthrie, *Reinventing Public Education: How Contracting Can Transform America's Schools* (University of Chicago Press, 1997), pp. 83–124.

85. Amy Gutmann, *Democratic Education* (Princeton University Press, 1987), p. 70.

86. *Minersville Board of Education* v. *Gobitis,* 310 U.S. 598 (1940). Frankfurter's reasoning justified a West Virginia regulation forcing Jehovah's Witnesses to salute the school flag, a decision that the Supreme Court reversed in *West Virginia State Board of Education* v. *Barnette,* 319 U.S. 624 (1943).

87. Paul E. Peterson, "Introduction: Technology, Race, and Urban Policy," in Paul E. Peterson, ed., *The New Urban Reality* (Brookings, 1985), pp. 1–29.

88. National Center for Education Statistics, "Findings from 'The Condition of Education 1997: Public and Private Schools: How Do They Differ?'" (Government Printing Office, 1997).

89. William T. Bogart and Brian A. Cromwell, "How Much More Is a Good School District Worth?" *National Tax Journal,* vol. 2 (June 1997), pp. 215–32; David Weimer and Michael Wolkoff, "School Performance and Housing Values: Using Non-Contiguous District and Incorporation Boundaries to Identify School Effects," *National Tax Journal,* vol. 54 (June 2001), p. 231–53. Economists have shown that the quality of a community's public schools informs the value of its property. Sandra E. Black, "Do Better Schools Matter? Parental Valuation of Elementary Education," *Quarterly Journal of Economics,* vol. 114 (May 1999), pp. 577–99; Kathy J. Hayes and Lori L. Taylor, "Neighborhood School Characteristics: What Signals Quality to Homebuyers?" Federal Reserve Bank of Dallas *Economic Review,* vol. 4 (February 1996), pp. 2–9; Katherine L. Bradbury, Christopher J. Mayer, and Karl E. Case, "Property Tax Limits, Local Fiscal Behavior, and Property Values: Evidence from Massachusetts under Proposition 2(1)/(2)," *Journal Of Public Economics,* vol. 80 (May 2001), pp. 287–311. See also Del Jones, "Location, Location, Location: Better Schools Mean Higher Property Values: Home Buyers Go Shopping for Schools," *USA Today,* May 15, 1996; Jennifer Babson, "With Schools as a Lure, Realtors Take Notice of Test Scores," *Boston Globe,* December 14, 1998.

90. Caroline Minter Hoxby, "The Effects of School Choice on Curriculum and Atmosphere," in Susan B. Mayer and Paul E. Peterson, eds., *Earning and Learning: How Schools Matter* (Brookings, 1999), pp. 281–316; Caroline Minter Hoxby, "Does Competition among Schools Benefit Students and Taxpayers?" *American Economic Review,* vol. 90 (December 2000), pp. 1209–38; Caroline Minter Hoxby, "Analyzing School Choice Reforms That Use America's Traditional Forms of Parental Choice," in Peterson and Hassel, *Learning from School Choice,* pp. 133–51. For the effects of explicit school choice interventions on public schools, see Caroline Minter Hoxby, "School Choice and School Productivity (or, Could School Choice Be a Tide That Lifts All Boats?)" and Thomas J. Nechyba, "Introducing School Choice into Multi-District Public School Systems," both papers prepared for the conference on the Economics of School Choice, National Bureau of Economic Research, Cambridge, Mass., February 23, 2001.

91. Gewirtz, Ball, and Bowe, *Markets, Choice, and Equity in Education,* pp. 9–10.

92. *Statistical Abstract of the United States 2000,* table 744, p. 470.

93. Michael E. Davern and Patricia J. Fisher, "Household Net Worth and Asset Ownership: Household Economic Studies," in *Current Population Reports: The Survey of Income and Program Participation* (U.S. Dept. of Commerce, Economics and Statistics Administration, 2001), pp. 70–71.

94. Raphael W. Bostic and Brian J. Surette, "Have the Doors Opened Wider? Trends in Homeownership Rates by Race and Income," Working Paper (Washington: Federal Reserve Board, April 2000).

95. U.S. Bureau of the Census, *American Housing Survey for the United States 1999* (U.S. Dept. of Commerce, 1999), table 2-1, p. 42. African Americans also have on average just $29,000 of equity in their homes, compared with $36,000 for His-

panics and $50,000 for whites. Patrick A. Simmons, *Housing Statistics of the United States,* 1st ed. (Lanham, Md.: Bernan Press, 1997), table 1.37, p. 58.

96. Simmons, *Housing Statistics of the United States,* figure 8, p. xvii.

97. Robert D. Bullard, "Race and Housing in a 'New South' City: Houston," in Robert Bullard, J. Eugene Grigsby III, and Charles Lee, eds., *Residential Apartheid: The American Legacy* (University of California Press, 1994), table 7.6, p. 194.

98. *Statistical Abstract of the United States 1998,* table 1218, p. 727. In absolute terms, whites pay considerably more for housing than do African Americans. In one survey, 15 percent of African Americans reported paying more than $1,000 a month in housing costs, compared with 24 percent of whites.

99. Stephanie M. Wildman, *Privilege Revealed: How Invisible Preference Undermines America* (New York University Press, 1996), p. 50.

100. *American Housing Survey for the United States 1999,* table 2-1, p. 42.

101. Ibid., table 2-8, p. 58.

102. Ibid.

103. Bullard, "Race and Housing in a 'New South' City."

104. See, for example, Alicia H. Munnell and others, "Mortgage Lending in Boston: Interpreting HMDA Data," Working Paper WP-92-7 (Federal Reserve Bank of Boston, October 1992), p. 2. See also Munnell and others, "Mortgage Lending in Boston: Interpreting HMDA Data," *American Economic Review,* vol. 86, no. 1 (March 1996), pp. 25–53. Subsequent studies have criticized Munnell and others. See, for example, Raphael W. Bostic, "The Role of Race in Mortgage Lending: Revisiting the Boston Fed Study," Finance and Economics Discussion Series 1997-2 (Washington: Board of Governors of the Federal Reserve System, January 1997).

105. Bullard, Grigsby, and Lee, *Residential Apartheid,* p. 4.

106. Jamshid A. Momeni, *Race, Ethnicity, and Minority Housing in the United States* (Greenwood Press, 1986), table 4.1, p. 55.

107. Franklin J. James, "Minority Suburbanization in Denver," in Bullard, Grigsby, and Lee, *Residential Apartheid,* table 4.1, p. 99.

108. These data were provided by Terry Moe. For a complete description of his survey, see Moe, *Schools, Vouchers, and the American Public.*

109. Charles T. Clotfelter, "Are Whites Still Fleeing? Racial Patterns and Enrollment Shifts in Urban Schools, 1987–1996," *Journal of Policy Analysis and Management,* vol. 20 (2001), p. 202.

110. William Raspberry, "A Reluctant Convert to School Choice," *Washington Post,* May 30, 1997, p. A25.

111. Gary Orfield, *Must We Bus? Segregated Schools and National Policy* (Brookings, 1978).

112. Moe, *Schools, Vouchers and the American Public,* table 7-3.

113. Joint Center for Political and Economic Studies, *2000 National Opinion Poll* (Washington, 2000).

114. Terry M. Moe, "Hidden Demand: Who Would Choose Private Schools?" *Education Matters: A Journal of Opinion and Research,* vol. 1 (Spring 2001), pp. 50–51.

Chapter Two

1. These totals do not include partial-tuition tax-credit programs or special contracts with private schools to provide educational services to special needs students on a case-by-case basis.

2. Children First America, "68 Private Programs and Counting," *School Reform News* (October 1999), insert, p. B.

3. Quite different voucher programs in Vermont and Maine date back to 1869 and 1954, respectively. The Vermont program provides full tuition reimbursement to parents who live in a district that lacks a public school and who consequently choose to enroll their children in an area private school. Parents initially were allowed to send their children to any private school, secular or religious. In 1999, however, the Vermont Supreme Court ruled that government reimbursements to parents of children enrolled in religious schools violated the state constitution. Rural Vermont parents continue to use the tuition program to send their children to secular private schools. An estimated 400 students received aid to attend private schools in Vermont during the 1998–99 school year. Nina Shokraii Rees, *School Choice: What's Happening in the States* (Washington: Heritage Foundation, 2000), p. 167. Maine's tuition program shares many characteristics with Vermont's, although it operates on a much larger scale. Parents are reimbursed if they send their children to private schools because their community lacks a public school. Religious private schools initially were eligible to participate, although subsequent state laws disqualified them. The exclusion of religious schools was challenged in state court in 1997, and the Maine Supreme Court eventually ruled their exclusion to be constitutional. The U.S. Supreme Court refused to review the case. *Bagley* v. *Raymond School Department,* 728 A.2d 127 (1999). During the 1998–99 school year, 5,295 students received aid to attend private schools under the Maine program. Rees, *School Choice,* pp. 71–72.

4. For a summary of the political wrangling that preceded the enactment of the Milwaukee voucher law, see John F. Witte, *The Market Approach to Education: An Analysis of America's First Voucher Program* (Princeton University Press, 2000).

5. Witte, *The Market Approach to Education.* The book summarizes and extends results initially reported in the following papers: John F. Witte, "Achievement Effects of the Milwaukee Voucher Program," paper presented at the annual meeting of the American Economics Association, New Orleans, January 1997; John F. Witte, "First Year Report: Milwaukee Parental Choice Program," University of Wisconsin-Madison, Department of Political Science and the Robert M. La Follette Institute of Public Affairs (November 1991); John F. Witte, Andrea B. Bailey, and Christopher A. Thorn, "Second Year Report: Milwaukee Parental Choice Program," University of Wisconsin-Madison, Department of Political Science and the Robert M. La Follette Institute of Public Affairs (December 1992); John F. Witte, Andrea B. Bailey, and Christopher A. Thorn, "Third Year Report: Milwaukee Parental Choice Program," University of Wisconsin-Madison, Department of Political Science and the Robert M. La Follette Institute of Public Affairs (December 1993); John F. Witte and others, "Fourth Year Report: Milwaukee Parental Choice Program," University of

Wisconsin-Madison, Department of Political Science and the Robert M. La Follette Institute of Public Affairs (December 1994); John F. Witte, Troy D. Sterr, and Christopher A. Thorn, "Fifth Year Report: Milwaukee Parental Choice Program," University of Wisconsin-Madison, Department of Political Science and the Robert M. La Follette Institute of Public Affairs (December 1995); John F. Witte, "Achievement Effects of the Milwaukee Voucher Program," paper presented at the 1997 annual meeting of the American Economics Association.

6. Jay P. Greene, Paul E. Peterson, and Jiangtao Du, "School Choice in Milwaukee: A Randomized Experiment," in Paul E. Peterson and Bryan C. Hassel, eds., *Learning from School Choice* (Brookings, 1998), pp. 335–56; Jay P. Greene, Paul E. Peterson, and Jiangtao Du, "Effectiveness of School Choice: The Milwaukee Experiment," *Education and Urban Society,* vol. 31 (February 1999), pp. 190–213; Cecilia Rouse, "Private School Vouchers and Student Achievement: An Evaluation of the Milwaukee Parental Choice Program," *Quarterly Journal of Economics,* vol.113 (May 1998), pp. 553–602.

7. *Jackson* v. *Benson,* Wisc. S. Ct., No. 97-0270.

8. State of Wisconsin, Legislative Audit Bureau, *An Evaluation: Milwaukee Parental Choice Program,* report 00-2 (Madison, 2000); Caroline M. Hoxby, "Rising Tide: New Evidence on Competition and the Public Schools," *Education Next* (Winter 2001), pp. 68-75; Frederick M. Hess, "Hints of the Pick-Axe: The Impact of Competition on Public Schooling in Milwaukee," in Paul E. Peterson and David E. Campbell, eds., *Charters, Vouchers, and Public Education* (Brookings, 2001).

9. *Doris Simmons-Harris* v. *John Goff,* Docket no. 96 CVH 10/721 (July 31, 1996).

10. *Zelman* v. *Simmons-Harris,* 528 U.S. 983 (November 5, 1999).

11. *Simmons-Harris* v. *Zelman,* 72 F. Supp. 2d 834 (December 20, 1999).

12. *Simmons-Harris* v. *Zelman,* 234 F. 3d 945 (December 11, 2000).

13. Jay P. Greene, William G. Howell, and Paul E. Peterson, "Lessons from the Cleveland Scholarship Program," in Peterson and Hassel, *Learning from School Choice,* pp. 357–92; Jay P. Greene, William G. Howell, and Paul E. Peterson, "Lessons from the Cleveland Scholarship Program," occasional paper (Harvard University, Program on Education Policy and Governance, September 1997); Paul E. Peterson, William G. Howell, and Jay P. Greene, "An Evaluation of the Cleveland Voucher Program after Two Years," occasional paper (Harvard University, Program on Education Policy and Governance, 1999); Kim K. Metcalf and others, "A Comparative Evaluation of the Cleveland Scholarship and Tutoring Grant Program: Year One, 1996–97" (Indiana University, School of Education, Smith Research Center, March 1998); Kim K. Metcalf and others, "Evaluation of the Cleveland Scholarship Program: Second-Year Report (1997–98)" (Indiana University, School of Education, Smith Research Center, 1998); Kim K. Metcalf, "Evaluation of the Cleveland Scholarship and Tutoring Grant Program, 1996–1999" (Indiana University, School of Education, Indiana Center for Evaluation, Smith Research Center,1999); Kim K. Metcalf, "Evaluation of the Cleveland Scholarship Program: 1998–2000 Summary Report" (Indiana University, School of Education, Indiana Center for Evaluation, Smith Research Center, 2001).

14. "Florida Begins Voucher Plan for Education," *New York Times*, August 17, 1999, p. A15.

15. Jay P. Greene, "An Evaluation of the Florida A-Plus Accountability and School Choice Program," occasional paper (Harvard University, Program on Education Policy and Governance, February 2001). For a criticism of this report, see Gregory Camilli and Katrina Bulkley, "Critique of 'An Evaluation of the Florida A-Plus Accountability and School Choice Program,'" *Education Policy Analysis Archives*, vol. 9, no. 7 (2001), available at 〈http://epaa.asu.edu/epaa/v9n7 [November 5, 2001]〉.

16. J. David Greenstone and Paul E. Peterson, *Race and Authority in Urban Politics: Community Participation and the War on Poverty* (Russell Sage, 1973).

17. Paul E. Peterson, *Making the Grade: A Report of the Twentieth Century Fund Task Force on Federal Elementary and Secondary Education Policy* (Twentieth Century Fund, 1983), pp. 83–135.

18. For an evaluation of the privately funded program in Indianapolis and an earlier voucher program in San Antonio, see David J. Weinschrott and Sally B. Kilgore, "Evidence from the Indianapolis Voucher Program," in Peterson and Hassel, *Learning from School Choice*, pp. 307–34; R. Kenneth Godwin, Frank R. Kemerer, and Valerie J. Martinez, "Comparing Public Choice and Private Voucher Programs in San Antonio," in Peterson and Hassel, *Learning from School Choice*, pp. 275–306. For the evaluation of the Charlotte program, see Jay P. Greene, "Vouchers in Charlotte," *Education Matters: A Journal of Opinion and Research*, vol. 1 (Summer 2001), pp. 55–60.

19. The actual take-up rates in New York (as opposed to the take-up rates among participants in the follow-up testing sessions) were 74, 62, and 53 percent in Years I, II, and III, respectively.

20. These students also were excluded from the evaluation.

21. The Washington Scholarship Fund began offering scholarships in 1993 and operated on a small scale until it was expanded in 1998.

22. *Children's Scholarship Fund: Giving Parents a Choice, Giving Children a Chance,* pamphlet (New York: Children's Scholarship Fund, no date), p. 7.

23. Unless otherwise indicated, all Edgewood enrollment and demographic information included in this book is taken from State of Texas, Texas Education Agency, Academic Excellence Indicator System, 1997–98, *District Report for Edgewood Independent School District* (District # 015905), available on the website of the Texas Education Agency (www.tea.state.tx.us [November 2, 2001]).

24. Students who chose a private school outside Edgewood received scholarships equivalent to the tuition at that school or the amounts noted, whichever was less. If the vouchers exceeded tuition at an Edgewood private school, the school was allowed to keep the difference. A more complete description of the program may be found in Robert B. Aguirre, *A Report on the First Semester of the Horizon Voucher Program* (San Antonio, Tex.: Children's Educational Opportunity Foundation, 1999).

25. The average reported is based on the assumption that Horizon students paid the school's maximum tuition charges. Information was available for 710 Horizon students. Memorandum from CEO Foundation to evaluation team, July 1999. The

evaluation team does not have information on the amount of money Edgewood private schools receive from nontuition sources.

26. Aguirre, *A Report on the First Semester of the Horizon Voucher Program*, p. 10.

27. William Mendenhall, *Introduction to Probability and Statistics*, 7th ed. (Boston: PWS-Kent, 1987), p. 654.

28. Lawrence F. Katz, Jeffrey R. Kling, and Jeffrey B. Liebman, "Moving to Opportunity in Boston: Early Results of a Randomized Mobility Experiment," *Quarterly Journal of Economics*, vol. 116, no. 2 (2001), pp. 607–54.

29. Jens Ludwig, Greg J. Duncan, and Paul Hirschfield, "Urban Poverty and Juvenile Crime: Evidence from a Randomized Housing-Mobility Experiment," *Quarterly Journal of Economics*, vol.116, no. 2 (2001), pp. 655–79.

30. Jens Ludwig, Helen F. Ladd, and Greg J. Duncan, "Urban Poverty and Educational Outcomes," *Brookings-Wharton Papers on Urban Affairs, 2001*, pp. 147–202.

31. They, too, use the results from a lottery as an instrument to detect the effects of actually receiving the prescribed treatment, a topic we discuss at greater length later.

32. Robert Boruch and Frederick Mosteller, "Overview and New Directions," and Robert Boruch, Dorothy de Moya, and Brooke Snyder, "The Importance of Randomized Field Trials in Education and Other Areas," in Frederick Mosteller and Robert Boruch, eds., *Evidence Matters: Randomized Trials in Education Research* (Brookings, 2002).

33. Thomas D. Cook and Monique R. Payne, "Objecting to the Objections to Using Random Assignment in Educational Research," in Mosteller and Boruch, *Evidence Matters*, pp. 150–78.

34. W. Steven Barnett, "Benefit-Cost Analysis of the Perry Preschool Program and Its Policy Implications," *Educational Evaluation and Policy Analysis*, vol. 7 (Winter 1985), pp. 333–42.

35. Papers from this conference are published in Mosteller and Boruch, *Evidence Matters*.

36. Lawrence H. Summers, Remarks at President's Weekend Dinner, Harvard University Graduate School of Education, November 2, 2001, available at ⟨www.president.harvard.edu/speeches/2001/gse.html⟩.

37. 106 H.R. 4875

38. Frederick Mosteller, "The Tennessee Study of Class Size in the Early School Grades," *Future of Children*, vol. 5 (Summer/Fall 1995), pp. 113–27; Alan B. Krueger, "Experimental Estimates of Education Production Functions," *Quarterly Journal of Economics*, vol. 114 (May 1999), pp. 497–532.

39. Jeffrey Henig, "School Choice Outcomes," in Stephen Sugarman and Frank Kemerer, eds., *School Choice and Social Controversy: Politics, Policy, and Law* (Brookings, 1999), pp. 90–91.

40. Jay P. Greene, Paul E. Peterson, and Jiangtao Du, "Effectiveness of School Choice: The Milwaukee Experiment," occasional paper (Harvard University, Program on Education Policy and Governance, March 1997); Rouse, "Private School Vouchers and Student Achievement," pp. 553–602.

41. Witte, *The Market Approach to Education*.

42. The following papers and publications give interim results from the random-ized field trials. For the evaluation of the School Choice Scholarship Foundation pro-gram in New York City, see Paul E. Peterson and others, "Initial Findings from the Evaluation of the New York School Choice Scholarships Program" (Harvard Univer-sity, Program on Education Policy and Governance, November 1997); Paul E. Peter-son, David Myers, and William G. Howell, "An Evaluation of the New York City School Choice Scholarships Program: The First Year," occasional paper (Harvard University, Program on Education Policy and Governance, October 1998); Paul E. Peterson and others, "The Effects of School Choice in New York City," in Susan B. Mayer and Paul E. Peterson, eds., *Earning and Learning: How Schools Matter* (Brook-ings, 1999), pp. 317–40; William G. Howell and others, "Test-Score Effects of School Vouchers in Dayton, Ohio, New York City, and Washington, D.C.: Evidence from Randomized Field Trials," occasional paper (Harvard University, Program on Education Policy and Governance, September 2000); David Myers and others, "School Choice in New York City after Two Years: An Evaluation of the School Choice Scholarships Program," occasional paper (Harvard University, Program on Education Policy and Governance, September 2000); Paul E. Peterson and William G. Howell, "Exploring Explanations for Ethnic Differences in Voucher Impacts on Student Test Scores," in Tom Loveless and John E. Chubb, eds., *Ending the Test-Score Gap* (Brookings, forthcoming). All Program on Education Policy and Governance papers are available at (www.ksg.harvard.edy/pepg [November 2, 2001]).

For additional reports from the evaluation of the WSF program in Washington, D.C., see Paul E. Peterson and others, "Initial Findings from an Evaluation of School Choice Programs in Washington, D.C., and Dayton, Ohio," occasional paper (Har-vard University, Program on Education Policy and Governance, October 1998); Patrick J. Wolf, William G. Howell, and Paul E. Peterson, " School Choice in Wash-ington, D.C.: An Evaluation after One Year," occasional paper (Harvard University, Program on Education Policy and Governance, February 2000); Patrick J. Wolf, Paul E. Peterson, and Martin R. West, "Results of a School Voucher Experiment: The Case of Washington, D.C., after Two Years," occasional paper (Harvard University, Program on Education Policy and Governance, 2001).

For additional reports from the evaluation of Dayton, see William G. Howell and Paul E. Peterson, "School Choice in Dayton, Ohio: An Evaluation After One Year," occasional paper (Harvard University, Program on Education Policy and Governance, February 2000); Paul E. Peterson, David Campbell, and Martin West, "An Evalua-tion of the Dayton Voucher Program after Two Years," occasional paper (Harvard University, Program on Education Policy and Governance, 2001).

43. The assessment used in this study is Form M of the Iowa Tests of Basic Skills, 1996 (Itasca, Ill.: Riverside Publishing Co.), coordinated by the University of Iowa.

44. In 90 to 95 percent of the cases, the parents filled out the questionnaires. To simplify discussion, we present all responses as if they were responses of the parents.

45. Also, the program operators in New York decided in advance that 85 percent of the scholarships would be awarded to students from public schools whose test scores were lower than the city median. Because 70 percent of applicants met that cri-

terion, they were assigned a higher probability of winning a scholarship. In the analysis reported here, results have been adjusted by weighting cases to account for these features of the lottery process. For a complete discussion on weighting procedures in New York, see Myers and others, "School Choice in New York City After Two Years."

46. Those are the numbers of students who were offered vouchers and included in the study. A handful of additional families were offered vouchers, but they were not included in the evaluation for lack of baseline information.

47. While in most cases parents brought their children to the testing sessions, occasionally other family members or friends did so.

48. Patricia Luevano, "Response Rates in the National Election Studies, 1948–1992," Working Paper 44 (Ann Arbor, Mich.: Inter-University Consortium for Political and Social Research, March 1994).

49. In each year of the STAR experiment, there was sizable attrition from the preceding year's treatment groups, and those students were replaced with new students. In first grade, 2,314 new students were added; in second grade, 1,791 new students were added; and in third grade, 1,389 new students were added. Of the initial experimental group that started in kindergarten, 48 percent remained in the experiment for the entire four years. See Eric A. Hanushek, "Some Findings from an Independent Investigation of the Tennessee STAR Experiment and from Other Investigations of Class-Size Effects," *Educational Evaluation and Policy Analysis*, vol. 21 (Summer 1999), pp. 143–68. The original evaluation of the STAR study reports a 29 percent response rate after one year. Elizabeth Word and others, *Student/Teacher Achievement Ratio (STAR), Tennessee's K–3 Class Size Study: Final Summary Report, 1985–1990* (Nashville: Tennessee State Department of Education, 1990).

Alan Krueger, who performed secondary analyses on the data, does not report response rates in any year. In "The Effect of Attending A Small Class in the Early Grades on College-Test Taking and Middle School Test Results: Evidence from Project STAR," Working Paper 7656 (Cambridge, Mass.: National Bureau of Economic Research, 2000), Krueger and Diane Whitmore report a sample of roughly 11,600 students, a number generated from the base sample plus those students who were added in each year due to sample attrition. (Paper available at www.nber.org [January 14, 2002]).

50. Those numbers were calculated by John Witte and his research team. See Witte, "First Year Report: Milwaukee Parental Choice Program," table A1. Witte reports response rates for both the test and control populations only for the first year; in addition, he reports response rates "based on delivered surveys" and not necessarily on those returned surveys that were complete for data analysis. See Witte and others, "Fourth-Year Parental Report: Milwaukee Parental Choice Program," p. 25. See also Jay P. Greene and others, "The Effectiveness of School Choice in Milwaukee: A Secondary Analysis of Data from the Program's Evaluation," Occasional Paper 96-3 (Harvard University, Program on Education Policy and Governance, August 1996), p. 36.

51. In New York and Washington, families in the control group were automatically entered in a new lottery if they attended follow-up testing in the first and second years. In Dayton, control group families were entered in a new lottery only after

the first year of the program. For the second year, they were offered higher compensation instead. Families who began the study as members of a control group were dropped from the evaluation if they subsequently won a follow-up lottery. Excluding those families was necessary to preserve the random design of the evaluation and had the effect of reducing the size of the control groups slightly.

52. While program administrators included that provision in some letters to parents in order to boost response rates, they did not in fact drop any voucher recipients for not attending follow-up sessions. After the first year, parents in Dayton and Washington were not required to participate in order to retain the scholarship.

53. Response rates for parent and student surveys were similar, although not identical, to student test response rates. See reports on individual cities for details.

54. The biggest difference in response rates of the treatment and control groups was seen in the second year of the evaluation in New York, when the treatment group's response rate was seven points higher than the control group's.

55. While nonrespondents in both groups were more likely to be African American and to have lower education levels, they were less likely to receive welfare. Differences in test scores, religious affiliation, residential mobility rates, church attendance, satisfaction with their school, and family size were insignificant.

56. However, the CSF program was not advertised equally in all parts of the country, scholarships were not available in proportionate numbers everywhere, and application rates were not uniform in all parts of the United States.

57. Because no baseline data were collected for the national evaluation of CSF, it is impossible to verify this conclusively.

58. The sampling procedure ensured that samples of test and control groups were similar for geographic areas and that both were proportional to the scholarship offer rate among geographic areas.

59. To facilitate comparisons, parents were asked about the experiences of only one of their children in grades 1 through 8. If the family had more than one child in this age cohort, they were asked to report on the child who was next to have a birthday (a technique that maintains randomization and comparability). Provided that they were in grades 4 through 8, those children were interviewed. Parents and students were asked a variety of questions about their school experiences.

60. In accordance with the recommendations of the American Association for Public Opinion Research, we have calculated an adjusted response rate. See American Association for Public Opinion Research, *Standard Definitions: Final Dispositions of Case Codes and Outcome Rates for Surveys* (Ann Arbor, Mich.: 2001), also available at (www.aapor.org [November 2, 2001]).

As detailed in *Standard Definitions*, this response rate uses as its denominator an estimate of the percentage of eligible cases among the unknown cases. We generated that estimate by assuming that the percentage of ineligible households among those we interviewed was the same as the percentage among those we did not interview (43 percent). The treatment group response rate was 45.0 percent, and the control group rate was 47.0 percent, generating an overall response rate of 45.6 percent. In *Standard Definitions*, this is Response Rate 4 (RR4).

61. For a few demographic measures—education level, race, and religious affiliation (percent Catholic)—there were slight differences between the treatment and control groups that reach or approach statistical significance. Because the response rates for the treatment and control groups were very similar, it is unlikely that those differences were due to anything more than chance (recall that only chance determined whether a family received a scholarship). To account for the differences, we have employed standard poststratification weighting. See appendix B for additional discussion of weighting procedures.

62. Robert P. Berrens and others, *The Advent of Internet Surveys for Political Research: A Comparison of Telephone and Internet Samples* (University of Wisconsin, 2001).

63. Alan Gerber, "Estimating the Effect of Campaign Spending on Senate Election Outcomes Using Instrumental Variables," *American Political Science Review,* vol. 92 (June 1998), pp. 401–11. Similarly, Mark Schneider and others use instrumental variables to estimate the effect of school choice on social capital; their choice of instruments, although creative, suffers from some of the same limitations as Gerber's do. See Mark Schneider and others, "Institutional Arrangements and the Creation of Social Capital: The Effects of Shool Choice," *American Political Science Review,* vol. 91 (March 1997), pp. 82–93.

64. Alan S. Gerber and Donald P. Green, "The Effects of Canvassing, Telephone Calls, and Direct Mail on Voter Turnout: A Field Experiment," *American Political Science Review,* vol. 94 (September 2000), pp. 653–63.

65. Joshua D. Angrist, "Estimating the Labor Market Impact of Voluntary Military Service Using Social Security Data on Military Applicants," *Econometrica,* vol. 66 (March 1998), pp. 249–88; Joshua D. Angrist and Alan B. Krueger, "Does Compulsory School Attendance Affect Schooling and Earnings?" *Quarterly Journal of Economics,* vol. 106 (November 1991), pp. 979–1014; Joshua D. Angrist and Alan B. Krueger, "Why Do World War II Veterans Earn More than Nonveterans?" *Journal of Labor Economics,* vol. 12 (January 1994), pp. 74–97; Thomas Lemieux and David E. Card, "Education, Earnings, and the Canadian GI Bill," Working Paper 6718 (Cambridge, Mass.: National Bureau of Economic Research, September 1998); Joshua D. Angrist and Alan B. Krueger "Estimating the Payoff to Schooling Using the Vietnam-Era Draft Lottery," Working Paper 4067 (Cambridge, Mass.: National Bureau of Economic Research, May 1992); Joshua D. Angrist and Alan B. Krueger, "The Effect of Age at School Entry on Educational Attainment: An Application of Instrumental Variables with Moments from Two Samples," *Journal of the American Statistical Association,* vol. 87 (June 1992), pp. 328–36.

66. Thomas J. Kane, Douglas O. Staiger, and Jeffrey Geppert, "Randomly Accountable: Test Scores and Volatility," *Education Next,* vol. 2 (Spring 2002), pp. 56–61.

67. It is a convention among statisticians that if Type I error confidence levels are set at 0.95, then Type II confidence levels are set at 0.80. See, for example, Jacob Cohen, *Statistical Power Analysis for the Behavioral Sciences,* 2d ed. (Hillsdale, N.J.: Lawrence Erlbaum, 1988).

68. In Years II and III, we report the impact of attending a private school for the full two and three years, respectively. To estimate this effect, the instrument we use assumes that the impact of attending a private school is, on average, zero for those who never did attend a private school as well as for those who switched to a private school for one or two years and then returned to public school. If students benefit from switching back and forth between public and private schools, then our results overestimate true impacts. If, on the other hand, moving back and forth between public and private schools has negative educational consequences, then the impacts we report in this book underestimate the true impacts of attending a private school for two and three years. Thus, we compare those students who attended a private school for a specific duration to those students in the control group who would have attended a private school for the specified duration had they been offered a voucher.

69. Paul E. Peterson, David Myers, and William G. Howell, "An Evaluation of the Horizon Scholarship Program in the Edgewood Independent School District, San Antonio, Texas: The First Year," occasional paper (Harvard University, Program on Education Policy and Governance, October 1999).

Chapter Three

1. *Brown* v. *Board of Educatiosn,* 347 U.S. 483 (1954).

2. Dirk Johnson, "Chicago Schools' Answer to Tug of the Suburbs," *New York Times,* June 2, 2000, p. A12.

3. Bruce Fuller and others, *School Choice* (Policy Analysis for California Education, University of California, Berkeley, and Stanford University, 1999).

4. Only 10 percent of elementary and secondary students attend magnet schools (Fuller and others, *School Choice*).

5. The test score and poverty data for public schools came from data files made available by the New York State Department of Education, personal communication, September 1999. Catholic school data came from a data file made available by the Archdiocese of Manhattan, Bronx, and Staten Island, personal correspondence, September 1999.

6. John F. Witte, *The Market Approach to Education: An Analysis of America's First Voucher Program* (Princeton University Press, 2000), p. 53.

7. Amy Stuart Wells, "African-American Students' View of School Choice," in Bruce Fuller and Richard F. Elmore, eds., *Who Chooses? Who Loses? Culture, Institutions, and the Unequal Effects of School Choice* (Teachers College Press, 1996), p. 47.

8. National Center for Education Statistics, *Digest of Education Statistics 1999,* NCES 2000-031 (U.S. Dept. of Education, Office of Educational Research and Improvement, 2000), table 62, p. 73; U.S. Department of Education, National Center for Education Statistics, *Private School Survey 1997–98* (Government Printing Office, 1999). Tuition information was taken from the CSF survey.

9. National Center for Education Statistics, *Private School Universe, 1997–1998*

(U.S. Dept. of Education, 1999), table 16, p. 21, available at (www.capenet.org [November 9, 2001]).

10. Jay P. Greene, "Civic Values in Public and Private Schools," in Paul E. Peterson and Bryan Hassel, eds., *Learning from School Choice* (Brookings, 1998), pp. 93–98.

11. John Chubb and Terry Moe, "Politics, Markets, and Equality in Schools," in Michael Darby, ed., *Reducing Poverty in America* (Thousand Oaks, Calif.: Sage Publications, 1997), p. 145.

12. Gary Rosen and Critics, "Are School Vouchers the Answer?" *Commentary*, vol. 109 (June 2000), pp. 16, 20.

13. Henry M. Levin, "Educational Vouchers: Effectiveness, Choice, and Costs," *Journal of Policy Analysis and Management*, vol. 17 (June 1998), p. 379.

14. Focus group session, Washington, D.C., March 6, 1999.

15. Terry Moe, *Schools, Vouchers, and the American Public* (Brookings, 2001).

16. However, we were unable to determine the extent to which the large proportion of blacks among CSF applicants is a function of CSF's marketing strategy.

17. The sample size for applicants is smaller for the portions of the analysis that address parents' involvement with school, parents' satisfaction with school, and parents' reports of public school characteristics, because relevant data on those issues were available only for that portion of applicants who were not offered a voucher. Since our survey was administered one year after lottery winners received their vouchers, their answers would reflect their experiences after switching schools, not their experiences with their public schools at the time that they applied to CSF. Fifteen percent of the control-group families in our sample who did not receive a scholarship nevertheless enrolled their children in a private school and also were excluded from the analysis. Although the latter exclusion involves a departure from the random assignment research design, including them in the analysis did not change any of the substantive results reported in tables 3-2, 3-3, or 3-4. Since the families in the control group were randomly selected from the total set of applicants, these results may be generalized to the total population.

18. The specific questions were
—"How many parent-teacher conferences did you or someone else attend for [child's name] this school year?"
—"How many times did you or someone else speak with [child's name] principal or teacher on the telephone this school year?"
—"About how many hours have you or someone else volunteered in [child's name] school this past month? Is it none, one to two hours, three to five hours, or six or more hours?"
—"How often do you or someone else talk with families who have children at [child's name] school? Would you say very often, often, not very often, or never?"

19. The specific questions were
—"How far in school do you intend to go: probably won't graduate from high school, will graduate from high school, will go to college but might not graduate, will graduate from college, will go to more school after college."

—"How strongly do you agree or disagree with the following statements? Do you strongly agree, somewhat agree, somewhat disagree, or strongly disagree?

(a) Class work was hard to learn

(b) I had trouble keeping up with the homework

(c) I would read much better if I had more help."

The index is additive, with the measures simply summed. That total was then divided by its standard deviation, thus producing an index with a standard deviation of one.

20. See appendix A, this volume, p. 210.

21. These voucher usage rates are drawn from the population of students who attended the first-year testing sessions. For all three cities, the actual voucher usage rates were lower. See Paul E. Peterson, David Myers, and William G. Howell, "An Evaluation of the New York City School Choice Scholarships Program: The First Year," PEPG 98-12 (Program on Education Policy and Governance, Harvard University, 1998); Patrick J. Wolf, William G. Howell, and Paul E. Peterson., "School Choice in Washington, D.C.: An Evaluation After One Year," paper prepared for the Conference on Vouchers, Charters, and Public Education sponsored by the Program on Education Policy and Governance, Harvard University, March 2000.

22. Focus group session, Washington, D.C., March 25, 2000.

23. Focus group session, Washington, D.C., March 6, 1999.

24. Focus group session, Washington, D.C., March 25, 2000.

25. Focus group session, Dayton, Ohio, March 18, 2000.

26. Focus group session, Washington, D.C., April 15, 2000.

27. Focus group session, Washington, D.C., April 18, 1999.

28. Witte, *The Market Approach to Education*, p. 69.

29. In New York City, students had to be entering grades 1–4 to be eligible. In Dayton, applications were received from students entering grades K–8; however, Dayton's was the smallest voucher program that we evaluated, and the number of applicants from students entering grades 6–8 was too small to permit separate analysis. Because of that, all our findings for Dayton are for all students, regardless of grade level.

30. *Digest of Education Statistics 1999*, table 59, p. 71.

31. Ibid. Since the definition of moderate disabilities is imprecise and often subjective, some have argued that much of the increase in the number of students with moderate disabilities is due not only to possible increases in the actual incidence of those disabilities but also to the fact that school districts receive additional state and federal funds for every child so classified. Victoria Purcell-Gates, professor of education at Michigan State University, says that there is a problem with "overidentification," labeling students learning disabled to get larger shares of federal funds (Tamara Henry, "Diagnosing Learning Problems Can Be Difficult for Parents and Teachers," *USA Today*, June 18, 1997, Life section, p. 8.). Furthermore, some have suggested that "troublemakers" frequently are sent to special education programs by frustrated teachers eager to get rid of them, even though the student in question may not have given any indication of having a disability. In part because of such criticisms and to

preserve funding for those truly in need, in 1997 federal law was altered in order to loosen the connection between disability identification and funding—especially in borderline cases.

32. Wade F. Horn and Douglas Tynan, "Time to Make Special Education 'Special' Again," in Chester E. Finn Jr., Andrew J. Rotherham, and Charles R. Hokanson Jr., eds., *Rethinking Special Education for a New Century* (Washington: Fordham Foundation and Progressive Policy Institute, 2001), p. 26.

33. Matthew Ladner and Christopher Hammons, "Special but Unequal: Race and Special Education," in Finn, Rotherham, and Hokanson, *Rethinking Special Education for a New Century,* pp. 85–110.

34. Focus group session, Washington, D.C., March 6, 1999, afternoon session.

35. Wolf, Howell, and Peterson, "School Choice in Washington, D.C.: An Evaluation After One Year" and Peterson, Myers, and Howell, "An Evaluation of the New York City School Choice Scholarships Program: The First Year."

36. Focus group session, Dayton scholarship recipients, April 1, 2000.

37. Focus group session, Washington, D.C., March 4, 2000.

38. Kelley Shannon, "Texas Kids to Get School Vouchers," Associated Press news release, April 22, 1998, available at (www.reporternews.com/texas/voucher0423.html [December 27, 2001]).

39. *News Hour Online, A News Hour with Jim Lehrer,* "School Vouchers," November 27, 1998.

40. "Private Effort: No Public Funds in Private Voucher program, So Give It a Go," *Houston Chronicle,* April 27, 1998, p. 18.

41. Focus group, Horizon parents, San Antonio, March 17, 1999.

42. Ibid.

43. Edgewood Independent School District, "Initial Screening of the CEO Data File," February 3, 1999.

44. Ibid.

45. Ibid.

46. *News Hour Online,* "School Vouchers."

47. Laura M. Litvan, "A School Voucher Test Case?" *Investor's Business Daily,* January 21, 1999.

48. State of Wisconsin, Legislative Audit Bureau, *An Evaluation: Milwaukee Parental Choice Program* (February 2000), p. 37.

49. Witte, *The Market Approach to Education,* pp. 60–61, 67.

50. Jay P. Greene, William G. Howell, and Paul E. Peterson, "Lessons from the Cleveland Scholarship Program," in Peterson and Hassel, *Learning from School Choice,* pp. 357–92.

51. Kim K. Metcalf, "Evaluation of the Cleveland Scholarship and Tutoring Grant Program" (Bloomington: Indiana Center for Evaluation, University of Indiana, 1999), p. 14.

52. Ibid., pp. 9–10.

53. Adjusting to a new private school can sometimes be difficult, as focus group conversations revealed. Said one D.C. mother: "We transitioned him . . . out of . . .

public school. He could do better than what he's doing. . . . I was told [this was] the transitioning period for him since this is his first year. . . . And his grades kind of fluctuated. He likes his new friends. He had to adjust to that. But now he's fine. He likes going to school." The child's father added: "It did get to be a bit much. Mostly, because the level of things that they were doing was pretty heavy for an eight year old . . . when you're starting to read books and do book reports, and doing multiplication, all those things can weigh heavily on an eight year old all at once." (Focus group session, Washington, D.C., March 6, 1999.) Another D.C. parent echoed those remarks: "We left public school to go to private school. What was a straight A student is now a shocking C. That's a shock to a kid when it came. . . . It's sort of a wake up call." (Focus group session, Washington, D.C., March 6, 1999.)

54. Focus group session, Washington, D.C., March 25, 2000.

55. Focus group session, Washington, D.C., April 18, 1999.

56. See Daniel Mayer, Paul Peterson, David Myers, Christina Tuttle, and William Howell, "School Choice in New York City after Three Years: An Evaluation of the School Choice Scholarships Program," February 19, 2002 (www.mathematica-mpr. com/PDFs/nycfull.pdf).

57. Witte, *The Market Approach to Education,* p. 88.

58. Focus group session, Dayton, April 1, 2000.

59. Evaluations of other voucher programs find much the same thing. According to the evaluator of the Milwaukee voucher program, the mobility rates for the voucher students in Milwaukee "seem to be in line with the [mobility] rates in the public schools." Witte, *The Market Approach to Education,* p. 144.

60. These models predict the probability that an individual will take the voucher and then the probability that he or she will make it through two years of the program. For results from an alternative modeling techinque, see William Howell, "Dynamic Selection Effects in School Voucher Programs," PEPG report 02-01 (Program on Education Policy and Governance, Harvard University, 2002).

61. Jay Greene, "Choosing Integration," paper prepared for the School Choice and Racial Diversity Conference sponsored by the National Center for the Study of Privatization in Education, Teachers College, Columbia University, May 22, 2000.

Chapter Four

1. We present individual effects for each city as well as the average effect for the cities combined. To generate the average effect, the point estimate from each city is weighted by the inverse of its variance.

2. Edward Wyatt, "Success of City School Pupils Isn't Simply a Money Matter," *New York Times,* June 14, 2000, p. A1.

3. *Derolph et al.* v. *State of Ohio,* 89 Ohio St. 3d 1 (2000), p. 24. Also see, for example, *Claremont School District* v. *Governor,* 142 N.H. 462 (1997).

4. Eric A. Hanushek, "Student Resources and Student Performance," in Gary Burtless, ed., *Does Money Matter?* (Brookings, 1996), p. 69; see also Eric A. Hanushek, Steven G. Rivkin, and Lori L. Taylor, "Aggregation and the Estimated

Effects of School Resources," *Review of Economics and Statistics*, vol. 78, no. 4 (1977), 611–27.

5. See, for example, Larry V. Hedges and Rob Greenwald, "Have Times Changed? The Relation between School Resources and School Performance," and David Card and Alan B. Krueger, "Labor Market Effects on School Quality: Theory and Evidence," in Burtless, *Does Money Matter?*

6. National Center for Education Statistics, *Digest of Education Statistics 1999,* NCES 2000-031 (U.S. Dept. of Education, Office of Research and Improvement, 2000), table 403, p. 457, and table 419, p. 471.

7. National Center for Education Statistics, *Digest of Education Statistics 1998,* NCES 1999-036 (U.S. Dept. of Education, Office of Research and Improvement, 1999). When including expenditures for debt service, capital outlay, direct costs, community services, and property, this figure rises to $6,943.

8. Michael Garet and others, *The Determinants of Per-Pupil Expenditures in Private Elementary and Secondary Schools: An Exploratory Analysis,* NCES Working Paper 97-07 (U.S. Dept. of Education, National Center for Education Statistics, March 1997), table 3.

9. Michael Garet, Tsze Chan, and Joel Sherman, *Estimates of Expenditures for Private K-12 Schools,* NCES Working Paper 95-17 (U.S. Dept. of Education, National Center for Education Statistics, May 1995), table 4-6.

10. *Digest of Education Statistics 1999,* table 74. In 1998–99, the average private school teacher's salary was $30,000, compared with $40,000 for public school teachers. Garet and others, *The Determinants of Per-Pupil Expenditures in Private Elementary and Secondary Schools,* table 3; National Center for Education Statistics, *Digest of Education Statistics 2000,* NCES 2001-034 (U.S. Dept. of Education, Office of Research and Improvement, 2001), table 74, p. 83. We have adjusted 1990–91 salaries to 1998–99 levels by assuming that private school salaries increased at the same rate as the cost of living between 1990–91 (the last year for which reliable data on private school teachers' salaries are available) and 1998–99, the latest year for which public school teacher salaries are available.

11. Henry Levin, "Educational Vouchers: Effectiveness, Choice, and Costs," *Journal of Policy Analysis and Management* (Summer 1998), pp. 383–84.

12. City of New York, Board of Education, *School-Based Expenditure Reports, Fiscal Year 1997–98: Systemwide Summary 1999.* These data were supplemented by information from an electronic file made available to us by the New York State Board of Education, personal communication, September 1999.

13. Estimates are based on information about Catholic schools in three boroughs in New York City in an unpublished memorandum submitted to the Harvard Program on Education Policy and Governance by the New York archdiocese in August 1999 and from data provided in the National Center for Education Statistics, *Common Core of Data, School Years 1993–94 through 1997–98.* (U.S. Dept. of Education, 2000). Comparable data estimate excludes public school expenditures for student transportation, food services, enterprise operations, nonelementary/secondary programs, adult education, capital outlay, payments to other school systems, payments

to state governments, interest on school system debt, central support for planning research and management services, and unspecified support services. It is not clear whether Catholic school expenditures include monies provided for textbooks and compensatory education by the state of New York. We were unable to calculate expenditures separately for elementary and secondary schools.

14. Private school tuition rates were estimated in part from information provided in Lois H. Coerper and Shirley W. Mersereau, *Independent School Guide for Washington, D.C., and Surrounding Area*, 11th ed. (Chevy Chase, Md.: Independent School Guides, 1998). For schools not listed in that volume, information was obtained in telephone conversations with school staff. Some schools have a range of tuition charges, depending on the number of students from the family attending the school and other factors. The tuition used for this calculation is the maximum charged by the school; it also includes all fees, except the registration fee, which is ordinarily treated as partial payment toward tuition. Figures are weighted in proportion to the number of students in the evaluation attending a particular school. Public school expenditures include the costs of transportation and special education, which may not be provided by private schools.

15. Figures are in 1998 dollars. Data taken from National Center for Education Statistics, *Common Core of Data, School Years 1993–94 through 1997–98*. Comparable data estimate excludes public school expenditures for student transportation, food services, enterprise operations, nonelementary/secondary programs, adult education, capital outlay, payments to other school systems, payments to state governments, interest on school system debt, central support for planning research and management services, and unspecified support services.

16. Similarly, in the national CSF evaluation, private school parents were less likely to report having special education programs, a cafeteria, a nurse's office, programs for advanced learners, and guidance counselors. Public schools, meanwhile, were less likely to provide individual tutors and after-school programs. Paul E. Peterson and David E. Campbell, "An Evaluation of the Children's Scholarship Fund," PEPG Report 01-03 (Program on Education Policy and Governance, Kennedy School of Government, Harvard University, 2001), table 5.

17. The impact on the range of school programs—bilingual education, special education, gifted education—did not differ consistently among ethnic groups, however.

18. Focus group session, control group, Washington, D.C., March 25, 2000, 2d session.

19. Focus group session, Washington, D.C., March 6, 1999.

20. Valerie Strauss, "Ackerman Plans to Modernize D.C. Schools: $1 Billion Would Fix All Buildings by 2009," *Washington Post*, December 20, 1998, p. B1.

21. Focus group session, Washington, D.C., March 25, 2000.

22. Caroline M. Hoxby, "The Effects of Class Size on Student Achievement: New Evidence from Population Variation," *Quarterly Journal of Economics*, vol. 115, no. 4 (2000), pp. 1239–85.

23. Alan B. Krueger, "Experimental Estimates of Education Production Functions," *Quarterly Journal of Economics*, vol. 114 (May 1999), pp. 497–532.

24. Focus group session, Washington, D.C., March 25, 2000.

25. Duke Helfand, "Teacher Shortage Hitting Inner Cities Hardest, Study Says," *Los Angeles Times*, December 8, 2000, p. B1; Jessica Garrison, "A Welcome Back for Teachers: Big Raises, a Tight Job Market, and a Fat Cost-of-Living Increase in State Funds Result in Double-Digit Jumps in Many Districts," *Los Angeles Times,* September 25, 2000, p. B1. Class-size reductions in California may have generated a host of negative externalities, foremost among them being a shortage of qualified teachers. According to a recent report, "there simply are not enough qualified persons available and willing to take open teaching jobs" and "far too many of California's new teachers are not sufficiently prepared to help their students meet the state's new academic standards." See SRI International, *The Status of the Teaching Profession 2000,* report issued by the Center for the Future of Teaching and Learning, p. 4 (www.cftl.org [January 14, 2002]). The report goes on to note that poorer districts and those that serve predominantly minority populations have been the least successful in attracting and retaining fully credentialed teachers. The issue, then, is not just whether smaller classes are better but whether the investment's benefits outweigh its direct and indirect costs.

26. Elizabeth Bell, "Students Gaining from Smaller Classes, Study Says," *San Francisco Chronicle,* June 29, 2000, A19. Susan P. Choy, *Findings from the Condition of Education, 1996: Teachers' Working Conditions,* NCES 97-371 (U.S. Dept. of Education, National Center for Education Statistics, 1997).

27. James Conant, *The American High School Today: A Report to Interested Citizens* (McGraw-Hill, 1959).

28. Arthur Powell, Eleanor Farrar, and David Cohen, *The Shopping Mall High School: Winners and Losers in the Educational Marketplace* (Boston: Houghton Mifflin, 1985.)

29. See, for example, Ronald Corwin, "Innovation in Organizations: The Case of Schools," *Sociology of Education,* vol. 48 (Winter 1975), pp. 1–37.

30. Joseph Bledsoe, "An Analysis of the Relationship of Size of High School to Marks Received by Graduates in First Year of College," *Journal of Educational Sociology*, vol. 27 (May 1954), pp. 414–18; Randall W. Eberts, Ellen K. Schwartz, and Joe A. Stone, "School Reform, School Size, and Student Achievement," Federal Reserve Bank of Cleveland *Economic Review,* vol. 26, no. 2 (1990), pp. 2–15; Leanna Stiefel and others, "High School Size: Effects on Budgets and Performance in New York City," *Educational Evaluation and Policy Analysis*, vol. 22 (Spring 2000), pp. 27–39; William J. Fowler Jr. and Herbert J. Walberg, "School Size, Characteristics, and Outcomes," *Educational Evaluation and Policy Analysis*, vol.13 (Summer 1991), pp. 189–202; Valerie Lee and Susanna Loeb, "School Size in Chicago Elementary Schools: Effects on Teachers' Attitudes and Students' Achievements," *American Educational Research Journal,* vol. 37 (Winter 2000), pp. 3–32.

31. Lee Hoffman, *Key Statistics on Public Elementary and Secondary Schools and Agencies: School Year 1995–1996,* NCES 1999-324 (U.S. Dept. of Education, National Center for Education Statistics, 1999); Stephen Broughman and Lenore Colaciello, *Private School Universe Survey, 1997–98,* NCES 1999–319 (U.S. Dept. of Education, National Center for Education Statistics, 1999).

32. The average size of private schools as reported by parents in Dayton, Washington, D.C., New York City, and San Antonio was 260, 217, 352, and 285, respectively, compared with average public school sizes of 434, 438, 493, and 434, respectively.

33. There is an ongoing debate about the relative importance of school spending on student achievement. For a summary of the arguments, see Burtless, *Does Money Matter?*

34. George Madaus, Peter Airasian, and Thomas Kellaghan, *School Effectiveness: A Reassessment of the Evidence* (McGraw Hill, 1980), p. 174.

35. Stewart Purkey and Marshall Smith, "Effective Schools: A Review," *Elementary School Journal,* vol. 83, no. 4 (1983), pp. 427–52.

36. John E. Chubb and Terry M. Moe, *Politics, Markets, and America's Schools* (Brookings, 1990), p. 16.

37. For example, we were unable to obtain systematic information on school autonomy, though one focus group parent in Dayton thought it important: "The other advantage to Catholic schools that I've seen is . . . they're not governed by the Board of Education. . . . And there's no bureaucracy. If your child needs this service and the school's providing it and it's working, there's one little tiny group that you go to. . . . You try fighting the Board of Education. I've done it. It can be done, but most of us don't have the energy." Focus group afternoon session B, Dayton, Ohio, March 20, 1999.

38. Focus group session, Dayton, Ohio, April 1, 2000.

39. Ibid.

40. Peterson and Campbell, "An Evaluation of the Children's Scholarship Fund," table 11, p. 64.

41. Dayton focus group, April 1, 2000.

42. According to the U.S. Department of Education, 36 percent of central-city teachers in public schools say that lack of parental involvement is a serious problem, compared with 4 percent of central-city teachers in private schools. Office of Educational Research and Improvement, *Schools and Staffing in the United States: A Statistical Profile, 1993-94* (U.S. Dept. of Education, 1996), table 6-2, p. 112. One cannot tell from these data whether the problem is due primarily to the actions of parents or the actions of school teachers and administrators. But in an RFT, parents' characteristics are the same for the test and control groups.

43. Focus group session, afternoon, Dayton, Ohio, March 20, 1999.

44. Focus group session, Washington, D.C., April 8, 2000.

45. Michael Rutter, *Fifteen Thousand Hours: Secondary Schools and Their Effects on Children* (Harvard University Press, 1979).

46. Harris Cooper, *Homework* (New York: Littleton Press, 1989); also see Susan Black, "The Truth about Homework," *American School Board Journal,* vol. 183 (October 1996), pp. 48–51.

47. In Dayton, differences between public and private school parents were not significant.

48. Another voucher recipient gave much the same report: "Maybe once or twice a week at the most—that's when they would actually have homework in the public

schools. When they got to the private school, within a week after they started . . . they had homework just about every day." Focus group, Horizon parents, San Antonio, March 11, 1999.

49. Focus group session, Washington, D.C., March 4, 2000.

50. Ibid.

51. Data were not available for San Antonio or New York.

52. Data were not available for Dayton or Washington, D.C.

53. Focus group session, Horizon parents, San Antonio, March 20, 1999.

54. Ibid.

55. Information in this paragraph is taken from Paul E. Barton, Richard J. Coley, and Harold Wenglinsky, *Order in the Classroom: Violence, Discipline, and Student Achievement* (Princeton, N.J.: Educational Testing Service, Policy Information Center, 1998), pp. 21, 23, 25, 27, and 29. See also Office of Educational Research and Improvement, *Schools and Staffing in the United States.*

56. One public school father in Dayton reported on his wife's experiences as a public school volunteer: "My wife volunteers two days a week at the school. And she tells me some stories. And I'm just like—that stuff wouldn't fly just a few years ago . . . It's changed a lot since we were there. . . . Lutheran schools—they just wouldn't put up with it. . . . The discipline is a lot greater." Focus group session, Dayton, Ohio, March 20, 1999, afternoon session B.

57. Ibid.

58. Ibid.

59. Focus group session, Washington, D.C., March 27, 1999.

Chapter Five

1. For some items, data are available only from one or two of the cities.

2. John E. Brandl, *Money and Good Intentions Are Not Enough, or Why a Liberal Democrat Thinks States Need Both Competition and Community* (Brookings, 1998), p. 109.

3. Alan Bonsteel, "Schools of Choice as Communities," in Alan Bonsteel and Carlos A. Bonilla, eds., *A Choice for Our Children: Curing the Crisis in America's Schools* (San Francisco: Institute for Contemporary Studies, 1997), p. 157.

4. Andrew Coulson, *Market Education: The Unknown History* (New Brunswick, N.J.: Social Philosophy and Policy Center and Transaction Publishers, 1999), p. 297.

5. Paul E. Peterson and others, "Initial Findings from the Evaluation of the New York School Choice Scholarships Program," occasional paper (Program on Education Policy and Governance, Kennedy School of Government, Harvard University, November 1997); Paul E. Peterson and others, "Initial Findings from an Evaluation of School Choice Programs in Washington, D.C., and Dayton, Ohio," occasional paper (Program on Education Policy and Governance, Kennedy School of Government, Harvard University, October 24, 1998). Available at (http://ksg.harvard.edu/pepg/ [November 26, 2001]).

6. Paul E. Peterson and David E. Campbell, "An Evaluation of the Children's Scholarship Fund," PEPG Report 01-03 (Program on Education Policy and Governance, Kennedy School of Government, Harvard University, May 2001).

7. John Witte, *The Market Approach to Education: An Analysis of America's First Voucher Program* (Princeton University Press, 2000), p. 119.

8. R. Kenneth Godwin, Frank R. Kemerer, and Valerie J. Martinez, "Comparing Public and Private Voucher Programs in San Antonio," in Paul E. Peterson and Bryan C. Hassel, eds., *Learning from School Choice* (Brookings, 1998), p. 283.

9. James S. Coleman, Thomas Hoffer, and Sally Kilgore, *High School Achievement: Public, Catholic, and Private Schools Compared* (Basic Books, 1982); James S. Coleman and Thomas Hoffer, *Public and Private High Schools: The Impact of Communities* (Basic Books, 1987).

10. Anthony S. Bryk, Valerie E. Lee, and Peter B. Holland, *Catholic Schools and the Common Good* (Harvard University Press, 1993).

11. Joseph P. Viteritti, *Choosing Equality: School Choice, the Constitution, and Civil Society* (Brookings, 1999), p. 197.

12. In Mark Schneider and others, "Institutional Arrangements and the Creation of Social Capital: The Effects of School Choice," *American Political Science Review*, vol. 91 (March 1997), pp. 82–93, the authors find that within the public sector, social capital increases when school choice programs are established.

13. As cited by Coulson, *Market Education*, p. 8.

14. James G. Dwyer, *Religious Schools v. Children's Rights* (Cornell University Press, 1998), p. 15.

15. Peter McLaren, *Schooling as a Ritual Performance: Toward a Political Economy of Educational Symbols and Gestures*, 3d ed. (Lanham, Md.: Rowman and Littlefield, 1999), pp. 168, 179.

16. Focus group session, Horizon parents not using a voucher, San Antonio, February 20, 1999.

17. Jay P. Greene with Daryl Hall, "The CEO Horizon Scholarship Program: A Case Study of School Vouchers in the Edgewood Independent School District, San Antonio, Texas," Research Paper 8526-600 (Washington: Mathematica Policy Research, April 2001).

18. Focus group session, control group, Dayton, Ohio, March 18, 2000.

19. Similarly, the evaluation of the Edgewood school district voucher program found no impact on student self-esteem, as measured by an index constructed from a similar set of questions. Paul E. Peterson, David Myers, and William G. Howell, "An Evaluation of the Horizon Scholarship Program in the Edgewood Independent School District, San Antonio, Texas: The First Year," PEPG Report 99-03 (Program on Education Policy and Governance, Kennedy School of Government, Harvard University, 1999), tables 1-17 and 2-9.

20. Gerald D. Suttles, *The Social Order of the Slum: Ethnicity and Territory in the Inner City* (University of Chicago Press, 1970); James S. Coleman, *The Adolescent Society: The Social Life of the Teenager and Its Impact on Education* (Free Press, 1961).

21. A predominantly minority school is any school with 50 percent or more minority students. Gary Orfield and John T. Yun, "Resegregation in American Schools" (Civil Rights Project, School of Education, Harvard University, June 1999).

22. Andrew Mollison, "Voucher System Not Good for Diversity, Report Says: North Carolina Governor Claims Danger to School Integration," *Atlanta Journal-Constitution*, June 13, 1999.

23. David Berliner and others, "Will Vouchers Work for Low-Income Students?" Education Policy Project CERAI-00-37 (University of Wisconsin-Milwaukee, December 19, 2000).

24. Edward B. Fiske and Helen F. Ladd, *When Schools Compete: A Cautionary Tale* (Brookings, 2000), p. 305.

25. Clifford W. Cobb, *Responsive Schools, Renewed Communities* (San Francisco: Institute for Contemporary Studies, 1992), p. 103.

26. Jay P. Greene, "Civic Values in Public and Private Schools," in Peterson and Hassel, *Learning from School Choice*, pp. 83–106. For a discussion of the issue, see Gary Rosen, "Are School Vouchers Un-American?" *Commentary*, vol. 109, no. 2 (February 2000), pp. 26–31.

27. Terry M. Moe, *Schools, Vouchers, and the American Public* (Brookings, 2001); Terry M. Moe, "Hidden Demand: Who Would Choose Private Schools," *Education Matters*, vol. 1 (Spring 2001), pp. 48–55.

28. Peterson and Campbell, "An Evaluation of the Children's Scholarship Fund," table 8, p. 61.

29. Ibid, table 9, p. 62. The size of the effect for blacks was larger, but because of sample size the difference was not statistically significant.

30. Ibid, table 8, p. 61.

31. Jay P. Greene, "Civic Values in Public and Private Schools," in Peterson and Hassel, *Learning from School Choice*, table 4-3, p. 99. Data are taken from U.S. Department of Education, National Center for Education Statistics, National Education Longitudinal Study, 1992.

32. Jay P. Greene and Nicole Mellow, "Integration Where it Counts: A Study of Racial Integration in Public and Private School Lunchrooms," PEPG Report 98-13 (Program on Education Policy and Governance, Kennedy School of Government, Harvard University, 1998).

33. Peterson and Campbell, "An Evaluation of the Children's Scholarship Fund," table 8.

34. Peterson, Myers, and Howell, "An Evaluation of the Horizon Scholarship Program," table 1.8, p. 44.

35. Greene, "Civic Values in Public and Private Schools," p. 99.

36. Peterson and Campbell, "An Evaluation of the Children's Scholarship Fund," table 4, p. 48.

37. Henry Levin, "Education Vouchers: Effectiveness, Choice, and Costs," *Journal of Policy Analysis and Management*, vol. 17 (Summer 1998), p. 382.

38. Frances R. A. Paterson, "Building a Conservative Base: Teaching History and Civics in Voucher-Supported Schools," *Phi Delta Kappan*, vol. 82 (October 2000), pp. 150–56.

39. Cobb, *Responsive Schools, Renewed Communities*, p. 200.

40. Stephen Macedo, *Diversity and Distrust: Civic Education in a Multicultural Democracy* (Harvard University Press, 2000), p. 263.

41. Peter L. Berger and Richard John Neuhaus, "To Empower People," in Micahel Novak, ed., *To Empower People: From State to Civil Society* (Washington: American Enterprise Institute, 1996), pp. 206, 159, as quoted in Charles L. Glenn, *The Ambiguous Embrace: Government and Faith-based Schools and Social Agencies* (Princeton University Press, 2000).

42. Moe, *Schools, Vouchers, and the American Public*, p. 56.

43. David E. Campbell, "Making Democratic Education Work—Schools, Social Capital, and Civic Education," and Patrick J. Wolf and others, "Private Schooling and Political Tolerance," in Paul E. Peterson and David E. Campbell, eds., *Charters, Vouchers, and Public Education* (Brookings, 2001), pp. 268–90 and 241–67; David E. Campbell, "Bowling Together: Private Schools Serving Public Ends," *Education Next*, vol. 1 (Fall 2001), pp. 55–61; Kenneth Godwin, Carrie Ausbrooks and Valerie Martinez, "Teaching Tolerance in Public and Private Schools," *Phi Delta Kappan*, vol. 82 (March 2001), pp. 542–46; Greene, "Civic Values in Public and Private Schools," pp. 101–03; Jay Greene, Joseph Giammo, and Nicole Mellow, "The Effect of Private Education on Political Participation, Social Capital, and Tolerance: An Examination of the Latino National Political Survey," *Georgetown Public Policy Review*, vol. 5 (Fall 1999), pp. 53–76. The one exception to the pattern is the lower levels of toleration expressed by students in fundamentalist Christian religious schools.

44. For index construction, see David E. Campbell, "The Civic Side of School Reform," unpublished manuscript (Princeton University, Center for the Study of Democratic Politics, 2000).

45. About two-thirds of the applicants for the national CSF scholarships indicated that they had attended church at least once the previous week. By comparison, 40 percent of Americans said in 1994 that they had attended church in the last week. In 1996, 37 percent of Americans indicated that they had attended religious services in the last week. Tom W. Smith, "A Review of Church Attendance Measures," *American Sociological Review*, vol. 32 (February 1988), pp. 131–36. A 1998 study estimates average church attendance to be about 37 percent. Robert Putnam, *Bowling Alone: The Collapse and Revival of American Community* (Simon and Schuster, 2000), p. 71. An unpublished survey conducted by the Program on Education Policy and Governance, Kennedy School of Government, Harvard University, shows that 39 percent of all parents (both public and private school) attend religious services at least once a week. For public school parents only, the percentage is 36 percent; for private school parents it is 62 percent.

46. Kevin B. Smith and Kenneth J. Meier, *The Case against School Choice: Politics, Markets, and Fools* (Armonk, N.Y.: M. E. Sharpe, 1995), p. 123.

47. Ibid, p. 124.

48. Carnegie Foundation for the Advancement of Teaching, *School Choice: A Special Report* (Princeton, N.J., 1992), p. 13.

49. Mark Schneider and others, "The Empirical Evidence for Citizen Information and a Local Market for Public Goods," *American Political Science Review*, vol. 89 (September 1995), pp. 707–09. Also, see Mark Schneider and others, "Shopping for Schools: In the Land of the Blind, the One-Eyed Parent May Be Enough," *American Journal of Political Science*, vol. 42 (July 1998), pp. 769–94; Caroline M. Hoxby, "Analyzing School Choice Reforms Using America's Traditional Forms of Parental Choice," in Peterson and Hassel, *Learning from School Choice*, p. 144.

50. Mark Schneider, Paul Teske, and Melissa Marschall, *Choosing Schools: Consumer Choice and the Quality of American Schools* (Princeton University Press, 2000), p. 94.

51. Carol Ascher, Norm Fruchter, and Robert Berne, *Hard Lessons: Public Schools and Privatization* (New York: Twentieth Century Fund Press, 1996), pp. 40–41.

52. Dan Murphy, F. Howard Nelson, and Bella Rosenberg, *The Cleveland Voucher Program: Who Chooses? Who Gets Chosen? Who Pays?* (New York: American Federation of Teachers, 1997), p. 10.

53. Focus group session, Washington, D.C., March 1, 1999.

54. Focus group session, Dayton, Ohio, March 18, 2000.

55. Focus group session, control group, Dayton, Ohio, March 25, 2000.

56. Parents chose from the following response categories: child attended a neighborhood public school; the school was the only choice available; academic quality; school safety; religious instruction; convenient location; this child's friends; sports program; school facilities; discipline; teacher quality; what is taught in school; class size; extracurricular activities; special features of school (for example, tutoring or special programs for students).

57. Peterson, Myers, and Howell, "An Evaluation of the Horizon Scholarship Program," table 1.5, p. 41.

58. In Year I, parents in New York were asked if each reason was "not important," "important," or "very important" in selecting their school. The ranking of items is virtually identical to that reported in table 5-9.

59. State of Wisconsin, Legislative Audit Bureau, *An Evaluation: Milwaukee Parental Choice Program* (February 2000), p. 41.

Chapter Six

1. Christopher Jencks and Meredith Phillips, "Aptitude or Achievement: Why Do Test Scores Predict Educational Attainment and Earnings?" pp. 3–14, and Christopher Winship and Sanders D. Korenman, "Economic Success and the Evolution of Schooling and Mental Ability," pp. 49–78, in Susan E. Mayer and Paul E. Peterson, *Earning and Learning: Why Schools Matter* (Brookings, 1999).

2. Thomas J. Kane and Douglas O. Staigler, "Improving School Accountability Measures," Working Paper W8156 (Cambridge, Mass.: National Bureau of Economic Research, March 2001).

3. Thomas J. Kane, Douglas O. Staiger, and Jeffrey Geppert, "Randomly Accountable," *Education Next,* vol. 2 (Spring 2002), p. 58.

4. Anthony S. Bryk and others, *Academic Productivity of Chicago Public Elementary Schools: A Technical Report Sponsored by the Consortium on Chicago School Research* (March 1998), available at (www.consortium-chicago.org [January 10, 2002]).

5. James Coleman, Thomas Hoffer, and Sally Kilgore, *High School Achievement: Public, Catholic, and Private Schools Compared* (Basic Books, 1982).

6. See, for example, Arthur S. Goldberger and Glen G. Cain, "The Causal Analysis of Cognitive Outcomes in the Coleman, Hoffer, and Kilgore Report," *Sociology of Education,* vol. 55 (April-July 1982), pp. 103–22.

7. Thomas Hoffer, Andrew Greeley, and James Coleman, "Achievement Growth in Public and Catholic Schools," pp. 74–97; Douglas J. Wilms, "Catholic School Effects on Academic Achievement: New Evidence from the High School and Beyond Follow-up Study," pp. 98–114; and Christopher Jencks, "How Much Do High School Students Learn?" pp. 128–35, *Sociology of Education,* vol. 58 (April 1985).

8. Hoffer, Greeley, and Coleman, "Achievement Growth in Public and Catholic Schools," table 1–7, 1–8, pp. 80–81; these are the estimates of effects when controlling for background characteristics and years in Catholic school. Effect size is estimated from information provided in the article by Jencks, who estimates an average annual effect size of Catholic schools on all students of around 0.05 in math and reading but does not estimate an effect size for black or minority students separately. Hoffer, Greeley, and Coleman, however, estimate effects on minorities that are approximately three times those for whites.

9. Jencks, "How Much Do High School Students Learn?" p. 134.

10. Derek Neal, "The Effects of Catholic Secondary Schooling on Educational Achievement," *Journal of Labor Economics,* vol. 15, no. 1, part 1 (1997), pp. 98–123.

11. William N. Evans and Robert M. Schwab, "Who Benefits from Private Education? Evidence from Quantile Regressions" (Department of Economics, University of Maryland, 1993); David N. Figlio and Joe A. Stone, "Are Private Schools Really Better?" *Research in Labor Economics,* vol. 1, no. 18 (1999), pp. 115–140. Other studies finding positive educational benefits from attending private schools include Coleman, Hoffer, and Kilgore, *High School Achievement,* and John E. Chubb and Terry M. Moe, *Politics, Markets, and America's Schools* (Brookings, 1990). Critiques of those studies have been prepared by Goldberger and Cain, "The Causal Analysis of Cognitive Outcomes in the Coleman, Hoffer, and Kilgore Report."

12. Stephen Morgan, "Counterfactuals, Causal Effect Heterogeneity, and the Catholic School Effect on Learning," *Sociology of Education,* vol. 74 (October 2001), pp. 341–74.

13. Cecilia Elena Rouse, "School Reform in the 21st Century: A Look at the Effect of Class Size and School Vouchers on the Academic Achievement of Minority Students," Working Paper 440 (Princeton University, 2000), p. 19.

14. Jeffrey Grogger and Derek Neal, "Further Evidence on the Effects of Catholic Secondary Schooling," in *Brookings-Wharton Papers on Urban Affairs: 2000* (Brook-

ings, 2000), p. 153. The findings presented in this paper come from analyses conducted on the National Educational Longitudinal Study.

15. Morgan has calculated "propensity scores" to match comparable public and private school students with one another and thereby mitigate the problem of selection bias. See Morgan, "Counterfactuals, Causal Effect Heterogeneity, and the Catholic School Effect on Learning." When two-stage least squares models are estimated, one needs to find instrumental variables correlated with the type of school students attended but not directly related to test performance. Scholars have obtained different results, depending on the instrumental variables chosen. See, for example, Neal, "The Effects of Catholic Secondary Schooling," and Figlio and Stone, "Are Private Schools Really Better?"

16. According to an Indiana University evaluation, after two years those in third grade at the beginning of the program had higher test scores than a selected group of public school students in language and science. Kim Metcalf, "Evaluation of the Cleveland Scholarship and Tutoring Grant Program, 1996–1999" (Indiana Center for Evaluation, Smith Research Center, School of Education, Indiana University, 1999), p. 15. According to an evaluation by the Program on Education Policy and Governance at Harvard, gains were observed in Year I but not Year II in two newly created schools formed to serve just voucher recipients. Jay P. Greene, William G. Howell, and Paul E. Peterson, "Lessons from the Cleveland Scholarship Program," in Paul E. Peterson and Bryan C. Hassel, eds., *Learning from School Choice* (Brookings, 1998), pp. 357–92. Neither study was a randomized field trial.

17. Results from these evaluations are reported in Peterson and Hassel, *Learning from School Choice.*

18. John F. Witte, *The Market Approach to Education: An Analysis of America's First Voucher Program* (Princeton University Press, 2000); Paul E. Peterson and Chad Noyes, "Under Extreme Duress, School Choice Success," in Diane Ravitch and Joseph P. Viteritti, eds., *New Schools for a New Century: The Redesign of Urban Education* (Yale University Press, 1997), pp. 123–46.

19. The assessment used in this study is Form M of the Iowa Test of Basic Skills.

20. The following equations were used to conduct the two-stage least squares analyses that estimate the impact of switching from a public to a private school on test scores:

$$P = \alpha_1 + \beta_1 V + \beta_2 Y_{0R} + \beta_3 Y_{0M} + \mu_1$$

$$Y_t = \alpha_2 + \beta_4 P + \beta_5 Y_{0R} + \beta_6 Y_{0M} + \mu_2,$$

where Y_t represents the student's test scores in either Year I, II, or III, depending on the value of the subscript t; P is an indicator for attendance at a private school; V is an indicator for whether or not a student was offered a voucher; Y_{OR} and Y_{OM} are the baseline math and reading test scores; and B_4 is the estimated impact of switching from a public to a private school on student test scores. For further methodological information, see William G. Howell, Patrick J. Wolf, David E. Campbell, and Paul E. Peterson, "School Vouchers and Academic Performance: Results from Three Randomized Field Trials," *Journal of Policy Analysis and Management,* vol. 21 (Spring 2002), pp. 207–33.

21. Weights were constructed using the inverse of the estimates' variances.

22. In Washington, D.C., African American students in Year I in grades 6–8 who were offered a voucher scored significantly lower than members of the control group. By contrast, younger African Americans who were offered a voucher scored somewhat higher than members of the control group.

23. "Principal is Convicted of Assaulting Reporter," *New York Times,* August 11, 1997, p. A12; Valerie Strauss and Jay Matthews, "Charter Schools Strive to Get Ready," *Washington Post,* July 13, 1998, p. B1; Jay Matthews and Valerie Strauss, "Problems Vex Two Charter Schools," *Washington Post,* November 19, 1998, p. B1; Brian Gill and others, *What We Know and What We Need to Know about Vouchers and Charter Schools* (Santa Monica, Calif.: RAND, 2001), pp. 93–95.

24. Diane Ravitch, *The Great School Wars: New York City, 1805-1973* (Basic Books, 1974). Interestingly, the School Choice Scholarships Foundation was itself a direct consequence of a bishop's suggestion that the Catholic schools take 1,000 of the public schools' most difficult students. When the public school superintendent rejected the idea, this private foundation was established to open private school doors to public school students.

25. Raymond Domanico, "Catholic Schools in New York City" (Program on Education and Civil Society, New York University, 2001).

26. Because the New York City impact is more precisely estimated than the D.C. impact, the former is weighted more heavily than the latter when the weighted average across the two cities is calculated.

27. Alan B. Krueger, "Experimental Estimates of Education Production Functions," *Quarterly Journal of Economics* (May 1999), p. 525.

28. See Ann Flanagan, Jennifer Kawata, and Stephanie Williamson, *Improving Student Achievement: What NAEP Test Scores Tell Us* (Santa Monica, Calif.: RAND Corporation, 2000), p. 59.

29. Nonetheless, a number of analysts have objected to the apparent absence of controls for family background characteristics. For instance, Bruce Fuller and his colleagues at the University of California–Berkeley argued, "The experimental group may have been biased as some of the most disadvantaged voucher winners did not switch to a private school, and therefore were excluded from the group (possibly boosting mean achievement levels artificially)." An interest group, People for the American Way, lodged a similar complaint: "The . . . study's key finding improperly compares two dramatically different groups and may well reflect private-school screening-out of the most at-risk students." In the three cities, roughly half the students took the voucher that was offered to them (the takers) and about half did not (the decliners). However, we did not drop the decliners from the analysis. All voucher applicants were invited to follow-up testing sessions, and each of the families that participated was included in the analysis. To estimate the impact of switching from a public to a private school, we did not simply compare takers with the students who remained in public school (the decliners and those who did not win a voucher), as

Fuller and his colleagues have contended. Instead, as previously noted, we used the fact that the vouchers were awarded randomly to generate an instrumental variable that generates a consistent estimate of the effect of switching to a private school.

30. Patrick J. Wolf, William G. Howell, and Paul E. Peterson, " School Choice in Washington, D.C.: An Evaluation after One Year," paper prepared for the Conference on Charters, Vouchers, and Public Education 2000, sponsored by the Program on Education Policy and Governance, Kennedy School of Government, Harvard University (www.ksg.harvard.edu/pepg/ [January 11, 2002]).

31. Asbjorn Hrobjartsson and Peter C. Gotzsche, "Is the Placebo Powerless? An Analysis of Clinical Trials Comparing Placebo with No Treatment," *The New England Journal of Medicine*, vol. 344 (May 2001), pp. 1594–602.

32. The problem of using small numbers of cases in estimating value-added test scores is discussed further in appendix D, which also reports effects by grade level and baseline performance for each city.

33. Harry Brighouse, *School Choice and Social Justice* (Oxford University Press, 2000), p. 118.

34. Carol Ascher and others, *Hard Lessons: Public Schools and Privatization* (New York: Twentieth Century Fund, 1996), p. 9.

35. John Chubb and Terry Moe, "Effective Schools and Equal Opportunity," in Neil Devins, *Public Values, Private Schools* (London: Falmer Press, 1989).

36. Kate Zernike, "Gap Between Best and Worst Widens on U.S. Reading Test." *New York Times,* April 7, 2001.

37. It is calculated by dividing a sample's standard deviation by its mean. This statistic is preferable to a simple calculation of the variance or the standard deviation, because it adjusts for the fact that as the mean increases, so does the standard deviation (a measure of dispersion). For example, in an inflation-ridden economy, the standard deviation will increase more rapidly if calculated in current dollars than in constant dollars, whereas the coefficient of variation will generate similar estimates of changing income dispersion.

38. In New York and Dayton, the observed impacts for African American students and those from other ethnic groups differed along other dimensions as well. In Year II in New York, for instance, the impact of attending a private school on hallway monitoring was significantly smaller for Hispanics than it was for African Americans. The Year II impact on school resources, meanwhile, was larger. Given the sign of those differences, however, this can hardly explain why African American voucher students achieved the only test score gains. Could it be that African American students in private schools benefit because their hallways are less closely monitored and because they have fewer school resources than their public school peers? Probably not. Consequently, in the analyses that follow, we focus explicitly on those aspects of schooling that generated impacts that differed significantly for African Americans and other ethnic groups when the observed differences seem to have benefited black students.

39. Similar nonexplanations were obtained when similar models were used in an estimate of voucher impact on the test scores of Hispanic students in New York City.

40. Although it is not shown, the impact of the resources and programs of Day-

ton's schools on the test scores of white students was not statistically significant, nor did including those resources and programs in the model alter the negligible impact of switching to a private school on white students' test scores.

41. Private school impacts for Hispanics in New York City and whites in Dayton remained statistically insignificant when the comprehensive model was used to estimate effects.

42. See, for example, John Ogbu and H. D. Simons, "Voluntary and Involuntary Minorities: A Cultural-Ecological Theory of School Performance with Some Implications for Education," *Anthropology and Education Quarterly*, vol. 29, no. 2 (1998), pp. 155–88, and John Ogbu, "Differences in Cultural Frame of Reference," *International Journal of Behavioral Development*, vol. 16, no. 3 (1993), pp. 483–506.

43. It is possible, however, that the voucher impacts derive not from these characteristics considered separately or additively but through some complex interaction among some or all of the variables. Perhaps it is the interaction between school disruptions and school size that counts. Or the interaction between school-parent communication and class size? Indeed, different aspects of school life may come together in different ways for African American and other students, generating very different test scores. Future research may wish to explore that possibility by constructing models that account for the interaction of different school factors, rather than just the main effects of each taken one at a time.

44. Steven G. Rivkin, Eric A. Hanushek, and John F. Kain, "Teachers, Schools, and Academic Achievement," Working Paper 6691 (Cambridge, Mass.: National Bureau of Economic Research, April 2000).

45. To overcome the self-selection problems that plague research on peer effects, Caroline Hoxby has examined the impacts on individual student achievement that result from being in classes that differ in their racial and gender composition. She finds that "a credibly exogenous change of 1 point in peers' reading scores raises a student's own score of between 0.15 and 0.4 points." "Peer Effects in the Classroom: Learning from Gender and Race Variation," Working Paper 7867 (Cambridge, Mass.: National Bureau of Economic Research, August 2000).

46. Elijah Anderson, *Code of the Street: Decency, Violence, and the Moral Life of the Inner City* (W. W. Norton, 2000).

Chapter Seven

1. Lowell C. Rose and Alec M. Gallup, "Results from the 32nd Annual Phi Delta Kappa/Gallup Poll of the Public's Attitudes toward the Public Schools," *Phi Delta Kappan*, vol. 82 (September 2000), pp. 41–57. Similarly, a survey of parents whose children were attending the public school assigned to them found that 48 percent were "very satisfied." Fifty-two percent were "very satisfied" with their school's academic standards. National Center for Education Statistics, *The Condition of Education*, NCES 2000-062 (Government Printing Office, 2001), table 46-2, p. 163.

2. Steven A. Tuch and Ronald Weitzer, "Racial Differences in Attitudes toward the Police," *Public Opinion Quarterly*, vol. 61 (Winter 1998), pp. 642–63.

3. John R. Hibbing and Elizabeth Theiss-Morse, *Congress as Public Enemy: Public Attitudes toward American Political Institutions* (Cambridge University Press, 1995).

4. Robert L. Kahn and others, "Americans Love Their Bureaucrats," as quoted in Francis E. Rourke, *Bureaucratic Power in National Policy Making* (Boston: Little Brown, 1986), p. 290.

5. Richard Fenno, *Home Style: House Members in Their Districts* (Boston: Little Brown, 1978), p. 168; Glenn Parker and Roger Davidson, "Why Do Americans Love Their Congressman So Much More Than Their Congress? *Legislative Studies Quarterly*, vol. 4 (February 1979), pp. 52–61.

6. Morris Fiorina and Paul E. Peterson, *The New American Democracy*, 2d ed. (New York: Longman, 2001), p. 267.

7. Anthony P. Carnevale and Donna M. Desrochers, *School Satisfaction: A Statistical Profile of Cities and Suburbs* (Princeton, N.J.: Educational Testing Service, 1999), p. 46.

8. Ibid, p. 138.

9. National Center for Education Statistics, *The Condition of Education*, table 46-2, p. 163.

10. Terry M. Moe, *Schools, Vouchers, and the American Public* (Brookings, 2001), p. 96.

11. Kevin Smith and Kenneth Meier, *The Case against School Choice* (Armonk, N.Y.: M. E. Sharpe, 1995), pp. 123–24.

12. Michael D. Johnson and Claes Fornell, "A Framework for Comparing Customer Satisfaction across Individuals and Product Categories," *Journal of Economic Psychology*, vol. 12 (March 1991), pp. 267–86. Economists have found it hard to measure satisfaction precisely because of the difficulties of making comparisons across individuals and across products. However, some economists think that satisfaction can be measured across individuals, and therefore is valuable for policymaking and strategy formation. For them, satisfaction is understood to be a synonym for economic utility ("measuring satisfaction becomes equivalent to measuring utility") and answers to these questions "involve psychological as well as economic considerations." Therefore, Johnson and Fornell presented a model of utility that "views behavior (e.g. product performance and worth) and perceptions of economic conditions (e.g. performance expectations) as the primary antecedent of subjective well-being (i.e. satisfaction and utility)" (p. 274).

On a more abstract level, Princeton-trained economist Tom Warke has built on the Johnson and Fornell model of utility and argues that "those choices that maximize the self-perceived happiness of rational agents are also the right choices." Tom Warke, "Classical Utilitarianism and the Methodology of Determinate Choice in Economics and in Ethics," *Journal of Economic Methodology*, vol. 7 (November 2000), pp. 373–94. Finally, according to Anders Gustafsson and Michael Johnson, from the perspective of the consumer, "the primary antecedent or drivers of consumer satisfaction are the more abstract benefits that a product or service provides." The authors note that the benefits may be the information provided by a piece of technology, relations with a firm's salespeople, or the atmosphere within a restaurant. Such benefits constitute the lens through which consumers view and ascribe a value to a product or service. Anders

Gustafsson and Michael D. Johnson, "Bridging the Quality-Satisfaction Gap," *Quality Management Journal,* vol. 4 (July 1997), pp. 27–43, quote is from p. 29.

13. See, for example, David Varady, "Influences on the City-Suburban Choice: A Study of Cincinnati Homebuyers," *Journal of the American Planning Association,* vol. 56, no. 1 (1990), pp. 22–40. Increasing numbers of black families also have left central cities so that their children can attend suburban public schools. See Martin T. Katzman, "The Flight of Blacks from Central-City Public Schools," *Urban Education,* vol. 18, no. 3 (1983), pp. 259–83.

14. Focus group afternoon session, Washington, D.C., March 27, 1999.

15. Focus group session, Washington, D.C., March 6, 1999.

16. Focus group afternoon session, Washington, D.C., March 27, 1999.

17. Focus group session, Washington, D.C., March 6, 1999.

18. Focus group session, Horizon parents, March 11, 1999.

19. Focus group session, Washington, D.C., April 18, 1999.

20. Ibid.

21. We limited the sample to African Americans living in areas that were at least 90 percent urban.

22. Dayton control group, March 18, 2000.

23. Strictly speaking, this attenuation in satisfaction impacts may be caused by either a decline in the level of satisfaction expressed by the treatment group or an increase in the level reported by the control group. We show later in this chapter that the level of satisfaction reported by members of the control group remained relatively constant during the programs' first two years. A decline in impact, therefore, can be attributed to a decline in satisfaction reported by voucher users.

24. Martin Carnoy, *Do School Vouchers Improve Student Performance?* (Washington: Economic Policy Institute, 2001), p. 16.

25. National Center for Education Statistics, *The Condition of Education,* p. 163.

26. Kim K. Metcalf, "Evaluation of the Cleveland Scholarship and Tutoring Grant Program, 1996–1999," Indiana Center for Evaluation, Smith Research Center, School of Education, Indiana University, 1999, pp. 19–20.

27. John F. Witte, "Who Benefits from the Milwaukee Choice Program?" in Bruce Fuller, Richard F. Elmore and Gary Orfield, eds., *Who Chooses? Who Loses? Culture, Institutions, and the Unequal Effects of School Choice* (Teachers College Press, 1996), p. 132.

28. R. Kenneth Godwin, Frank R. Kemerer, and Valerie J. Martinez, "Comparing Public Choice and Private Voucher Programs in San Antonio," and David J. Weinschrott and Sally B. Kilgore, "Evidence from the Indianapolis Voucher Program," in Paul E. Peterson and Bryan Hassel, eds., *Learning from School Choice* (Brookings, 1998), pp. 275–306 and 307–34.

29. Anita D. Suda, *Education Reform in the Dayton Area: Public Attitudes and Opinions* (Washington: Thomas B. Fordham Foundation, October 1998), pp. 26–28.

30. All these estimates were adjusted for a variety of background characteristics.

31. Focus group session, Horizon parents, San Antonio, March 11, 1999.

32. Focus group session, Horizon parents, San Antonio, March 20, 1999.

33. Ibid.

34. Brian P. Gill and others, *Rhetoric versus Reality: What We Know and What We Need to Know about Vouchers and Charter Schools* (Santa Monica, Calif.: RAND, 2000), pp. 128–29, available at (www.rand.org).

Chapter Eight

1. For discussion of the legal issues, see Michael W. McConnell, "Legal and Constitutional Issues of Vouchers," and Elliott M. Mincberg and Judith E. Schaeffer, "Grades K–12: The Legal Problems with Public Funding of Religious Schools," in C. Eugene Steuerle and others, eds., *Vouchers and the Provision of Public Services* (Brookings, 2000); Stephen G. Gilles, "On Educating Children: A Parentalist Manifesto," *University of Chicago Law Review*, vol. 63 (Summer 1996), p. 937; Michael W. McConnell, "The Selective Funding Problem: Abortions and Religious Schools," *Harvard Law Review*, vol. 104 (March 1991), p. 989; Jesse H. Choper, "Federal Constitutional Issues," in Stephen D. Sugarman and Frank R. Kemerer, eds., *School Choice and Social Controversy: Politics, Policy, and Law* (Brookings, 1999), pp. 235–65.

2. Michael W. McConnell, "Legal and Constitutional Issues of Vouchers," in Steuerle and others, *Vouchers and the Provision of Public Services,* p. 381.

3. Mincberg and Schaeffer, "Grades K–12," p. 395.

4. *Zobrest* v. *Cataline Foothills School District,* 509 U.S. 1 (1993); *Rosenberger* v. *University of Virginia* 515 U.S. 819 (1995); *Good News Club* v. *Milford Central School* (99-2036) 202 F. 3d 502 (2001), reversed and remanded.

5. *Bagley* v. *Raymond School Department,* 728 A.2d 127 (Maine 1999). The Maine Supreme Court ruled that a program that provided private or public school tuition for children in rural school districts without their own public schools—but that expressly excluded religious schools—did not violate the First Amendment guarantee of free exercise of religion and the 14th Amendment guarantee of equal protection. The state trial court ruled in favor of the state, as did the Maine Supreme Court on April 23, 1999. In May 1999, the First Circuit Court of Appeals rejected a similar challenge to Maine's exclusion of religious schools brought in federal court by the American Center for Law and Justice. On October 12, 1999, the U.S. Supreme Court declined to review its decision. Also, see *Chittenden Town School District* v. *Vermont Department of Education,* 738 A.2d 539 (Vermont 1999).

6. State of Wisconsin, Legislative Audit Bureau, *Milwaukee Parental Choice Program: An Evaluation,* Report 00-2 (February 2000).

7. Chester E. Finn Jr., Bruce V. Manno, Gregg Vanourek, and others, "Charter Schools: Taking Stock," in Paul E. Peterson and David E. Campbell, eds., *Charters, Vouchers, and Public Education* (Brookings, 2001), pp. 19–42.

8. Free-lunch information was available for only thirty-seven of the school districts. Council of the Great City Schools, *Annual Report: 1999–2000* (Washington, 2000), tables 5, 7.

9. Compiled from information available in 2001 from the Center for Education Reform, Washington, D.C.

10. Jodi Wilgoren, "With Ideas and Hope, a School Goes to Work," *New York Times*, August 23, 2000, special section.

11. The story of the Bronx Preparatory Charter School is well told in Jodi Wilgoren, "In Building a Charter School, the Hard Job Is Getting It Built," *New York Times*, July 7, 2001, pp. A1, A14.

12. Albert Hirschman, *Exit, Voice, and Loyalty: Responses to Decline in Firms, Organizations, and States* (Harvard University Press, 1970).

13. Ibid., pp. 45–46.

14. James Brooke, "Minorities Flock to Cause of Vouchers for Schools," *New York Times*, December 22, 1997, p. A1; Jodi Wilgoren, "Young Blacks Turn to School Vouchers as Civil Rights Issue," *New York Times*, October 9, 2000, p. A1.; Jodi Wilgoren, "School Vouchers: A Rose by Any Other Name," *New York Times*, December 20, 2000, p. A1.

15. Moe, *Schools, Vouchers, and the American Public* (Brookings, 2001), p. 88.

16. An estimated 27 percent of the school-age population qualified for a voucher.

17. In seventeen of thirty states, including Arizona, laws require charter schools to be funded at the same per-pupil level as traditional public schools in the district. Bryan C. Hassel, "Charter Schools: A National Innovation, an Arizona Revolution," in Robert Maranto and others, eds., *School Choice in the Real World: Lessons from Arizona Charter Schools* (Boulder, Colo.: Westview, 1999), pp.83–84.

18. In 2001–02, charter schools received $6,600 per pupil, aside from special education services, which were separately funded.

19. Two economists have used existing information on the demand for private schools to estimate what would happen if vouchers were offered. Their results do not differ markedly from those observed in Milwaukee, especially if one assumes higher demand in central cities. According to their estimate, "A voucher equal to about 40 percent of public spending per student . . . would increase private enrollment by 9.5 percent." Danny Cohen Zada and Moshe Justman, "Demand for Public and Private Education: Theory and Evidence," Department of Economics, Ben-Gurion University, Beer Shaeva, Israel, January 2000.

20. Statement issued by Gregory S. Nash, president, National Education Association of New York, Albany, February 16, 2000.

21. Charles Ornstein, "Education Reforms Approved By House; GOP Fails in Bid for Vouchers," *Dallas Morning News*, May 24, 2001.

22. City of Milwaukee Public Schools, *The Comprehensive Annual Financial Report 2000*, p. 68.

23. Howard L. Fuller and George A. Mitchell, "The Fiscal Impact of School Choice on the Milwaukee Public Schools," *Current Education Issues*, vol. 99 (March 1999).

24. *Chittenden Town School District* v. *Vermont Department of Education*, 738 A.2d 539 (Vermont 1999).

25. National Center for Educational Statistics, *Digest of Education Statistics 2000*, NCES 2001-034 (U.S. Dept. of Education, Office of Research and Improvement, 2001), table 31, p. 34. Columbia University Teachers College economist Henry Levin estimates a cost increase of as much as 25 percent of current spending. In his view, "costs would rise because of public subsidies for existing private school students, record-keeping for each voucher student, school monitoring, school accreditation, student transportation, information systems on alternatives, and adjudication of disputes. Preliminary estimates suggest an excess public cost on the order of $75 billion per year nationally, about 25 percent of present spending, about $1,500 per year per student." Henry Levin, "Educational Vouchers: Effectiveness, Choice, and Costs," *Journal of Policy Analysis and Management*, vol. 17, no. 3 (1998), pp. 373–392. But surely it would not cost taxpayers an additional 25 percent to educate another 11 percent of the population. This analysis also ignores any efficiency gains in education. According to Eric Hanushek, "The most obvious way to introduce cost control pressures is through choice programs that institute competition among schools. If schools compete in part on the basis of their costs, more schools might find it in their interest to use alternative technologies to control costs." Eric Hanushek, *Making Schools Work: Improving Performance and Controlling Costs* (Brookings, 1994), p. 114. The $43 billion dollar figure does not take into account any efficiency gains that might occur.

26. *Digest of Education Statistics 2000*, table 31, p. 34.

27. Jessica L. Sandham, "Vouchers Stall as Florida Schools Up Their Scores," *Education Week*, vol. 19 (July 12, 2000), pp. 1, 32–33.

28. Jay P. Greene, "The Looming Shadow: Florida Gets Its F Schools to Shape Up," *Education Next* (Winter 2001), pp. 76–82.

29. Ladd argues that the gains Greene observed may "reflect schools' response to the shame of being labeled a failure, not the voucher threat per se." Letter to the editor, *Education Next*, vol. 2, no. 1 (Spring 2002), p. 4.

30. For discussion, see this volume, pp. 140–42.

31. Caroline Minter Hoxby, "Rising Tide: New Evidence on Competition and the Public Schools," *Education Next*, vol. 1, no. 4 (Winter 2001), pp. 68-75.

Appendix A

1. In New York City and Washington, D.C., families in the control group were entered in a new lottery if they attended follow-up testing in Year I and II. In Dayton, control group families were entered in a new lottery after the first year of the program; in Year II, they were offered higher compensation instead. Families that began the study as members of a control group were dropped from the evaluation if they subsequently won a follow-up lottery. While necessary to preserve the random design of the evaluation, excluding such families had the effect of reducing the size of the control groups slightly. Although families that did complete the surveys may be systematically different from those that did not, dropping the randomly selected subset of survey respondents should only decrease the efficiency of the estimates, not bias

the findings. In D.C. inYear III, all control group families and all those that did not use the initial vouchers offered them were offered a voucher.

2. The one exception here concerns the Year II evaluation in New York City, in which the treatment group's response rate was 7 points higher than the control group's rate.

3. When baseline information was missing, means were imputed.

4. In each study (in New York City and Washington and in Dayton after Year I) the models include slightly different independent variables.

5. The number of observations reported here is the same as that reported in table 5-3, minus the 99 African Americans who showed up in Year III but not in Year II. Note that here we are estimating the effect of an offer (or "intent to treat") and not the effect of actually switching from a public to a private school, which is reported in chapter 6.

6. Gary King and others, "Analyzing Incomplete Political Science Data: An Alternative Algorithm for Multiple Imputation," *American Political Science Review*, vol. 95, no. 1 (2001), p. 46–69. The point estimates reported come from weighted regressions—imputed weights for missing observations in Year III were constrained to have positive values. Impacts generated from unweighted regressions using imputed values and observables also are comparable.

Appendix D

1. Thomas Kane and Douglas Staiger, "Volatility in School Test Scores: Implications for Test-Based Accountability Systems," *Brookings Papers on Education Policy 2002* (forthcoming).

2. Anthony S. Bryk and others, "Academic Productivity of Chicago Public Elementary Schools: A Technical Report Sponsored by the Consortium on Chicago School Research" (March 1998), p. 28.

Index

African Americans: demand for vouchers, 62, 86–87; discrimination in real estate market, 24–25; household net worth, 24; incomes, 23; limits on residential selection, 23–25; parent communication with schools, 107; parent involvement in schools, 120; in religious schools, 60; support of vouchers, 26–27; views of public schools, 169; voucher recipients, 79. *See also* Racial disparities in education; Segregated schools

African American students, impact of vouchers, 113, 186–87; explanations, 152–53, 158–66; homework increases, 108; parent satisfaction with schools, 176, 177; parent-school relationship, 107; reduced class sizes, 100; reduced school sizes, 102; school climate differences, 109, 110; school facilities and services, 93, 96; test score improvements, 142–43, 144, 145–46, 148–50, 151, 166, 186–87

AFT. *See* American Federation of Teachers

Agnew, Spiro, 169

Agostini v. *Felton*, 189, 191

Aguirre, Robert, 78

Airasian, Peter, 102

Alum Rock, Calif., 14

American Federation of Teachers (AFT), 10, 135

A+ Education Plan. *See* Florida A+ Education Plan

Apple, Michael, 60–61

Arizona: charter schools, 12, 149, 199; tax credits and deductions for private school tuition, 13

Arkansas: high school graduation rates, 7

Ascher, Carol, 156

Asians and Pacific Islanders: in religious schools, 60

Berger, Peter L., 131

Berliner, David, 21, 127, 130

Blacks. *See* African Americans